KURSK

HISTORY'S GREATEST TANK BATTLE

NIK CORNISH

First published in the UK in 2002

This edition published in 2005 by Grange Books
Grange Books plc
The Grange
1–6 Kingsnorth Estate
Hoo
Near Rochester
Kent ME3 9ND
www.grangebooks.co.uk

ISBN 1-84013-799-1

Printed in China

Editorial and design:
The Brown Reference Group plc
8 Chapel Place
Rivington Street
London
EC2A 3DQ
UK
www.brownreference.com

This book is dedicated to James, Alex and Charlotte

Editors: Peter Darman, Vanessa Unwin, Anne-Lucie Norton
Picture Research: Andrew Webb
Design: Seth Grimbly
Maps: Darren Awuah
Production: Matt Weyland

PICTURE CREDITS
CENTRAL MUSEUM OF THE ARMED FORCES, MOSCOW: 11 (top), 12 (both), 14, 16 (both), 17, 18, 19, 20, 25, 26, 50, 51 (both), 53, 54, 55 (both), 62, 64 (both), 65, 66, 67, 68 (both), 69, 72, 73 (top), 74, 76 (top), 78, 81, 84 (top), 85 (bottom), 88, 91 (both), 95 (bottom), 97 (top), 98 (top), 100 (both), 101 (both), 102 (bottom), 103, 104 (both), 105 (both), 110 (both), 112, 113 (bottom), 114 (both), 116 (top), 119 (top), 120 (top), 121, 122, 123, 124 (both), 125 (top), 126, 128, 129, 130 (both), 131 (both), 132, 133 (top), 134 (both), 136 (both), 137, 138 (bottom), 139, 140 (top), 141 (bottom), 142, 146, 147 (both), 148 (both), 149 (both), 150, 152 (top), 153 (both), 154 (both), 157 (both), 158 (bottom), 159 (bottom), 159 (bottom), 176, 177 (both), 178 (top), 180, 183 (both), 184 (both), 185 (bottom), 186 (top), 187, 188 (both), 190, 191 (both), 192, 193 (both), 194, 195, 196 (both), 197 (top), 198, 199 (both), 200, 201 (both), 202, 203, 204, 205 (bottom), 206 (top), 207 (both), 208 (both), 209, 211, 212 (top), 213 (both), 214 (both), 215, 216.
FROM THE FONDS OF THE RGAKFD IN KRASNOGORSK: 7 (top), 13 (both), 21 (bottom), 24, 29 (bottom), 56, 57, 59, 63, 70, 75, 76 (bottom), 79 (both), 84 (bottom), 89, 90 (both), 92, 94 (both), 95 (top), 96, 98 (bottom), 99 (top), 102 (top), 107 (bottom), 111 (top), 113 (top), 115, 116 (bottom), 117 (both), 127 (top), 135 (bottom), 138 (top), 140 (bottom), 141 (top), 144, 145 (both), 152 (bottom), 155, 156, 158 (top), 159 (top), 178 (bottom), 179 (both), 181 (both), 186 (bottom), 189, 197 (bottom), 205 (top), 206 (bottom), 210, 212 (bottom).
NIK CORNISH AT STAVKA MILITARY RESEARCH: 15 (bottom), 120 (bottom), 125 (bottom), 127 (bottom), 143 (top).
Robert Hunt Library: 6, 7 (bottom), 8 (both), 9, 10, 11 (bottom), 15 (top), 21 (top), 22 (both), 23, 27, 28, 29 (top), 30, 31, 32 (both), 33, 34, 35, 36, 37, 39, 40, 41, 42, 43 (both), 44 (both), 45, 46, 46-47, 48, 49 (both), 58 (both), 71 (both), 73 (bottom), 80 (both), 82, 83, 85 (top), 86, 93 (both), 97 (bottom), 99 (bottom), 106, 107 (top), 108 (both), 109 (both), 111 (bottom), 118, 119 (bottom), 133 (bottom), 135 (top), 143 (bottom), 151 (both), 160, 161 (bottom), 162, 163, 165, 166, 167, 168, 169, 170, 173, 174, 175, 182, 185 (top).
TRH PICTURES: 161 (top).

CONTENTS

Introduction

The destruction of the Sixth Army at Stalingrad at the beginning of 1943 was a disaster for Germany. However, Manstein was able to restore the front in southern Russia, which allowed Hitler to plan for a new offensive on the Eastern Front.

"We have only to kick in the door and the whole rotten structure will come tumbling down."

Hitler's well-known comment, made on the eve of the invasion of the Soviet Union was, by the summer of 1943, sounding ominously hollow. When, in the early hours of 22 June 1941, Germany and her allies had unleashed Operation Barbarossa, the codename for the invasion of the Soviet Union, success looked like a foregone conclusion as the panzers tore across the vast, open steppes. By the end of November 1941 Leningrad and Sebastopol (base of the Soviet Black Sea Fleet) were under siege, the Ukraine and the Baltic States were occupied, and Moscow itself was in the frontline. In theory the vast bulk of the Soviet Union's Army and Air Force had been destroyed, captured or so badly disrupted as to be of little or no fighting value. However, the theory was at odds with the facts of the situation. Germany's lack of preparedness for a winter campaign and the Soviet Union's seemingly limitless supplies of men and equipment were factors that had been overlooked in the euphoria of the rapid advances of the summer. The horrors of campaigning in the depths of a Russian winter with no anti-freeze, protective clothing or roads worthy of the name came home

▼ The Hammer and Sickle flies over the ruins of Stalingrad after Axis forces surrender at the beginning of February 1943. Some 250,000 German troops had been killed or captured following the city's encirclement by the Red Army in November 1942.

with a vengeance to the men of the *Wehrmacht*. As Colonel-General Heinz Guderian, the panzer genius, wrote to his wife "this is the revenge of reality." With their men and machines a shadow of their former strength, the overstretched units of Army Group Centre faced the power of the Soviet counterattack, launched on 5 December 1941. During the winter of 1941 the temperature fell as low as minus 43 °C. Such was the force of the Soviet counterattack that Army Group Centre appeared to be on the verge of collapse, as position after position was overwhelmed by Red Army men used to the harsh conditions and equipped with machines and weapons designed for winter warfare.

Disgusted with the advice of his generals to withdraw from the outskirts of Moscow, Hitler demanded that they stand firm and give no ground without fighting. Replacing senior officers who dared to question his orders, Hitler took command of the army on the Eastern Front on 17 December 1941. Army Group Centre's line, although punctured and severely weakened, held and its fighting withdrawal did not degenerate into a rout. Both Army Group North, facing Leningrad, and Army Group South, completing the line down to the Black Sea, fell back to more defensible lines.

Although the Russians pressed hard they were unable to achieve their objective of driving the Germans back behind the River Dnieper. The onset of the thaw forced both sides to suspend their operations and take advantage of the time to rebuild their forces. The Soviet Union had survived the *Blitzkrieg* of 1941 bloodied, but unbroken. It was therefore essential to the Germans and their allies to defeat the Soviet Union during 1942 before Russian munitions factories, particularly those relocated beyond the Ural Mountains, increased production and outstripped those of the Axis powers.

▲ Lack of fuel immobilized the majority of the Sixth Army's motor vehicles, priority being given to tanks and ambulances. These armoured cars, an Sd Kfz 222 with its 20mm gun pointed skywards and an eight-wheeled Sd Kfz 232 *Funk* (radio), had been abandoned for just that reason.

The Russian counteroffensive had saved Moscow and crippled Hitler's plans for crushing the Soviet Union with one mighty blow. But despite its losses in men and materiel, the *Wehrmacht* was by no means a spent force. The objective for the German summer offensive of

▼ The grisly harvest of Stalingrad: a field of Axis corpses on the outskirts of the city. Many of the bodies have had their clothing removed by civilians to tailor for their own use. In the background a Soviet-produced Gaz lorry delivers another grim cargo.

▲ **G.K. Zhukov, who in August 1942 was named Deputy Commissar of Defence and First Deputy Commander-in-Chief of Soviet Armed Forces. He planned and directed the counteroffensive that encircled the German Sixth Army at Stalingrad.**

▼ **S.K. Timoshenko. Created a Marshal of the Soviet Union and Commissar for Defence in May 1940, his offensive in southern Russia in May 1942 to retake Kharkov was a total disaster. Forbidden by Stalin to withdraw his forces, he lost over 200,000 men.**

1942 was to be limited in scope when compared with Barbarossa, but highly ambitious in terms of its territorial and economic aspirations. Instead of an offensive from the Baltic to the Black Sea, only Army Group South would be totally committed.

Operation *Blau* (Blue)

The outline of the German plan for the summer of 1942 was laid down in Hitler's Directive 41 dated 5 April 1942. Essentially Hitler set his forces the task of clearing the Soviets from the region of the River Don, the Donbass industrial area, taking the Caucasian oilfields and occupying the passes through the Caucasus Mountains, thus accessing the Trans-Caucasian lands. It was anticipated that operations south of the Caucasus would bring neutral Turkey into the war on the side of the Axis. Operation *Blau*, the codename for Army Group South's general offensive, was to begin after Sebastopol had fallen and the Soviets' Izyum bridgehead on the right bank of the River Donets had been eliminated. Army Group South, in effect, was to become two commands, Army Group B to the north and connecting with Army Group Centre, and Army Group A completing the line to the Black Sea.

The operation was to be split into several phases. Phases one and two involved the north flank of Army Group South moving from Kursk to Voronezh, advancing down the River Don to link up with the Sixth Army, and encircling all Soviet forces within these two arms of a pincer before taking out the Izyum bridgehead. Phase three involved the right flank of Army Group South forcing the defences along the River Donets in the Voroshilovgrad area and moving up the River Don to meet up with other elements of Army Group South. At this point the designations Army Group A and B would be activated. This second pincer movement would close on Stalingrad and take the city or at least neutralize it as an industrial and communications centre. Stalingrad, standing on the banks of the River Volga, controlled river traffic, was an important industrial centre and, as such, was the major objective of Directive 41. The advance into the Caucasus was not dependent on Stalingrad's capture.

The date chosen to begin the first phase was 18 May. However, at dawn on 12 May, Field Marshal

Fedor von Bock, commander of Army Group South, was informed that his Sixth Army was under attack in the Kharkov area. It swiftly became clear that this was not a small-scale operation but one that involved dozens of infantry divisions and hundreds of tanks. Kharkov, fourth city in the Soviet Union, was the objective for the Red Army. The German counteroffensive was launched on 17 May with an attack on the Soviet left flank. Marshal S. K. Timoshenko, commanding the Soviet forces in the area, requested permission to withdraw and call off the attempt to retake Kharkov, but his request was refused by Stalin. Consequently the Red Army lost more than 200,000 men, some 1200 tanks and a little over 2000 guns. In practical terms, Operation *Blau* was now under way as the Izyum bridgehead was overrun by 28 May and a foothold had been established on the left bank of the River Donets. The following week the final push against Sebastopol began, and by 4 July it had fallen. Following the fall of Sebastopol, the Eleventh Army was thus released for inclusion in Operation *Blau*.

From Kursk to the Crimea, the Germans and their allies could muster some 73 divisions, of which 9 were armoured, 7 motorized (including 2 Waffen-SS) and 26 were allies, mainly Romanian and Italian. Although alerted by spies in Switzerland during April and by the recovery of German plans from a plane crash behind Soviet lines on 20 June (just eight days before the start date), Stalin refused to believe the evidence of a forthcoming Axis offensive. He was convinced that the main attack would be directed at Moscow and that any operations in the south would be feints.

▲ A German panzer nears a burning Russian village during Operation *Blau*, the German summer offensive in Russia in 1942. At first the *Blitzkrieg* carried all before it. The First Panzer Army, for example, drove 400km (250 miles) from its start line on 28 June and captured Rostov on 23 July.

On 28 June Army Group B attacked on a 140km (90-mile) front south of Orel with 23 divisions, including 3 armoured and 2 motorized. Two days later Colonel-General Friedrich Paulus' Sixth Army extended the offensive by another 80km (50 miles) with 18 divisions, including 2 armoured and 1 motorized. This northern pincer closed at Voronezh, trapping some 30,000 Soviet troops before the end of the first week in July.

▲ **Field Marshal Wilhelm List, commander of Army Group A during Operation *Blau*. He was dismissed by Hitler for displaying a lack of energy in pressing the offensive. In fact, the slow progress was due more to the exhaustion of the infantry divisions and losses in vehicles than bad leadership.**

On 7 July Timoshenko gave orders to his South-Western Front to withdraw as the threat from the Sixth Army was now obvious. Therefore when the leading units of Army Group A attacked two days later they met only Soviet rearguards when crossing the River Don. As Paulus advanced towards Rossosh, Army Group A began its part of Operation *Blau* and by 12 July the whole of the front was moving forwards in an attempt to encircle the retreating Soviet forces. On 17 July Voroshilovgrad fell and Stalin gave permission to the commander of South Front to fall back. It was at that point Hitler intervened. XL Army Corps was relocated from the drive on Stalingrad, leaving that area of operations to the Sixth Army alone instead of the two army groups originally allocated. Paulus was forced to mark time as the Soviets did everything in their power to organize their newly created Stalingrad Front.

The drive to Stalingrad

By 15 July units of Army Group South were half way to Stalingrad, having taken Millerovo. Rostov fell to the Germans on 23 July but without netting the hoped-for bag of prisoners. The Red Army was trading space for time and the *Wehrmacht* marched on into the seemingly endless steppes of the River Don lands, and the Sixth Army towards its appointment with destiny. On 23 July Hitler issued Directive 45 from his forward headquarters at Vinnitsa in the western Ukraine. The orders in Directive 45 launched Army Group A into the Caucasus and Army Group B into Stalingrad and along the banks of the Rivers Don and Volga to the north and south of the city. Thus Hitler was attempting to achieve both objectives simultaneously, and by doing so hoped to draw Japan as well as Turkey into the war with the USSR. To further complicate his generals' problems, Hitler removed several key units from Army Group South, including the SS Panzergrenadier Divisions *Totenkopf* and *Leibstandarte*, the 9th and 11th Panzer Divisions, and the recently upgraded Panzergrenadier Division *Grossdeutschland*. The majority of the Eleventh Army was distributed across the Eastern Front but, by way of compensation, a further 10 allied divisions had been drafted in (although most of them were incapable of more than garrison or security duties). The rapidity of the German advance had meant that fuel for the vehicles was taking so long to reach frontline units that Paulus was unable to exploit his successful action at Kalach on 4 August until 21 August.

Paulus' orders of 19 August assigned the south and centre of Stalingrad to LI Corps and the northern districts to XIV Corps. However, the first street fighting demonstrated how well the Soviets had organized the Stalingrad Front, and resistance was stronger and more determined than the Germans had anticipated.

As the push into the Caucasus continued, even more difficult to resolve than the worsening supply problem was that of exhausted men and worn-out vehicles. As a propaganda exercise, on 21 August a detachment of German mountain troops planted a swastika flag at the top of Mount Elbrus in the Caucasus range, one of the highest peaks in Europe. Angered by what he perceived as a lack of energy, Hitler replaced Field Marshal List as commander of Army Group A and took the responsibility upon himself. Progress was not made and the winter was fast approaching. In Stalingrad the fighting had taken on all the characteristics of a battle of attrition. Both sides committed men and

▲ Soviet infantrymen were notoriously ill-disposed to wearing helmets, believing them to be an indication of cowardice. They preferred the *pilotka* (side cap). This group of men are worming their way towards a German position through the debris of one of the many ruined factories in Stalingrad. The men are all armed with the PPSh submachine gun, an ideal weapon for close-quarter fighting.

◄ Fires rage in Stalingrad as the Germans and Soviets battle for control of the city. The defenders, the Soviet Sixty-Second Army under Lieutenant-General V.I. Chuikov, had been driven almost to the Volga by mid-October 1942, but managed to hold on.

▲The crew of this 37mm antiaircraft gun, probably men of the 9th Flak Division, fell victim to the rapid advance of the Soviet forces which overran Gumrak airfield on the morning of 22 January. The poor quality of their winter clothing is obvious.

▼ The ghastly conditions of the Russian Front during winter are vividly depicted in this stunning image of an unidentified artillery unit closing in on Stalingrad during December 1942. The gun is a 76mm ZiS-3 divisional piece, which was introduced in 1942. The relaxed manner in which the crew is perched on obviously freezing metal is testament to the quality of their winter clothing.

equipment to gain the advantage. Slowly and bloodily the Sixth Army fought its way towards the banks of the Volga. On 20 September German infantry pushed through to the river but were unable to hold more than a small part of the bank. The Red Army found that it could neutralize the air and artillery support enjoyed by the German ground forces by keeping in close contact with them and denying the Germans a clear target. Heavy bombing by General Wolfram von Richthofen's Air Fleet IV further exacerbated conditions on the ground by simply creating large areas of rubble which the infantry had to negotiate inch by inch. Conventional armoured vehicles were almost useless as their speed was reduced to a crawl, at which point they became ideal targets for Soviet infantry armed with Molotov cocktails, grenades and antitank rifles. To support the Sixth Army's efforts five battalions of combat engineers were airlifted in, and although their expertise was useful, their casualty rate necessitated them being amalgamated into one battalion. Soviet reinforcements were ferried into the city at night. However, by mid-November, some units of the Sixty-Second Army, Stalingrad's garrison commanded by Lieutenant-General V.I. Chuikov, had been driven back to within 200m (220yd) of the Volga. It seemed that one final effort would give Paulus victory.

On 15 November Army Group B had, on its order of battle, 76 divisions, but of these, 36 were

allied (Romanian and Italian) formations that were low in infantry and antitank weapons. These allied troops were placed on the flanks of the Sixth Army following the orders contained in Directive 41. Unfortunately these divisions were occupying positions of great responsibility for which they were entirely ill-equipped. As the daily slaughter in Stalingrad continued and the weather deteriorated, the Soviets began to assemble their forces for a counterattack which was designed to trap the Sixth Army.

The Soviet counteroffensive was codenamed Uranus and was to be commanded by Marshal G.A. Zhukov. Its aim was simply to encircle all Axis forces within its grasp by a gigantic pincer movement. The first pincer was to be launched by the South-West and Don Fronts to the north of Stalingrad on 19 November. The second pincer, to the south of the city, was Colonel-General Eremenko's Stalingrad Front, which was to attack on 20 November.

The northern pincer struck the Romanian Third Army, which rapidly collapsed and thus allowed a Soviet cavalry corps to pour into the breach. A similar breakthrough took place on the following day as the southern pincer attacked. The next day Eremenko's cavalry cut the Novorossisk–Stalingrad railway line. So rapid were the movements of the Soviet pincers that they linked up at the village of Sovietskiy during the morning of 23 November. Paulus and his men were encircled. That afternoon Hitler ordered Paulus to "take up a hedgehog position and await help from outside." During the evening of 23

▲ This T-34/76 Model 1943, of an unidentified unit, is one of a group firing on a column of German vehicles, some of which are just visible in the distance. The hastily applied whitewash camouflage is clearly beginning to wear thin. The open nature of the frozen steppe was ideal tank country, with almost limitless visibility.

▼ An Italian L6/40 light tank, one of the 55 available to the Italian Eighth Army on the Don Front at the time of Operation Saturn. The light armour and 47mm main gun were totally inadequate in the face of the massed T-34/76 tanks that poured across the frozen River Don.

November Paulus requested permission to break out, as he reasoned that the "enemy has not yet succeeded in closing the gap to west and south-west. But his preparations for attack are becoming evident."

Convinced by Hermann Göring, commander of the *Luftwaffe*, that it was possible to airlift at least 508 tonnes (500 tons) of the 711 tonnes (700 tons) of supplies required daily by the Sixth Army, Hitler did not rescind his stand-fast orders, despite the protests of several of his senior officers. Following discussions with his staff, Paulus ordered his men to dig in, and the Stalingrad pocket – some 45km (37 miles) from the city to its western extremity and 30km (25 miles) from north to south – was created. Inside the pocket were some 250,000 Axis troops.

To deal with this crisis Hitler created Army Group Don, commanded by Field Marshal Erich von Manstein, specifically to drive through the Soviet lines and relieve the Sixth Army. On 12 December Manstein's attack went in, but its spearhead only reached to within 55km (40 miles) of Stalingrad and, to avoid encirclement, Army Group Don began to withdraw on Christmas Eve.

▼ The Red Army relied on cavalry to act as scouts on the vast, open steppes of southern Russia. These two men are part of the screen searching for the small groups of Germans that attempted to break out of the Stalingrad pocket. Russian horses were renowned for their stamina and capacity to survive under the most extreme conditions.

▲ **Some of the extensive Soviet antiaircraft batteries that ringed Stalingrad. One of the reasons Hitler forbade the Sixth Army to retreat was Göring's promise that his *Luftwaffe* aircraft could supply the encircled troops, but Göring was woefully wrong.**

◄ **Warmly clad in *ushanka* (fur cap), sheepskin coat and fur-lined mittens, this Red Air Force man is checking the ammunition of the main armament for the legendary Il-2 *Shturmovik* ground-attack aircraft, two 23mm cannon. Strangely, given the snow-covered terrain, the aircraft does not appear to be camouflaged for winter operations.**

A further Soviet offensive, this time aimed at the Italian Eighth Army and the remnants of the Romanian Fifth Army, began on 16 December. Within 48 hours the Axis front had collapsed and again the Red Army poured in to exploit the breach. Moreover what little chance the *Luftwaffe* had had of supplying the Sixth Army was reduced even further by the loss of its forward airfields, and each transport plane's journey increased to a round trip of some 480km (300 miles) through

◀ **The face of defeat. Field Marshal Friedrich Paulus pictured on the day of his surrender to the victorious Red Army following the crushing defeat at Stalingrad. Paulus was suffering from depression and dysentery at this time. His promotion from Colonel-General had been announced on the day he went into captivity, 31 January 1943. He apologized to his Russian interrogators that circumstances made it impossible for him to change his uniform to reflect his promotion.**

increasingly effective Soviet air defences. The fate of the Sixth Army was sealed. Now it remained to be seen how long it could occupy the attention of the Red Army and allow Axis forces in the Caucasus time to escape as the Soviets prepared to drive farther to the west. Abandoning Krasnodar, Field Marshal Ewald von Kleist's Army Group A withdrew into the Taman peninsula, situated opposite to the Crimea, nursing the hope of renewing their Caucasian ambitions at a later date.

▼ **A mixed bag of German and Romanian prisoners. The Germans had cut the rations of the Romanians in order to give their own troops more supplies. The lack of winter equipment, other than fur caps, can be seen clearly from this photograph, as can the apathetic mood of the men.**

▲ **For many Germans their first sighting of the River Volga was as a frozen bridge into captivity. Later in the year POWs were used to raise vessels that had been sunk by the *Luftwaffe*. The likelihood of any of the prisoners attempting to escape is slight, as the number of guards reflects.**

Chuikov offered Paulus the opportunity to surrender but this was not taken, and on 22 January the final Soviet attack began. Inexorably, and in bitter weather, the Red Army advanced and the pocket became smaller. In a futile effort to prevent surrender, as no German field marshal had ever been taken prisoner, Hitler promoted Paulus to the rank of field marshal on 31 January, but on that day he was captured. Two days later the last German detachments in the city surrendered. To the west Manstein was desperately creating a defence line along the banks of the River Mius, having abandoned Rostov on 14 February.

Now the Soviets began to overreach themselves. Flushed with success, they launched Operation Gallop, commanded by General M.M. Popov, on 29 January. Gallop was a large-scale raid undertaken by several tank corps moving in different directions, with the objective of exploiting the empty spaces and confusion behind the Axis lines and keeping them off balance. Scraping together what little armour he could, Manstein succeeded in driving back Popov's main force and destroying another tank corps which had almost reached the River Dnieper at Zaporozhye, near Manstein's headquarters, during the last days of February 1943.

The Soviets opened a second improvised offensive, Operation Star, on 2 February, with the cities of Belgorod, Kursk and Kharkov as its objectives. Following the surrender of Stalingrad six Soviet armies were released for use elsewhere. These troops were to be deployed as part of an ambitious plan to encircle German forces in and

around the city of Orel. When this had been achieved the next objective was to link up with other Soviet forces in a pincer movement and trap the Germans between Smolensk and Briansk. The ultimate goal of all these actions was to reach the River Dnieper by the middle of March and thus destroy the remains of Army Group Don, the southernmost part of Army Group South.

Colonel-General K.K. Rokossovsky was to command the Central Front, which was to be created from formations that had fought at Stalingrad. However, the difficulties in moving men and equipment some 200km (150 miles) along a single track railway led to Rokossovsky's participation in the offensive being postponed until 25 February. The Briansk and Western Fronts had attacked before Rokossovsky's arrival and ran into solid resistance. Rokossovsky's men, arriving and attacking piecemeal, broke through German and Hungarian units on 25 February allowing XI Tank Corps to exploit the gap. XI Tank Corps, operating with cavalry and partisans, penetrated over 200km (125 miles) into the German rear,

▲ Ambush! A pair of T-34/76s in fading whitewash camouflage wait in hiding for any panzers unwary enough to drive incautiously into this small village during the advance after the fall of Stalingrad. Attached to the turret is the standard Russian rifle, the Mosin-Nagant 7.62mm. The radio aerial indicates that the vehicle is probably the troop commander's tank.

reaching the River Desna on 7 March. By this time Rokossovsky's forces were spread out along the few serviceable roads, presenting a clear target for the counteroffensive that the Germans were developing from the south.

Manstein had concluded that the Red Army could be held and then driven back by adopting a mobile defensive strategy. This involved allowing the Soviets to advance until they had outrun their supply lines and then confronting them from prepared defensive positions. Inevitably this doctrine meant giving up ground, which was anathema to Hitler. However, Manstein felt confident that Hitler would find his ideas acceptable. The two met on 6 February and Hitler grudgingly gave his permission for a withdrawal to the line of the River Mius. Now Manstein could go ahead and assemble his forces in the western Donbass for a counteroffensive. German divisions, including SS Panzer Corps, which comprised the three SS Panzergrenadier Divisions, *Leibstandarte Adolf Hitler*, *Das Reich* and *Totenkopf*, had been moving to the Eastern Front from the west since early January. SS Panzer Corps had then been used to cover the retreat of Axis forces east of the River Donets before retiring in turn to take up positions in preparation for Manstein's counterblow.

In such a fluid situation the Germans formed short-lived battle groups from whatever forces were available to stem the Soviet advance. For their part the Red Army commanders viewed the Axis movements as the prelude to a wholesale withdrawal from the eastern Ukraine. Nothing suggested that Manstein was methodically regrouping his armoured forces. By the middle of February Kharkov was in imminent danger of falling to the Russians. Hitler issued yet another stand-fast order, directing SS Panzer Corps not to retire from the city. SS-Obergruppenführer Paul Hausser, SS Panzer Corps' commander, decided that he must disobey his Führer and withdraw in order to save his men and their equipment. Kharkov was taken by the Russians on 15 February and SS Panzer Corps regrouped at Krasnograd.

With Hitler's agreement, Manstein proceeded with further regrouping and preparations for the

▼ Into action with the tank *desant* troops. Well-equipped for the brutal conditions of winter warfare in thickly padded snowsuits, these men blend in with the terrain. Tank *desant* troops rode into battle clinging to the outside of tanks and jumped off when close enough to engage the enemy or occupy abandoned positions.

▲ These Soviet cavalrymen, riding past an abandoned German Model 35/36 37mm antitank gun, are part of VII Guard Cavalry Corps. Involved in the rapid, confused pursuit of the Axis forces towards the River Donets, VII Guard Cavalry Corps was isolated and severely mauled by SS Panzer Corps during February 1943.

counteroffensive, which was to consist of three clearly defined phases:

1. SS Panzer Corps was to regroup near Krasnograd, XL and LVII Panzer Corps near Krasnomeyskoye, and XLVIII Panzer Corps near Zaporozhye, from where they would converge against the right flank of South-Western Front and hurl it back over the northern River Donets.

2. They would then regroup south-west of Kharkov, and strike at Voronezh Front, pushing it back across the northern Donets before recapturing Kharkov and Belgorod.

3. The offensive would continue towards Kursk, and Second Panzer Army, from Army Group Centre, would collaborate by striking southwards from the Orel area to meet Manstein's troops coming up from the south.

The counteroffensive was to be under the control of the staff of the Fourth Panzer Army. The forces assembled included seven panzer divisions, the 5th SS *Wiking* Motorized Infantry Division, whose personnel were mainly Scandinavian and western European volunteers, and four army infantry divisions.

Manstein launched SS Panzer Corps at Kharkov on 6 March. The Soviet leadership was slow to realize the seriousness of their situation. Initially two of Rokossovsky's armies (Sixty-Second and Sixty-Fourth) were sent to reinforce the Voronezh and South-Western Fronts in the Kharkov region and along the Donets respectively.

▲ A view of Kharkov's Red Square. This great prize was the second city of the Ukraine and the fourth largest in the Soviet Union, and its liberation was a major coup for the Red Army. However, Manstein's brilliant counteroffensive not only recaptured the city in March, it also meant that the Germans had regained the Donets–Mius line.

▼ The liberation of Kharkov on 15 February 1943. The Soviet reoccupation lasted one month. Here, two T-34/76s drive through the city's central plaza sRed Square. The Germans had withdrawn swiftly, hence the relatively undamaged appearance of the buildings. The architecture is typical of the Soviet municipal style of the period.

▲ **A StuG III assault gun armed with a long-barrelled 75mm gun on the outskirts of Kharkov in March 1943. This vehicle belongs to General Paul Hausser's SS Panzer Corps which, by 10 March, was to the east of the city and ready to batter its way in.**

▼ **The SS rolls into Kharkov: infantry and a Panzer III of the *Leibstandarte* Division move through the suburbs. The SS men had been forced to abandon the city in February 1943, but a month later were back to exact a bloody revenge on the Red Army.**

New orders were issued to Rokossovsky to reduce the depth of the planned encirclement around Briansk. The Soviet attack began on 7 March, coinciding with the German Second Army's attack on the River Desna. On 17 March the Fourth Panzer Army and Second Army advanced on Belgorod, Kharkov having been taken by the SS on 15 March. By the end of March, the Voronezh Front was back on the eastern bank of the Donets.

Manstein's master stroke

On 14 March Stalin, concerned by the deteriorating situation in the south, summoned Deputy Supreme Commander, Marshal of the Soviet Union G.K. Zhukov, to Moscow. Zhukov was despatched to the HQ of Voronezh Front to assess the situation. In his report to Stalin, Zhukov was blunt.

"We must move everything we can from the STAVKA [Soviet equivalent of combined chiefs of staff] Reserve and the reserves of the neighbouring Fronts at once, because if we do not the Germans will capture Belgorod and develop their offensive towards Kursk."

Within hours the Twenty-First and Sixty-Fourth Armies were moving towards Belgorod, but they were too late to prevent its capture. Belgorod fell on 18 March, confirming Zhukov's predictions. The Twenty-First and Sixty-Fourth Armies established strong defensive positions to the east of the city. The speed of the Soviet redeployment had frustrated one of Manstein's objectives: the move on Kursk.

However, Manstein had the bit between his teeth and did not care to surrender the initiative in the Kharkov-Kursk-Orel region. Although his men and machines were reaching the end of their capacities Manstein attempted to persuade Field Marshal Günther von Kluge, commander of Army Group Centre, to cooperate in an attack on Rokossovsky's forces in the newly formed Kursk salient. Kluge, insisting that his men were in no fit condition to do more, refused. Indeed Army Group Centre had been involved in its own operation, the withdrawal from the Rzhev salient in front of Moscow, which shortened the line by some 300km (200 miles). This area had been the focus of Zhukov's attention for several months and he had planned an operation, codenamed Mars, which was designed to emulate the success of

▲ Field Marshal Erich von Manstein, one of the finest German commanders. His mastery of mobile warfare saved the southern wing in early 1943, but Hitler's insistence on not yielding ground led to his dismissal in 1944.

Operation Uranus (the encirclement of Stalingrad). Operation Mars began on 25 November 1942. However, Army Group Centre was in far better shape than Army Group South and Mars was a failure that cost the Red Army some 300,000 men and 1400 tanks. On the Soviet side of the line, Rokossovsky's opportunity to advance on Orel passed as troops were diverted south and STAVKA cancelled all further offensives other than those of a purely local nature.

With the onset of the April thaw, both sides settled down to consider their next move. The Axis forces were back in almost the positions they had held before Operation *Blau*, but the Red Army had proven itself capable of inflicting a large-scale, unprecedented defeat on the once-invincible

▲ **With its winter whitewash fading fast, a T-34/76 moves at speed across country during the spring of 1943. To extend its operating range the T-34 was often fitted with supplementary external fuel tanks. The handles on the turret are grips for tank *desant* men. Casualties amongst these troops were consistently high and the relationship between them and their tank crews was particularly close.**

Wehrmacht. The ingredients were mixing that would give rise to what promised to be an interesting summer in Russia. As the troops of both sides drew breath, their commanders began to plan. Both STAVKA and OKH (*Oberkommando des Heeres,* the headquarters responsible for the Eastern Front) were aware that the summer campaign of 1943 would be decisive. The Germans had particular need to worry. It was essential that Germany kept a firm grip of the initiative on the Eastern Front to retain Nazi influence over the neutrals of Europe.

The defeat at Stalingrad had lost Germany the tungsten of Portugal and the chrome of Turkey, both vital elements in munitions production and thus a highly significant factor in Hitler's strategic thinking (which placed the possession of such raw materials at the top of his military agenda). Furthermore Sweden, a major supplier of iron ore which had until this point pursued a policy of "benevolent neutrality", now adopted a less compliant stance. Indeed, such was Hitler's concern in respect of Swedish raw materials that reinforcements were sent to Norway in case the situation should require the occupation of Sweden. Hitler had hoped that Turkey would invade the Soviet Union through the Caucasus. In the aftermath of Stalingrad, Germany's recovery notwithstanding, it became clear that this would not happen. The support of Germany's partners on the Eastern Front was also becoming less than wholehearted. Both Italian confidence in Germany's ability to win the war and Mussolini's faith in Hitler had been seriously eroded. Finland, regarding itself as Germany's ally more by chance than choice, was in need of peace and now made no secret of that fact. Romania, having sustained heavy casualties as a result of the Soviet breakthroughs around Stalingrad, requested that its remaining troops in Russia be withdrawn from the frontline. The Hungarian forces became less amenable to following German orders and their role was restricted to security duties in the rear.

▼ With the beginnings of the thaw in April 1943, conditions deteriorated rapidly, the melting of the frozen ground causing problems even for the wide-tracked T-34/76s and the KV-1s of the Red Army. The tracks of the T-34 were 478mm (19in) wide, which gave them a distinct advantage over their opponents.

▲ **The *rasputitsa*, or muddy season, posed problems for the Russians as well as the Germans. The troops of both the *Wehrmacht* and the Red Army relied heavily on horse-drawn transport, and extensive use was made of the peasant wagon, which was ideally suited for the local conditions.**

Finally, Japan was now highly unlikely to violate the non-aggression pact with Stalin and move into the Soviet Far Eastern provinces and Siberia. Therefore it was with a sense of increasing urgency that the German High Command began planning the summer campaign.

As early as 13 March OKH had issued Operation Order 5. This order, for security reasons, had only a circulation of five copies. The earlier sections of Order 5 called for the construction of strong lines of defence along areas of the front that would not be involved in offensive activity and against which: "We must let them crash, and bloody them."

Part one of this document dealt with the Kuban bridgehead and the Crimea, that were to remain passive. Part four covered the defensive preparations on the Leningrad front. It is parts two to four that are particularly relevant:

2. Army Group South.
A strong panzer army has to be formed on the northern flank of the army group immediately and no later than mid-April so that it will be ready for commitment at the end of the mud period, before the Russian offensive. The objective of this offensive is the destruction of enemy forces in front of Second Army by attacking out of the Kharkov area in conjunction with an attack group from Second Panzer Army.

3. Army Group Centre.
First, the situation between Second and Second Panzer Armies must be straightened out; then the defensive fronts are to be strengthened and equipped with antitank weapons as planned. This is especially important near Kirov, in the region north and north-west of Smolensk, as well as Velikie Luki. Then an attack group is to be formed to attack in conjunction with the northern flank of

Army Group South. The forces are to be obtained by the *Beuffelbewegung* (the operation to abandon the Rzhev salient).

4. Army Group North.
Since there is no plan for a major offensive operation during the first half of the summer in the Army Group North area of operations, the main effort will be applied to the defence ...

An operation against Leningrad is planned for the second half of the summer (after the beginning of July).

From this order it is clear that the Kursk salient was to be the object of a panzer-led pincer movement. Later in March operations to drive the Red Army from the industrial areas of the Donets, south-west of Kharkov, were considered, but these were later shelved in favour of concentrating on Operation Citadel, or *Fall Zitadelle* as it was called by the Germans.

On 15 April, Operation Order 6 was issued and this was with a less-restricted circulation of 13 copies (perhaps an ominous omen). The order begins, "I have decided to conduct Citadel, the first offensive of the year, as soon as the weather permits." The purpose of Operation Citadel was clearly defined in a detailed list of numbered objectives:

1. The objective of this offensive is to encircle enemy forces located in the Kursk area by means of rapid and concentrated attacks of shock armies

▼ German wounded from the fighting in southern Russia in early 1943. The disaster at Stalingrad and its aftermath had cost the Axis war effort in the East five armies, one of which, the German Sixth, had been particularly formidable. In addition, the Red Army had become more effective and its commanders more able than in 1941.

from the Belgorod area and south of Orel and to annihilate the enemy in concentrated attacks. During the offensive a new, abbreviated front, which will save strength, will be established.

2. We must ensure that:

a. The element of surprise is preserved and the enemy be kept in the dark as to when the attack will begin.

b. The attack forces are concentrated on a narrow axis, in order to provide local overwhelming superiority of all attack means ... to ensure contact between the two attacking armies and the closure of the pocket.

c. The attack wedge is followed by forces from the depths to protect the flanks, so that the attack wedge itself will only have to be concerned with advancing.

d. By prompt compression of the pocket, the enemy will be given no respite and will be destroyed.

e. The attack is conducted so quickly that the enemy will be denied the opportunity of either breaking out of the encirclement or of deploying strong reserves from other fronts.

f. Additional forces, particularly mobile formations, are freed up by quickly constructing a new front.

▲ Adolf Hitler (left) with Benito Mussolini in happier times for the Axis alliance. Stalingrad had shaken the Italian dictator's faith in his pact with Germany. Hitler desperately needed a victory in the East in 1943 to reassure Mussolini and other wavering allies.

3. Army Group South will jump off with strongly concentrated forces from the Belgorod–Tomarovka line, break through the Prilery–Oboyan line, and link up with the attacking armies of Army Group Centre at east of Kursk.

4. Army Group Centre will launch a concentrated attack from the line Trossna north of Maloarkhangelsk with the main effort on the eastern flank, break through the line Fatezh–Veretenovo, and establish contact with the attacking army from Army Group South near and east of Kursk ... The line Tim–east of Shchigry–Sosna sector is to be reached as soon as possible.

5. The earliest date for the attack will be 3 May.

12. The final objectives of the operation are:

a. The shifting of the boundary line between

Army Groups South and Centre to the general line Konotop (South)–Kursk (South)–Dolgoe (Centre).

b. The transfer of the Second Army with three corps and nine infantry divisions, as well as the attached Army troops, from Army Group Centre to Army Group South.

c. The assembly of three additional infantry divisions from Army Group Centre to be made available to the OKH in the area north-west of Kursk.

d. The removal of all mobile formations from the front for use elsewhere.

Thus was the die cast. All that now remained for Germany was to build up the strength of the *Wehrmacht*, and in particular its panzer arm, in preparation for the titanic struggle that would soon burst over the Eastern Front like a summer thunderstorm.

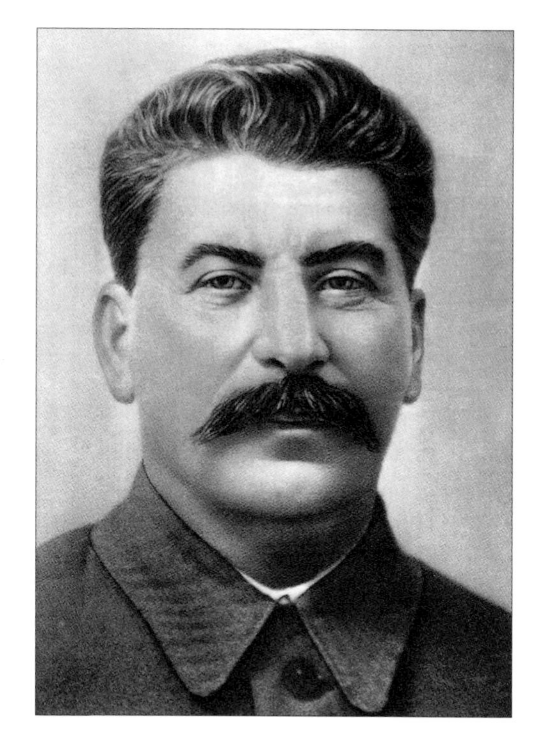

▲ Soviet dictator Josef Stalin. Totally ruthless, he did at least take the advice of his subordinates at times. Prior to Kursk, for example, General N.F. Vatutin persuaded him that the German Army could be ground down in a series of defensive battles in the salient.

▼ As both armies recuperated after the fighting of early 1943, fresh men and machines were brought in. Here, a British-built Churchill Mark 3 drives past a wrecked *Wehrmacht* Sd Kfz 232 sporting the remains of its winter camouflage scheme. The Churchill was unpopular with its Soviet crews as it was weakly armed and slow in comparison with their own tanks.

Rearming the *Wehrmacht*

Despite the losses incurred by the* Wehrmacht *during Operation Barbarossa in 1941 and the defeat at Stalingrad between 1942 and 1943, the German Army was able to rearm for Operation Citadel and field a number of new weapon systems.

At the outbreak of war in September 1939 German military theory was dominated by the concept of *Blitzkrieg*: Lightning War. *Blitzkrieg* as implemented by the German Army involved the use of speed, firepower and mobility, especially tanks, mobile artillery and aircraft, to inflict a total defeat on the enemy. Attacking forces avoided areas of strong resistance to sustain the momentum of the assault, which concentrated on the enemy's rear areas to sever his lines of communication and supply. Having achieved this, less mobile forces – infantry – could then surround and destroy isolated pockets of resistance.

In a series of short, sharp campaigns, first Poland, then Denmark and Norway, and finally France and the Low Countries had been overcome. The operations in Yugoslavia and Greece had been fought in a similar manner but not on such a grand scale or over ground that was as suited to

▼ Much was expected of the new Panzer V Panther that the Germans rushed off the production line to take part in the Kursk offensive. Designed as a result of German experiences with the T-34, the Panther had well-sloped hull and turret armour.

▲ **A German *Sturmgeschütz* (assault gun) III – StuG III – on the edge of the Kursk salient in the spring of 1943. Originally designed as a armoured self-propelled gun to support infantry attacks, the StuG III was later used in the antitank role.**

tank warfare. Naturally men and materiel were lost during these years but Germany's armaments industry was able to make good the losses. During the campaign in France the armoured forces of Germany had been outnumbered but, by supplementing their own machines with Czech 38(t) tanks and superior tactics, the Germans had nevertheless emerged victorious.

When Operation Barbarossa began the Germans deployed 17 panzer divisions with a total strength of just over 3000 tanks. The tanks ranged from the Panzer I, which was little more than a machine-gun carrier and clearly obsolete, the Panzer II, lightly armed with a 20mm gun and again obsolete, through the various marks of Panzer III and IV that were the vehicles on which the Germans relied in tank-to-tank actions.

With the element of surprise, total air superiority, tactical ingenuity and two years of successful campaigning behind them, it is hardly surprising that the panzer forces achieved such spectacular results as they did in 1941. But the essence of Hitler's earlier conquests had been speed; rapid drives through countries with clearly defined borders and highly developed road and rail systems that could be easily integrated into those of the Reich and facilitate the smooth flow of weapons from its factories. By contrast, the Soviet Union that the *Wehrmacht* and its allies set out to crush covered one-sixth of the earth's land mass, was possessed of a much more primitive transport network, and was considerably farther from the essential munitions plants. Indeed, the Soviet rail-track gauge was broader than those elsewhere in western Europe, and this in itself was to create delays in a land where roads were little more than well-defined cart tracks that dissolved into mud after any rainfall.

As a result of pre-Barbarossa battle experience, production of both Panzers I and II had been ended other than for the manufacture of self-propelled guns and specialist antitank vehicles which used their chassis. The majority of Panzer IIIs had had their main armament upgraded from 37mm to 50mm guns. The heavy tank, the Panzer IV, retained its short-barrelled 75mm gun. Although adequate for the campaigns before the invasion of the Soviet Union, these weapons were found to be at a great disadvantage when faced

with the heavily armoured Soviet T-34 and KV-1 tanks which they first encountered in July 1941. In June 1941 the Red Army fielded over 900 T-34 and 500 KV-1 tanks, many of which were lost due to inexperienced crews and faulty tactical deployment. When they were used properly they created terror amongst the Axis troops, who had no antitank guns capable of penetrating their armour, particularly the sloping front-plate of the T-34. One gun that could stop them was the legendary 88mm, an antiaircraft gun which the Germans discovered to be a highly effective tank killer. The other was the long 75mm antitank gun, but this was not available in large numbers at the time.

By the autumn of 1941 the Germans had recognized the fact the Panzer III and IV were in need of further improvement if they were to retain the edge over the Soviet tank forces that their training and experience had given them. Both types were to be produced with thicker armour and the Panzer IV was to have the long 75mm gun as its main armament; the turret of the Panzer III was too small to accommodate this piece.

Useful as these measures were in improving the quality of the tank arm, they were only stop gaps; it was vital that these vehicles were produced in sufficient quantities to match the Red Army in numbers. Soviet tank production was greater than that of the Axis, even when disrupted by the German advances between 1941 and 1942. Tank factories were evacuated by rail to locations beyond the Ural Mountains, off-loaded and back in production within an incredibly short space of time, though what the cost was in human terms can never be calculated. The Panzer IVs lost during 1941 had been replaced by April 1942, but there had been no real increase in numbers overall. The

◄ Colonel-General Heinz Guderian was created Inspector of Armoured Forces in February 1943. Working closely with Albert Speer, he increased the rate of monthly panzer production. He also initiated many corrections to panzers in person, travelling around factories and tank-shooting ranges.

▼ Minister of Armaments, Albert Speer, who was responsible not only for armaments production, transportation and placement, but also for raw materials and industrial production. He kept the German war machine going, but only by using slave labour.

low rate of production was, in part, due to Hitler's desire not to allow any radical disruption of German civilian life, in particular the employment of German women in munitions factories. However, during the second half of 1942, with the *Wehrmacht* crying out for more men and munitions of all sorts, there was only one way to overcome the labour shortfall: the employment of "volunteer" workers recruited from the conquered territories of Europe. Initially this workforce was assembled voluntarily, but rapidly it became a matter of conscription and coercion. The effects of such workers being taken on by the most sensitive and essential of Germany's industries can only be judged by the number of defective weapons that found their way into the hands of the unsuspecting combat troops. But the importation of foreign labour did allow Germany to finally abandon one-shift working in many armament factories. Even with the increases in production, only 100 Panzer IVs were produced in November 1942, a drop in the ocean beside the 1000 T-34s that rolled off the line during the same month.

Administrative changes

Another factor that improved Germany's industrial production was the replacement of Fritz Todt as Minister of Armaments by Albert Speer. Speer demonstrated a flair for organization and was primarily responsible for the rapid increase in munitions production that began in 1942 and was to continue until well into 1944. The other significant appointment that Hitler made during his period of post-Stalingrad rationality was that of General of Panzer Troops Heinz Guderian as Inspector of Armoured Forces. Guderian had been ordered into retirement by Hitler, along with other senior officers of Army Group Centre, for failing to take Moscow in late 1941. On 17 February 1943 Guderian was summoned to meet Hitler at Vinnitsa in the Ukraine. Guderian broke his journey at Rastenburg to discuss the terms of his possible reinstatement with Hitler's adjutant, Colonel Rudolf Schmundt, and found them acceptable.

Following a meeting with Hitler, Guderian was officially appointed to his new post on 28 February 1943. He was horrified at the condition into which the armoured forces had sunk. Returns for the 18 panzer divisions on the Eastern Front gave

▲ The mighty Tiger entered production in August 1942. Heavily armoured and armed with the formidable KwK 36 88mm gun, it could engage and knock out any Soviet tank before the latter could get within firing range. However, the Tiger was slow and was very expensive to build.

the number of 495 battleworthy tanks, just over twice the number of tanks in a fully equipped panzer division at the start of Barbarossa. Guderian was granted wide-ranging powers and would work closely with Speer. It was expected that together they would bring order and good sense to the

apparent chaos that dogged German tank development and production. However, even these measures did not prevent the absurd request by OKH, early in 1943, to end all tank production except that of Tigers and Panthers. At a meeting on 9 March Guderian ruled out such suggestions and it was decreed that production of the Panzer IV should continue as it was the backbone of the armoured forces. Panzer III production facilities had been turned over to the assault guns, the *Sturmgeschütz* (StuG) III, on the express order of Hitler himself in December 1942.

1943 was to see the introduction of new German tanks that had been under consideration for some time. The two German tanks most closely associated with the battle of Kursk are the Tiger and the Panther. Of these, the Tiger had been "blooded" in action on the Leningrad Front in late 1942 where it had performed badly in country unsuited for armoured warfare. The Tiger was the culmination of several years of development influenced by battlefield experience gained in Russia. Two designs had been commissioned, one from Porsche (of Beetle and sports car fame) and one from the Henschel company. On Hitler's birthday, 20 April 1942, both prototypes were demonstrated and the Henschel design was chosen. An order was placed and production was to begin in August. The vehicle was designated Panzer Kampfwagen VI Tiger Ausf H (Sd Kfz 181).

▲ The debut of the Panther at Kursk was inauspicious. Because of technical problems associated with the gearbox, transmission and suspension, plus a number of engine fires, many broke down before and during the battle. From the original 250 Panthers, only 43 were still in service by 10 August 1943.

The Tiger

Experience had taught the Germans that the weapon which was most effective against all Soviet armour was the 88mm KwK 36, a derivative of the legendary Flak 88. This gun was chosen to be the Tiger's main armament. Thus armed, a Tiger could stand off and destroy Soviet tanks at ranges over 1500m (1200yd), which put them out of danger from the Soviet tank guns. Co-axially mounted with the 88 was a 7.92mm MG 34, with a similar machine gun in a ball mounting on the front vertical plate for use by the radio operator/machine gunner. Armour plate was up to 100mm (4in) thick with the belly armoured to 26mm (1in) to reduce damage by mines and exploding dogs. The tracks were wide to distribute the vehicle's 57 tonnes (56 tons) evenly over soft ground and snow. The maximum road speed was 36km/h (23mph); off-road this was reduced to 19km/h (12.5mph). The five-man crew consisted of the commander, gunner, loader, radio operator/machine gunner and driver.

However, the Tiger was expensive in labour terms, requiring more than 300,000 man hours to make; also, if disabled, it was difficult to recover. A version of the Tiger was produced specifically to recover disabled Tigers and other heavy vehicles. The Tiger was designated a "breakthrough tank" (*Durbruchswagen*) and in this role it was to prove its worth. In the hands of a tank ace such as Michael Wittmann it would demonstrate time and time again its combat power.

The Panther was almost a direct result of the *Wehrmacht*'s early encounters with the T-34; consequently its design was a radical departure from those of the Panzer III and IV. With a sloping front-plate 80mm (3in) thick, its long overhanging gun and road speed of 54km/h (34mph), the Panther was clearly a product of the T-34 theory of combining armament, armour and mobility. Again two competing designs were produced, one by MAN and one by Daimler-Benz. It was the MAN design that was adopted and, in November 1942, Panther production began with the official designation of Panzer Kampfwagen V Panther Ausf D (Sd KFz 171). Such was the mood of desperation to get the Panther into frontline service that the initial production programme called for an output of 250 per month from the outset. This sense of urgency was rewarded with a rapid display of teething troubles, due in part to the increased weight which was greater than the original specification laid down. This led to excessive wear of gears and a more powerful engine that stretched the transmission to its limits. These

▼ Soldiers of the *Grossdeutschland* Panzergrenadier Division prior to their participation in the Battle of Kursk. One of the élite units in the German Army, the division was liberally equipped with tanks, assault guns and armoured personnel carriers.

problems and defects in the suspension were the major weaknesses of the early production Panthers, but these were the vehicles that were used at Kursk.

At the March meeting, Guderian had emphasized that under no circumstances could the Panther be expected to enter service earlier than July 1943. This statement was confirmed by trials held in Germany, where mechanical breakdowns and engine fires occurred with monotonous and disturbing regularity. However disconcerting the field tests had proved to be, and despite the warnings of the experts as voiced by Guderian, Panthers could be produced twice as quickly as Tigers and had a gun that was capable of knocking out Soviet armour almost as easily as the Tiger's 88. The main armament was the 75mm 42L/70, an improved version of the gun fitted to the Panzer IV model G. In addition there were two MG 34s, one co-axially mounted in the gun mantlet and one on the front-plate. The crew numbered five but, due to its poor test performance and reputation for spontaneous combustion, the tank was regarded by the armoured troops with little optimism.

The chassis of the Porsche contender in the Tiger competition was adopted in a modified form as the basis for a self-propelled carriage for the 88 L/71. The final official designation was 88mm 43/2 L/71 Ausf *Panzer Jäger* Tiger (P) *Elefant Fruher Ferdinand*. This 69-tonne (68-ton) unit was not a subtle weapon: lacking a turret, the gun was mounted in a high, boxlike superstructure. The gun, a longer-barrelled version of the 88, was the only armament. The lack of a machine gun proved to be a severe weakness at Kursk, leaving the slow-moving *Elefant* prey to Soviet tank-hunting infantry squads. Some 76 *Elefants* were used during Citadel by the Ninth Army in the 653rd and 654th Heavy Tank Destroyer Detachments.

▼ Panzer IVs equipped with armoured side skirts. These tanks are Ausf H models, whch differed from the Ausf G variant in having the SSG77 transmission and a host of minor modifications including all-steel rollers and external air filters. A total of 3774 H models were built starting in April 1943.

▲ **German troops hitch a lift aboard a Panzer III. The Panzer III was outclassed by the T-34 on the Eastern Front from the end of 1941, but because of armour shortages it remained in service. At Kursk, for example, panzer units were equipped with 155 Ausf N models.**

To extend the combat life of the Panzer IIIs and IVs, armoured side skirts (*schurzen*) were issued to protect the running gear, tracks and turret against light antitank weapons. A total of 841 Panzer IV Model Gs constituted the mainstay of the panzer arm at Kursk. This upgunned version was capable of dealing with the T-34 at battlefield ranges. Some 432 Panzer IIIs were also available for Citadel, rearmed with the long 50mm gun which, again at close quarters, could penetrate the heavy front-plate of the T-34. These tanks provided a useful supplement to the heavier types. Some 60 Panzer IIIs were converted to flamethrower tanks, and these vehicles were used with particularly deadly effect, as the hot weather had thoroughly dried the vegetation.

In addition to the various tanks, both old and new, considerable reliance was placed on the assault guns (*Sturmgeschütz*). Guderian had no influence on the design and production of these as they remained under the control of the artillery chain of command, which jealously guarded its power. Originally the majority of assault guns were based on the proven Panzer III chassis. The basic concept behind the assault gun was to provide close, mobile artillery support for the infantry. The original armament was the short-barrelled 75mm gun housed in a turretless structure with limited traverse. By 1943 assault guns had proved to be highly effective tank destroyers, particularly the up-gunned version which was armed with the long 75mm 40L/48 gun. The addition of 5mm (0.19in) thick armour plates to protect the tracks and wheels gave these vehicles a rather boxlike appearance.

Finally, Citadel saw the first widespread use of tank destroyers and self-propelled guns based on different panzer chassis. These vehicles included the "Grizzly Bear" (*Brummbär*), which was a Panzer IV chassis with a heavily armoured superstructure that protected a short-barrelled 150mm howitzer. Produced to destroy fortifications, this self-propelled gun served with Panzer Battalion 216 as a part of the Ninth Army. Another adaptation of the Panzer IV chassis was the "Rhinoceros" (*Nashorn*), a tank hunter/destroyer with a similar boxy appearance to the Grizzly Bear. The Rhino's main armament was the 88mm gun, a more than adequate weapon when faced with T-34s. The Rhino was earlier known as the "Hornet" (*Hornisse*). The Panzer IV chassis was also used for the "Bumble Bee" (*Hummel*), a self-propelled gun that carried a long-barrelled 150mm howitzer in an open-topped armoured body. The Bumble Bee was employed as mobile artillery support for the 20th and other panzer divisions.

The obsolete Czech-made Panzer 38(t) chassis was given a new lease of life as the basis for the "Wasp" (*Wespe*) self-propelled 105mm light howitzer, another piece of artillery support for the tanks. Neither was the chassis of the Panzer II ignored. A long 75mm antitank gun was mounted in a simple body and another effective tank hunter/destroyer was available to the *Wehrmacht*. It was known as the "Marten" (*Marder* II).

Greater production, repair and refurbishment increased most panzer divisions' strength to approximately 100–130 tanks each by June 1943. But there had been a change in the priorities of allocation. The campaign in Russia had demonstrated the courage, skill and fighting efficiency of the Waffen-SS, Nazi Germany's "Imperial Guard". The rewards for the Waffen-SS came during 1942 when Hitler ordered that they receive the latest equipment, from tanks and assault guns to armoured troop carriers. In the teeth of *Wehrmacht* opposition, the three original Waffen-SS divisions, *Leibstandarte Adolf Hitler*, *Das Reich* and *Totenkopf*, although officially designated panzergrenadier divisions, were increasingly equipped and used as panzer formations.

Luftwaffe support

A little over two-thirds of the aircraft available on the Eastern Front, some 1800 machines, were scheduled for use in the Citadel operation. In order to allow the increasingly vulnerable Stuka to carry out its classic dive-bomber role unimpeded by the Red Air Force, large numbers of Messerschmitt Bf 109 G-6s and Focke-Wulf Fw 190 A-5s were assigned to provide fighter cover. In terms of expertise and the quality of its machines, the *Luftwaffe* still maintained an edge, even though the Soviets had achieved numerical and qualitative parity at least. Operation Citadel was supported by two *Luftflotte* (air fleets), one operating in support of the northern pincer, one in support of the southern pincer.

The *Luftwaffe* was to deploy – for the first time in large numbers – the Henschel Hs 129 B-2R2 antitank aircraft. This machine was the first purpose-built German "tank buster". The Hs 129 carried an impressive array of weapons, including two 7.92mm machine guns and two 20mm cannon in the nose, but the main armament was a 30mm cannon mounted in a gondola under the cockpit. German ground-attack units (*Schlachtsgeschwader*) also used the Focke-Wulf Fw 190 carrying anti-personnel fragmentation bombs, in addition to their wing-mounted 20mm cannons and machine guns.

► A StuG III coated with *Zimmerit* anti-magnetic paste and protected by armoured side skirts. *Zimmerit* was first used in mid-1943 to defeat the Soviet tactic of sticking magnetic mines to the vertical surfaces of panzers. It worked by putting a barrier between the mine and the tank's surface.

The bomber force utilized the tried and trusted Heinkel He III and Junkers Ju 88, as well as small numbers of the long-range Heinkel He 177. Some bombing of Soviet positions was carried out prior to the opening of Citadel, as were several raids on tank production facilities beyond the Ural Mountains. However, the pre-offensive *Luftwaffe* effort was not impressive. In part this was due to a shortage of aviation fuel that was being conserved for the major ground-support operations.

As well as carrying out their dive-bombing role, many Stukas had been armed with two underwing, pod-mounted 37mm cannons which, when used against the more vulnerable areas of Soviet armour such as the engine compartment, could destroy their target with relative ease. But whatever the achievements of the tank and aircraft units might be, the *Wehrmacht* still had to contend with the formidable Soviet infantry, and it was to be the *Landser*, the German infantryman, who would pick up this challenge.

▲ Waffen-SS troops on board Panzer IIIs. By July 1943 II SS Panzer Corps had been built into a powerful formation. The three divisions of the corps – *Leibstandarte, Totenkopf* and *Das Reich* – fielded a total of 390 tanks and 104 assault guns.

German infantry divisions had been restructured during the course of 1942. The new organization led to a reduction in strength that was not compensated for by increased firepower. The infantry divisions were cut from nine to six rifle battalions and the artillery component by a quarter. The effective strength was thus between 6000–8000 men. From the early days of Barbarossa, it had become common practice for many Axis units on the Eastern Front to enlist former members of the Red Army in non-combatant roles such as cooks and labourers. Collectively known as *Hiwis* (helpers) these men, technically deserters, were under no illusions as to their fate and that of their families should they be recaptured or the Soviet Union prove victorious. Therefore it was in their interest that Germany prevail. Aside from the Cossacks and other nationalist combat formations, there are numerous instances of *Hiwis* being armed and fighting alongside the Germans. However, it is unclear if *Hiwis* fought during Operation Citadel.

Provision of antitank guns was poor. Although many infantry divisions had been issued with a small number of the effective 75mm guns, the main weapon was still the 37mm model, which was of little or no use against the T-34. Operation Citadel was notable for the introduction of the *Panzerfaust*, a highly potent antitank weapon. Between 1943 and 1945, thousands of these weapons were produced and used with great effect, proving deadly in the hands of an experienced operator.

Manpower, following the loss of over 200,000 troops as a result of the Stalingrad débâcle, was at a premium. On 13 January 1943, Hitler had issued an order, "On general mobilization of men and women for the defence of the Reich", which extended total mobilization to all men between 16 and 45 and all women between 17 and 45. The number of reserved occupations was reduced and men within the age-range were drafted into the armed forces, being replaced by older folk or labour from other sources. By 30 May 1943 these efforts had increased the strength of Germany's armed forces to 9.5 million, their highest of the war.

Theoretically a 1943 panzer division had 130–180 tanks, organized into a two- or three-battalion tank regiment, a panzergrenadier brigade, an artillery regiment and divisional support units. However, practice did not match theory, certainly in the case of the *Wehrmacht* panzer divisions, which were lucky if they counted 100 tanks on their establishment. The condition of the Waffen-SS formations was rather better. The three units that formed II SS Panzer Corps were very well provided for, as was the élite *Grossdeutschland* Panzergrenadier Division of the *Wehrmacht*.

The unit returns for 5 July 1943 noted the Waffen-SS divisions averaged 130 tanks and 35 assault guns each, with *Grossdeutschland* weighing in with 160 tanks and 35 assault guns. Each of these divisions was provided with a "heavy" tank

▼ The *Hummel* self-propelled howitzer first entered service in March 1943. Some 100 were in service by the time of Citadel, in the heavy self-propelled howitzer batteries in the panzer divisions. Each *Hummel* carried only 18 rounds of ammunition, and so special *Hummel* ammunition carriers were built.

company of 14 Tigers; the remaining Tigers were issued to specialist Heavy Tank Battalions allocated at army or corps level and used where and when the necessity arose. *Grossdeutschland*'s 1st Tank Battalion was equipped with Panthers, as were two other army battalions that combined to form the 10th Panzer Brigade. The Waffen-SS divisions operated small numbers of Panthers.

Some 533 assault guns were made available for Citadel. Many were integrated into the panzer divisions, but the majority went into separate assault gun brigades of, on average, 30 vehicles. However, as OKH was very well aware, it was not simply a matter of quality or quantity of tanks and aircraft but the methods which they employed that would determine the battle's outcome.

▲ The *Marder* III self-propelled antitank gun comprised the 75mm Pak 40/3 gun mounted on a Panzer 38(t) chassis. From May 1943 onwards they were deployed to the antitank detachments of both infantry and panzer divisions. Production of the *Marder* III began in February 1943 and ended in May 1944.

With the introduction of new models such as the Tiger and the Panther, it looked – certainly at least when outlined on paper – that once again German tactics would prevail, even in the face of a more numerous enemy. Consequently, the basic application of *Blitzkrieg* methods would, with slight modifications, again be used during Operation Citadel.

The tactics that had proved so successful throughout four years of war had depended on bombing, artillery bombardment and a powerful attack by tanks against a specific point of the enemy's line. Once a breach was made the tanks and motorized infantry would drive on, regardless of danger to their flanks, to keep the foe off-balance and preceded by Stukas acting as flying artillery support until the objective was reached. The changes made for Operation Citadel were mainly to do with using the Tigers in their role of breakthrough tanks at the point of an armoured wedge (*Panzerkeil*), but care was to be taken that the wedge did not disregard its flanks or advance

▲ The *Wespe* was a light self-propelled gun armed with a 105mm field howitzer. Its task was to provide mobile formations with indirect artillery support. *Wespes* operated behind the front and avoided engagements, though they carried armour-piercing shells in case of an encounter with enemy tanks.

▼ The *Sturmpanzer* IV (*Brummbär*) assault infantry gun was armed with a 150mm gun. It was very effective against dug-in infantry positions, buildings and strongholds. The first *Brummbär*s were issued to *Sturmpanzer Abteilung* (Battalion) 216 just before Kursk.

▲ **A Heinkel He 111 medium bomber photographed in the skies over Orel in 1943. This twin-engined aircraft was used extensively at Kursk, but by mid-1943 was obsolete. It was very vulnerable to enemy fighters when lacking an escort.**

▼ **The Focke-Wulf Fw 190 A-5 was an excellent fighter. It had superb manoeuvrability, good speed, and its range and endurance were markedly superior to the Bf 109. In addition, visibility with the full-view canopy was also exceptional for the pilot.**

too far beyond infantry and artillery support. The flanks of the wedge would be Panzer IVs supported by Panzer IIIs. Panzergrenadiers, mounted in armoured personnel carriers, would be in close support with mortars and light artillery. The wedge was intended to bludgeon its way through the Soviet defensive zones supported by selective air strikes and artillery barrages. Orders were issued to tank commanders that immobilized vehicles were to be left behind; these would then act as fire support for the mobile elements and await recovery after the offensive had rolled forward. The need to maintain the impetus was essential to the success of the operation. Interestingly, the tactics adopted by Colonel-General Walter Model, commander of the Ninth Army, and Manstein differed from one another. To the north of the salient Model wished to conserve his tanks to exploit, not create, a breakthrough. This is unsurprising as his reputation was founded on his skill as a defensive general. Manstein, at the south of the salient, was determined to use the juggernaut of the wedge from the outset. In the environment of Operation Citadel, Model was more keenly aware of the formidable strength of the Red Army's defensive system. Furthermore, STAVKA had devoted marginally more to the defences of its northern flank as it had anticipated that it would have to bear the brunt of the German onslaught there.

▲ The Junkers Ju 87 G-2. Nicknamed the "tank cracker" (*Panzerknacker*) or "cannon bird" (*Kanaonenvogel*), it was armed with a pair of underwing Flak 18 37mm guns, with 12 rounds of ammunition per gun. The 37mm guns proved capable of destroying all but the heaviest Soviet tanks with their tungsten-cored rounds.

The process of assembling the large number of tanks required for Operation Citadel led to its

▲ **The Heinkel He 177 *Greif* was a long-range bomber that had a poor combat record. The aircraft was overweight, had structural weaknesses and frequently suffered from engine fires. Around 20 were used during the Stalingrad relief operation.**

opening being postponed several times. Five armies were allocated to Citadel under the authority of Army Group Centre (Kluge) and Army Group South (Manstein).

Army Group Centre

The offensive on the northern shoulder of the salient was to be carried out by the Ninth Army, under the command of Colonel-General Model.

Model's forces numbered some 335,000 men, and these men formed 21 German and 3 Hungarian divisions. The Hungarian divisions were used for anti-partisan and security duties and therefore were not regarded as part of the offensive force. Of the 21 German divisions, six – the 2nd, 4th, 9th, 12th, 18th and 20th – were panzer formations, the 10th Panzergrenadier Division and 14 infantry divisions completing the line-up. The divisions were allocated to army corps for the purpose of higher command.

XLVII Corps
2nd, 9th and 20th Panzer Divisions, 6th Infantry Division, and 21st Panzer Brigade. The armoured divisions of this corps were equipped with Panzer IIIs and IVs and StuG IIIs, but the 21st Brigade had 3 Tiger companies in the 505th Panzer Detachment with 45 Tigers and 15 Panzer IIIs, and the 909th Assault Gun Detachment, which was equipped with a total of 36 vehicles.

XLVI Corps
This comprised the 4th and 12th Panzer Divisions, as well as the 10th Panzergrenadier Division with a total of 184 tanks. At the outset of Citadel, this corps was held in reserve.

XLI Corps
This comprised the 18th Panzer Division, as well as the 86th and 292nd Infantry Divisions. It also comprised the 653rd and 654th Heavy Tank Destroyer detachments, recently formed and equipped with the entire production run, to date, of Porsche *Ferdinands* and a small number of Panzer IVs. Additional firepower was provided by the StuG IIIs of the 177th and 244th Assault Gun Brigades, and the 66 Grizzly Bears of 216th Panzer Battalion.

XX Corps
To the west; it consisted of four infantry divisions.

XXIII Corps
To the east; it consisted of three and one-third infantry divisions.

▼ The Junkers Ju 88 was one of the most versatile aircraft of World War II. It began as a dive-bomber and reconnaissance aircraft, and was later used as a torpedo-bomber, night fighter, day fighter and antitank aircraft. A total of 10,774 were built, including 104 prototypes and experimental versions.

In total the Ninth Army fielded 590 tanks and 424 assault guns.

The forces that connected Army Group South and Army Group Centre consisted of eight infantry divisions, three antitank detachments, four security divisions and the 8th SS Cavalry Division *Florian Geyer*. All these units were short of heavy weapons, armoured fighting vehicles and antitank weapons. However, these formations, collectively known as Second Army, were to remain on the defensive throughout Citadel under the command of Colonel-General Walter Weiss.

Army Group South

On the southern shoulder was an altogether more powerful German force. Fourth Panzer Army, commanded by Colonel-General Hermann Hoth, and Army Detachment Kempf, commanded by General Walter Kempf, constituted the main striking power. The strength of Manstein's command was nearly 350,000 men, 1269 tanks and 245 assault guns, and these huge numbers excluded the reserves.

LII Corps, on the left, consisted of three infantry divisions, which would assume a mainly defensive posture.

▲ A battery of *Hummels* in a rear assembly area prior to Operation Citadel. As can be seen, crews of these tanks travelled in open-topped, high-silhouette compartments with all their weather-related disadvantages.

XLVIII Panzer Corps, in the centre, comprised the 3rd and 11th Panzer Divisions, the 167th Infantry Division, and the *Grossdeutschland* Panzergrenadier Division, which included the 200 Panthers of the 10th Panzer Brigade; in all some 535 tanks and 66 assault guns.

II SS Panzer Corps, to the south, was made up of the three SS Panzergrenadier Divisions – *Leibstandarte*, *Das Reich* and *Totenkopf* – with 390 tanks and 104 assault guns, including 42 of Army Group South's 102 Tigers.

Army Detachment Kempf was tasked with guarding the right flank of the Fourth Panzer Army, and consisted of three army corps.

III Panzer Corps

This was made up of the 6th, 7th, and 19th Panzer Divisions with 299 tanks; 228th Assault Gun Detachment with 25 StuG IIIs; and the 168th

▲ **A German machine-gun team scans enemy frontline positions. The weapon is a tripod-mounted MG 34, the standard German infantry squad machine gun of World War II. It fired between 800 and 900 rounds per minute.**

Infantry Division. The cutting edge of III Panzer Corps was the 503rd Panzer Detachment which numbered 45 Tigers.

XI Corps (Corps *Rauss*)
This corps consisted of the 106th and 320th Infantry Divisions and the 905th and 393rd assault gun detachments with 25 StuG IIIs each.

XLII Corps
The 39th, 161st and 282nd Infantry Divisions plus the Hornet-equipped 560th Heavy Panzer Destroyer Detachment with 40 tank destroyers, and Heavy Tank Destroyer Detachment C with approximately 40 assault guns.

In support of this mighty array was XXIV Panzer Corps, a force which included the 17th Panzer Division and the 5th SS Motorized Division *Wiking*, equipped with 112 tanks. Yet even with this formidable assembly of men and machines at his disposal, Hitler still had sufficient qualms about the success of Operation Citadel to declare, prior to the battle, that the very thought of what was to come "turned my stomach". Well it might, since the period before the opening shots were fired had not been wasted by the commanders of the Red Army.

► **By the end of June 1943 *Wehrmacht* forces around the Kursk salient were in a high state of readiness. Morale and equipment levels were strong among the infantry and panzer divisions, as were expectations of victory. But the troops did not realize the depth of the Soviet defences they were facing.**

Soviet Preparations

Hundreds of thousands of civilian workers were drafted to work on the Soviet defences in the Kursk salient, where they constructed trenches, antitank ditches and other field fortifications to turn the area into a vast killing ground.

The victory at Stalingrad shattered the myth of the *Wehrmacht*'s invincibility and imbued the Red Army with a new-found sense of faith in its own capabilities: defeat no longer seemed inevitable. The morale of both the armed forces and the Russian people had been given a huge fillip. Slowly at first, but with gathering momentum, the Soviet propaganda machinery churned out less Communist Party exhortations and more appeals to Russian patriotism, love of the *Rodina* (motherland) and family. To further reinforce the sense of patriotism and fighting for Russia, the Red Army reintroduced traditional Russian items of uniform and insignia, discredited since the years of revolution and civil war, namely the peasant style shirt – the *gymnastiorka* – and the *pogoni,* or shoulder straps. The shoulder straps had been banned as symbols of counter-revolution and Tsarist oppression during 1918, and their rehabilitation was not greeted favourably by all. However, these changes were accepted, albeit with reservations in some quarters.

Although chastened by the success of the *Wehrmacht* in recapturing Kharkov and stabilizing the front of Army Group South, Stalin and some

▼ A mainly female working party labours to repair a railway line near the station at Ashkoljava. During the *rasputitsa,* the muddy season that followed the thaw, the railways proved the most effective method of transportation.

Nagant Model 1930 7.62mm piece, this formidable fighter is typical of the thousands of partisans operating behind the German lines in central Russia. Great numbers of Axis troops were tied down in an attempt to contain the activities of the highly organized partisan formations during the build-up to Operation Citadel.

of his more optimistic senior officers, such as Army General N.F. Vatutin (commander of the Voronezh Front), wanted to resume the offensive to pre-empt any further German activity. However, the more restrained arguments of Marshal of the Soviet Union G.K. Zhukov, Deputy Supreme Commander and second only to Stalin himself, as well as others, won the day. The Red Army halted and began to consolidate its positions and assess the situation.

One look at the map would draw the observer's eye to the most prominent feature on the Eastern Front, the vast salient that bit into the Axis line south of Orel and north of Kharkov, both occupied by the Germans, with its centre the Russian-held city of Kursk. All three cities were important railway junctions, and railways were the mainstay of the transport infrastructure in the Soviet Union; without them it would be impossible to wage a victorious campaign, whatever the season. With the ending of serious operations by the Red Army in late March, the Soviet formations that held the perimeter of the Kursk salient were, from north to south, as follows: above Orel lay the Western Front (Colonel-General V.D. Sokolovsky), facing Orel the Briansk Front (Colonel -General M.M. Popov). The northern flank of the salient was held by the Central Front (Colonel-General K.K. Rokossovsky) and the southern flank by the Voronezh Front (Army General N.F. Vatutin). The head of the salient was defended by formations of both Central and Voronezh Fronts. To the south of the salient was South-Western Front (Colonel-General R.I. Malinovsky).

Intelligence reports poured in to Moscow, and these indicated very clearly that the Germans were planning to launch a powerful offensive aimed at the Kursk salient. The source of these reports was either the Red Army, the Red Air Force or partisan groups operating behind the Axis lines. Further evidence was provided for Stalin by the Soviet spy, the so-called "Lucy" operating from neutral Switzerland, who had access to the discussions of

▼ The Red Air Force in the Kursk area was built up massively in an effort to deprive the *Wehrmacht* of the air cover essential to its operations. Here, Lavochkin La 5 fighters are being moved by rail. Interestingly, their only protection seems to be from the weather as no camouflage is in evidence.

the German High Command (OKW) through anti-Nazi elements. As a result of "Lucy's" activities Stalin was appraised of the contents of Hitler's Operation Order 6, the Citadel order. The British Military Mission in Moscow also provided information regarding the German's offensive intentions culled from the monitoring of *Luftwaffe* radio transmissions and decoded using the captured Enigma machine at Bletchley Park in England.

With these reports of the *Wehrmacht* assembling large forces – particularly to the north of the salient – in mind, Stalin ordered his Front commanders and advisers to prepare their own analyses of German intentions. Furthermore, during the first week of April, orders were issued to intensify Soviet intelligence-gathering operations from both in front of and behind the German lines. The behind-the-lines operations were coordinated by the office of the Central Partisan HQ in Moscow.

▲ The Eastern Front on the eve of the Battle of Kursk. By destroying Red Army forces around Kursk, Hitler believed he could forestall any future Soviet offensives and win a much-needed victory in the East.

STAVKA's intelligence

Strategic assessment reports from members of STAVKA demonstrate a remarkably accurate picture of German intentions: a pincer movement from north and south that would amputate the Kursk salient and destroy the Soviet forces trapped inside, thus shortening the German line by some 250km (160 miles). Almost all were agreed that the German offensive would begin during the early days of May. However, the Kursk salient was such an inviting target that it was almost too obvious. Consequently, in order to avoid being caught unawares by activity elsewhere, STAVKA carefully monitored Axis movements along the entirety of the Eastern Front. The weight of evidence was such that Stalin agreed to the Red Army adopting a defensive stance to await the forthcoming attack.

Zhukov's report to Stalin on 8 April contained the following words:

"I consider that it would be pointless for our forces to go over to the offensive in the near future in order to pre-empt the enemy. It would be better for us to wear out the enemy on our defences, to smash his tanks and then by introducing fresh reserves and going over to a general offensive to beat the main enemy force once and for all."

On 12 April the decision was taken that Kursk was to be defended from the outset and in so much depth that it would be virtually impregnable. In the words of Major-General S.M. Shtemenko, First Deputy of the General Staff's Operational Directorate, written after the momentous events of 1943:

"Ultimately it was decided to concentrate our main forces in the Kursk area, to bleed the enemy forces here in a defensive operation, and then to switch to the offensive and achieve their full destruction. To provide against eventualities, it was considered necessary to build deep and secure defences along the whole strategic front, making them particularly powerful in the Kursk area."

On 21 April, in an order to all fronts concerned, which was signed by Stalin, STAVKA instructed them to:

1. Establish a frontal zone ... and, by the 10th of May of this year complete the evacuation of the entire civilian population to the rear beyond the bounds of a 25km [15.5 miles] zone from the formerly occupied frontlines ...

▲ **The officer addressing the civilian labourers is Lieutenant Krenitz. Motivational speeches on the need to construct the defensive belts were frequently given by combat troops to emphasize the urgency of the task and to foster a bond of solidarity between soldiers and civilians.**

Establish the rear boundary of the frontal zone.

2. Immediately set about constructing two (to) three military defensive lines, following one after another, in the frontal zone and accommodate all population points in this zone for defence.

Prepare all towns and population points in the frontal zone from which the civilian population must have been evacuated for defence irrespective of their distance from the frontlines ...

3. Immediately report fulfilment of this directive.

The defensive belts of trenches and other earthworks that were to be constructed to absorb the German attack were remarkable for their sheer size. It was on these fortifications as much as the tanks, aircraft and guns that the success or failure of the Red Army would rest. A major part of the provision for Shtemenko's "eventualities" was the creation, on 15 April, of a large strategic reserve (known initially as Steppe Military District) and commanded by Colonel-General I.S. Konev.

On 23 April Konev received his instructions:

1. During the period of its formulation, simultaneous with its missions of combat training, Steppe Military District forces are assigned the following missions.

a. In the event the enemy assumes the offensive before the District's forces are ready, care must be taken to cover firmly the following axes ...

In accordance with the force grouping the commander of district forces will organize careful study by unit and formation commanders and their staffs of these axes and the capabilities for developing positions.

b. Undertake, study and prepare to defend a line along the left bank of the Don River from Voeikovo, through Lebedan', Zadorsk, Voronezh, Liski and Pavlovsk to Bochugar. The line must be ready by 15 June 1943.

c. Carry out reconnaissance of a defensive line along the line of the Efremov ... to the Northern Donets River to determine the state of defensive installations along it ... and to select that line correctly.

▲ **An unidentified unit of women marches to a position near Kursk itself. Female soldiers were not new in Russia. During World War I several battalions of women were formed and this practice was continued, albeit on a larger scale, during World War II. Many women were employed as snipers and tank drivers and saw widespread combat.**

2. Forces, HQ and commanders will prepare mainly for offensive battle and operations, for penetrating enemy defensive zones as well as executing powerful counterstrokes with our forces, for rapidly fortifying positions which we have captured, for repelling enemy counterstrokes, for countering massive tank and air strikes and for night operations.

Thus was Steppe Military District instructed to cover all potential lines of German attack for Operation Citadel. It was also to provide the main line of defence should the Germans break through and threaten to encircle the Soviet forces in the salient and feed in reserves as necessary during the coming offensive.

The Soviet fronts that were expecting to bear the brunt of German fury were Voronezh, Central, South-Western and Briansk, and they too planned to build up their defences in such depth that the panzers would be a spent force before reaching open country. Once Stalin and STAVKA had decided on an initial defensive stance it was a question of how long they had to prepare their defences before the *Wehrmacht*'s onslaught began. With the consensus of opinion being a May deadline, it was imperative that work began immediately. Any time beyond the supposed deadline would be a bonus that could only work in the favour of the Soviets.

The Red Army

The ghastly losses that the Russians had suffered between 1941 and 1942 had taught costly lessons from which they learnt and went on to profit during 1943. The purges of the 1930s had created a mentality amongst the officer corps that abhorred flexibility of thinking and tactical creativity. It was these attributes that in part contributed to the slaughter of men and the destruction of vast quantities of equipment during the first 18 months of the war in the East; initiative was not a quality that Stalin encouraged in his subordinates. Stalin, though possessed of almost limitless powers of life and death in both the military and civilian domains, was a realist if only as a result of the

▲ Infantry reinforcements, many armed with the legendary PPSh ("Pee Pee Sha") submachine gun, make their way to positions "somewhere in the Kursk salient." The T-34/76 model 1942 nearest to the camera bears the legend "For the Motherland" and would appear to have recently arrived from the factory.

military reverses the Soviet Union had endured. Unlike Hitler, Stalin was prepared to listen and, more and more as success bred success, take the advice of his senior commanders as to the conduct of the war. The blunt approach of men like Zhukov and Lieutenant-General P.A. Rotmistrov (commander of the Fifth Guards Tank Army) who dared to place reality in Stalin's lap, had its own rewards with the successes at Moscow in 1941 and Stalingrad in 1942. That the operations which followed in the wake of these achievements were not as successful as their overly ambitious planners had hoped led in turn to analysis of their shortcomings. Such consideration was to bear fruit at Kursk. However, the analysis of defeat and victory can be of little value without the men and machines to fight, and it was numerically, in the latter particularly, that the Russians were beginning to gain the upper hand.

Driven by philosophy and pragmatism, Russian tank design was consolidated into the refinement of a limited number of proven vehicles. Of all the different tanks employed by the Red Army the T-34 medium tank and the KV-1 heavy tank were clearly superior to anything fielded by the Axis between 1941 and 1942. Thanks to the foresight of its designers the T-34 was, with minor modifications but significant up-gunning, to remain virtually unchanged throughout the war. The result of this concentration on one main vehicle was that a massive increase in tank production took place. Indeed, despite the cruel losses in 1941, the number of Russian tanks, of all available types, rose from 7700 in January 1942 to 20,600 in early 1943. The cornerstone of the Russian tank armada was the T-34 armed with a

▼ To increase their mobility and the scope of their operations, many partisan formations "saddled up". In an attempt to curb these horsemen the Germans committed the 8th SS Cavalry Division *Florian Geyer* which had been commanded by Hermann Fegelein, the brother-in-law of Hitler's mistress, Eva Braun.

▲ **Pictured here are two of the 1386 Lend-Lease M3A5 Lee tanks provided by the USA. Inadequate in performance, armour and weaponry, these tanks gained a poor reputation with their Russian crews. The distribution of these machines during Operation Citadel has been difficult to analyze.**

76.2mm gun and two 7.62mm machine guns. With its sloping front and side armour – 45mm (1.75in) and 60mm (2.3in) respectively – and a top speed of 55km/h (31mph), the T-34 provided very effective protection for its four-man crew, as well as a relatively stable gun platform.

Conversely the KV-1, although heavily armoured and carrying the 76.2mm gun, was relegated to an infantry support role. Thought was given to ending the production of the KV-1 in favour of the T-34 in late 1942, but the idea was shelved. Again, during 1942, time was given to considering a combination of the best features of the T-34 and the KV-1. However, with the appearance of the Tiger at the end of 1942 this plan was promptly cancelled. The KV-1 was not popular with Soviet tankers (tank crews) due to its lack of mobility, poor obstacle-crossing capabilities and its weight: at 44.7 tonnes (44 tons) it had a tendency to destroy bridges as it rolled over them. Furthermore, the KV-1was felt to provide little return in terms of firepower to compensate for its many shortcomings.

The chassis of the KV-1 was adapted for use with the 152mm gun-howitzer, which it was hoped would prove powerful enough to take on the Tiger's 88mm gun and thick armour at long range. From design to production took a mere 25 days during January 1943, and the SU-152 (*samokhadnaia ustanovka* – mechanized mounting) was born. By May 1943 the first four tank destroyer units were issued with 12 SU-152s each. The Russian troops' nickname for this vehicle, following the Kursk battles, was *Zveroboi* (animal hunter) because of its success in action against Tigers, Panthers and Elephants. The Germans nicknamed the SU-152 the *Dosenoffer* (can opener), as one hit from its gun could take the turret off a Tiger. Its 60mm (2.5in) of armour plating proved too strong for the majority of German antitank weapons.

The futility of producing light tanks such as the T-60 and the slightly improved T-70 had been recognized towards the end of 1942. Lend-Lease types produced by Britain and the USA, particularly the Anglo–Canadian Valentine, adequately filled their role as reconnaissance vehicles. The industrial capacity released was given over to producing the Red Army's first assault gun, the SU-76M, which married the 76.2mm ZiS-3 divisional gun to the T-70 chassis in a simple, thickly armoured superstructure. Initially these vehicles were unpopular with the tankers who derisively named them "crippled tanks". However, events were to prove the efficacy of this marriage as the SU-76 proved its capabilities as an antitank weapon, as well as an infantry support piece.

Lend-Lease vehicles were viewed as a mixed blessing by the Soviet troops who were issued with them. On the one hand, the tens of thousands of American lorries such as the Studebaker and Chevrolet and the Willys Jeep ensured the Red Army's mobility as well as freeing up production lines. By mid-1943 over 100,000 soft-skinned vehicles had been supplied to the USSR by the USA alone. On the other hand, tanks such as the Churchill Mark 3 and the M3 Lee had acquired a poor reputation with Russian tank men. Indeed, such was their dread of the American M3 that it was ghoulishly nicknamed "the grave for seven brothers" or "the field crematorium". Nevertheless, in 1943 some 20 percent of Soviet tank brigades were using Lend-Lease machines and over 10 percent were equipped entirely with them.

Assault guns and tank destroyers were being produced, though not in such quantities as tanks. The first such Russian vehicle was the massive, slab-sided KV-2 produced from 1940 that weighed in at 52.8 tonnes (52 tons). Built on a standard KV chassis, the KV-2 was basically a monstrous turret that gave it an overall height of 3m (11ft), carrying either a 122mm or 152mm gun that was intended to give fire support for infantry or armoured formations. The abysmal combat record of this dinosaur was such that production ended, with little regret, in 1941. At approximately the same time as the SU-152 was introduced, production began of the SU-122 which mounted a short-barrelled 122mm howitzer on a T-34 chassis.

▼ Another British vehicle, in this instance the Universal Carrier, was used in the reconnaissance role. Armed with an antitank rifle and open-topped, the value of such machines in a combat situation would have been marginal. The troops pictured here are involved in surveying potential sites for antitank defences.

▲ **Soviet KV-1 heavy tanks. At the beginning of the war against Germany the Red Army possessed 639 KV-1s. Armed with a 76.2mm main gun, the KV-1 could knock out all but the heaviest German tanks. However, because of mechanical problems, it was unreliable.**

▼ **The Soviet 45mm antitank gun Model 1942. Each Red Army rifle regiment in a rifle division had an antitank battery equipped with six 45mm guns. Its armour-penetration was only adequate at best, though it remained in service for the rest of the war.**

▲ **Freshly dug mounds of soil, bare bushes and trees suggest that these mortar emplacements were being prepared during the spring of 1943. The mortars are the 82mm Model 1941. Two men moved these weapons on a two-wheeled carriage similar to a modern golf trolley; the wheels are just visible. The barrel is protected from the elements by a dust cap.**

The superstructure was boxlike in shape but with the advantage of a smoothly sloped front-plate which caused shells to bounce off. This design was to remain a feature of such Soviet vehicles. Again the dual role of infantry support and antitank fire was envisaged, but its performance in the latter role was marred by the antitank round proving to be lacklustre at best.

The tank units of 1942 had undergone reorganization during the early months of 1943. On 28 January 1943 the State Defence Committee, the ultimate military authority, issued Decree 2791 ordering the creation of Tank Armies composed of units that had the same cross-country ability as one another to enable all vehicles to perform equally well in all terrain.

Theoretically a tank army was made up of two tank corps, one mechanized corps and supporting units, which gave a strength of 450–560 tanks and 48,000 men. In practice the composition of the five tank armies varied, often considerably, depending on the nature of their mission or the supply situation. The success of the long-range tank raids following the fall of Stalingrad had demonstrated how effective such forces could be in wrong-footing even the most experienced foe.

A tank corps consisted of three tank brigades, a motorized rifle brigade and various technical troops. Self-propelled guns were often included in their own units. Tank brigades numbered 53–65 tanks in 2 or 3 battalions, giving a tank corps 200–230 tanks.

The Soviets fielded their new self-propelled guns in a variety of configurations. The heavy self-propelled artillery regiments included 12 SU-152s, the medium regiments 16 SU-122s and 1 T-34 tank, the light regiments 21 SU-76s or 16 SU-85s and 1 T-34, and the older composite regiments 17

SU-76s and 8 SU-122s. The 152mm-equipped regiments were normally assigned to armies undertaking breakthrough operations and to selected tank armies. The 76mm and 85mm self-propelled gun regiments were assigned to tank corps and the composite (mixed calibre) regiments to mechanized corps. This system was not completely in place at the beginning of Operation Citadel.

Soviet artillery

Losses suffered by the Red Army during 1941 had led to the amalgamation of such specialist units as antiaircraft, antitank, infantry support tanks, engineer and field artillery simply to preserve them. Control of these formations was held at army level. The increased production of the weapons needed by these branches of service led to a similar expansion, in much the same proportions, as that of the tank forces. During the spring and early summer of 1943 antiaircraft, antitank and artillery penetration divisions were being formed. Such multi-battalion units could bring colossal firepower to bear in support of either attack or defence. Field artillery pieces such as the 76.2mm F22 and its successor from 1942, the 76.2mm ZiS-3, were fine weapons, as were the ML-20 152mm and the 122mm A-19, but the most devastatingly effective weapon on the Red Army's artillery register was the multiple rocket launcher, known to the Soviet troops as *Katyusha* (Katy) and to the Germans as "Stalin's Organ". The *Katyusha* was available in heavy and light versions, the M-30 and the M-13 respectively, and fired salvos which had a terrifying effect on enemy morale. The launch frames for the rockets were mounted on the backs of lightly armoured trucks and, like so much Soviet weaponry, were simple to produce and maintain but highly effective. The basic formation was eight rocket launchers.

Antitank guns were a weak area for the Red Army and it was not until the late summer of 1943 that antitank units began to receive supplies of the 57mm ZiS-2 antitank gun. Prior to that the main weapon was the 45mm gun of 1932 vintage which, although modified between 1942 and 1943, was a wholly inadequate piece. Great reliance was placed on the PTRD 14.5mm antitank rifle, which was capable of damaging the more thinly armoured, older German tanks. The Red Army employed specially trained dogs to run underneath tanks with packs of explosives strapped to their backs. The resulting inevitable explosion was usually fatal for both tank and dog.

Red Army infantry formations were known as "rifles" and a rifle division numbered, at full strength, a little over 9000 officers and men. The élite Guards rifle divisions were stronger, with an establishment of over 10,000 officers and men. Remarkably, the majority of rifle divisions in July 1943 stood at almost these levels. However, as the Soviet General Staff Study of the Kursk battles testifies, the strength of many formations had been made up by new recruits and trawling through the rear echelons and hospitals. The returns for the Voronezh Front are cited as an example:

"Thus 27 percent of the Voronezh Front's total requirement for replacements was satisfied by mobilization of those eligible for military service in liberated territory, 9 percent by return to duty of those who had recovered and were released from army and front hospitals, 33 percent by taking those fit for duty in rear units and installations and 31 percent by march replacements [those who had been called to the colours in the normal manner]." Aside from the military build-up, a huge army of civilians was mobilized to create the vast network of trenches, antitank ditches, bunkers and artillery positions. Operating under the guidance of army engineers, by the end of June 1943 there were some 300,000 civilians, mostly women and children, working feverishly on defence lines.

The defensive web that they created was truly awesome and based on minefields and antitank positions. A typical antitank strongpoint included an antitank company or battalion armed with antitank rifles, an engineer platoon with explosives, an antitank gun company with up to six guns and two or three tanks or self-propelled guns. The heavier German tanks were to be dealt with by carefully emplaced 85mm antiaircraft guns, with 122mm and 152mm howitzers providing rapid and heavy direct fire support. Furthermore, some strongpoints concealed dug-in T-34s exposing only their turrets. The troops manning these positions were given special training to deal with the new German tanks and would chant in unison the methods of destroying Tigers and their weak spots. As Nikita Khrushchev (at this time the Political

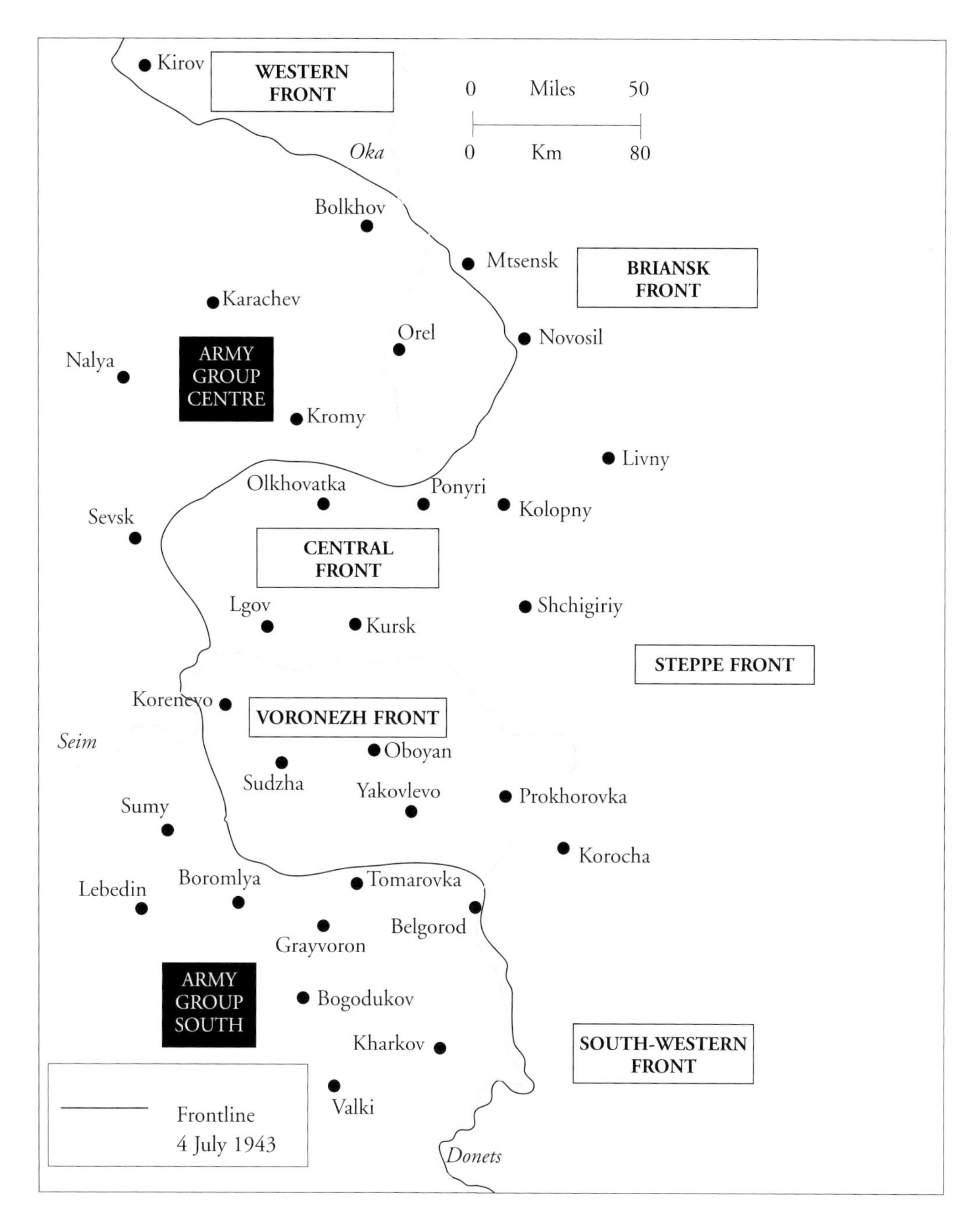

Commissar for the Voronezh Front) said, these facts would be as well-known as the Lord's Prayer had been in pre-communist days.

At points noted by the Soviet planners as particularly vulnerable, "Pakfronts" concealing up to a dozen antitank guns were dug to give concentrated fire against armour that had been channelled in their direction by the minefields.

▲ "Operation Citadel emerged as the most important in a series of limited offensives designed to consolidate the German defenses while inflicting sufficient damage on the Red Army to delay any Soviet offensive. Citadel in particular was expected to destroy two Soviet fronts while shortening the German defensive line by 120 kilometers." (David Glantz)

Three or four of these strongpoints were to co-operate and cover a single axis of approach and formed an antitank region. Rifle regiments constructed 3 or 4 such strongpoints, giving 9–12 for each division. Thousands of miles of trenches connected the strongpoints to give protection to riflemen, machine gunners and parties of engineers. It is appropriate to quote the figures for the Voronezh Front as noted in the Soviet study of the Kursk operations:

"On the Voronezh Front alone, from 1 April through 1 July, more than 4200 kilometres [2610 miles] of trenches, communications trenches, and ditches were dug ... and around 500 kilometres [310 miles] of antitank obstacles were constructed."

On the Voronezh and Central Fronts the results of these massive works was as follows:

▲ Music while you work! The civilian population was mobilized in huge numbers and generally employed in building defences in and around their homes. The vast majority of the labourers were women and young men not yet conscripted into the Red Army.

"During the three months [April–June] of preparation, three army defensive belts, three principal front defensive lines, and several intermediate and cut-off positions were established in the Central and Voronezh Fronts.

"Thus up to six defensive lines, successively echeloned into the depth, were created within the fronts along the assumed enemy attack axes [Maloarkhangel'sk and Schigry in the Central Front, and Belgorod and Oboyan in the Voronezh

Front]. The least-developed defensive system was at the junction of the Central and Voronezh Front, in the heights of the Kursk bulge [the Russian expression for the Kursk salient], where the distance between the army rear belt and the first front defensive line reached 60km [40 miles], while at the same time in other sectors of the bulge, the

▼ Dressed in their new 1943 uniforms, complete with the controversial throwback to the Tsarist officer corps shoulder boards, a group of officers from different branches of the Red Army listen intently to a Guards officer lecturing them on the complexities of the defensive belts on the Voronezh Front.

▲ Due to the repressive anti-partisan activities of the Axis forces, entire communities took to the countryside and joined in the widespread guerrilla warfare being waged. Armed with a variety of Soviet and captured weapons, the value of the partisans' contribution to the Red Army's success during the summer of 1943 has yet to be fully explored.

◀ The gathering of information was carried out ceaselessly. These Russian reconnaissance troops, dressed in their specialist camouflage suits, are bringing in a recently taken German prisoner. Missions were carried out to capture what the Russians termed "tongues", men captured with the specific purpose of being made to talk.

distance between defensive lines on average did not exceed 15–20km [12–17 miles]."

As much advantage as possible was taken of the terrain. The rivers Psel, Seim, Svapa, Northern Donets, Tim, Kshen' and Don were all incorporated into the defensive works, even though they were generally not very wide, little more than 130m (100yd) and up to only 3m (10ft) deep. The marshy nature of many of the river banks was another asset. The hilly ground on the northern shoulder of the salient reached heights of up to 290m (1000ft); the region was also sharply cut by a large number of ravines that reached depths of 40–70m (100–200ft), again valuable assets.

It was in the use of mines, both antipersonnel and antitank, that the Russians demonstrated a lethal flair. Hundreds of thousands of mines were carefully laid to channel tank attacks into artillery killing zones. Any ground that apparently offered some security would be mined, with devastating results for the foot soldiers who took shelter there. Similar traps were laid for tanks.

The figures for minefields are staggering. Up to 2400 antitank and 2700 antipersonnel mines were laid per mile in the Sixth Guards Army sector, which amounted to 69,688, and 64,340 mines in

▼ Partisans interrogating a German prisoner. This photograph is typical of the crudest type of Soviet propaganda. The "feel" of the image is wrong and it is very obviously posed. For example, the alleged prisoner is wearing his Iron Cross in the wrong place, and why are the men positioned on a slope?

its first line of defence alone. In the second and subsequent defence belts the density of mines fell off sharply, but the basic principle of channelling the advancing tanks was not ignored. On the Voronezh Front alone were laid 60,000 mines of all types. Interestingly, the Soviet analysts, following the battle, calculated that it took 350–400 mines to blow up one tank in the frontline, but only 120–150 in the rear areas. The discrepancy being due, apparently, to the fact that "mining during the process of withdrawal occurred along already designated axes, while along the forward edge a considerable proportion of the minefields were in sectors where no enemy tanks operated at all."

The length of the frontline was close to 450km (300 miles) but the depth was almost 190km (110 miles), dividing roughly into eight lines. Across the "neck" of the salient, the line to

▲ The dogs of war gather. One of the stranger antitank "weapons" that the Red Army experimented with was a specially trained dog, of no particular breed, which would run under an approaching German tank with an explosive charge strapped to its back. The explosion would disable the tank, easily penetrating the thin belly armour. The effect on the dog was predictable.

be held by Steppe Military District, lay another defensive belt with yet another running along the River Don to the north and south of Voronezh. Over 20,000 guns and mortars, 6000 antitank guns and hundreds of *Katyusha* rocket launchers were distributed throughout the Red Army's warren-like defences.

Attention was given to training the soldiers, of all branches of service, in the methods of defence that were to be used. This was an essential feature of Soviet preparations, given the large numbers of recently enrolled, raw and nervous troops. Infantry training took place every other day; alternate days were given over to construction work as they were for other branches of service, and was focused on "overcoming the soldiers' fear of tanks and on the ability to control antitank rifles, grenades and Molotov cocktails to perfection and boldly enter battle against enemy infantry following behind the tanks, isolate them from the tanks and destroy them."

In the meantime, the tankers were engaged in practising night marches, defensive fire, planned counterattack routes and "participated in exercises with rifle units". Sapper (combat engineer) forces trained newly formed detachments to lay and remove mines and mobile obstacles, all the while carrying out such work for real. Chemical warfare training was also given, with troops spending up to eight hours a day in gas masks.

As the anticipated date of the German attack approached, there were those in the higher echelons of the Soviet command who counselled for a pre-emptive attack. However, again the arguments of Zhukov prevailed and the defensive preparations continued. Hitler was not the only one who hoped that postponing the start date for Operation Citadel would enhance its chances of success. Every day the Red Army continued to

▼ A vital role undertaken by women soldiers was traffic control. This smartly clad traffic control officer stands in front of her sentry box which is decorated with a picture of Molotov, the Soviet Commissar for Foreign Affairs during World War II. The man is filling his cup with boiled water.

▲ **Dressed in a mixture of military and civilian dress, this group of female partisans relaxes for the camera. Even though they undertook the traditional female activities such as cooking, nursing the wounded and child care, the women were also expected to fight alongside the men when circumstances required. The weapons on show are the ubiquitous PPSh and Nagant pistols.**

▼ **The larger partisan formations were guided in their political thinking by a *Politruk* or political officer. The *Politruk* in this group is casually rolling a cigarette. The man on the right is armed with a German Mauser modified to take a box magazine; such field alterations were common amongst the partisans, some establishing underground workshops to carry out such work.**

pour men and materiel into the salient as quickly as possible. Nature itself lent a hand to the Russians by covering the spoil heaps and trench lines in fresh plant growth, thus aiding the Soviet efforts at *Maskirovka* (deception and camouflage), which included the establishment of hundreds of false gun positions complete with dummy (mock-up) guns. Again the Voronezh Front statistics for the huge *Maskirovka* preparations are interesting:

"Special engineer units carried out the following measures: prepared 883 prefabricated dummy tanks and 220 prefabricated dummy aircraft; organized three false tank concentration regions with 95 dummy tanks erected in them; and constructed 13 false airfields with dummy aircraft constructed in them."

Attrition was to be the order of the day as the Soviet defences absorbed the impetus of the German attack. The countryside over which the fighting was to take place was mainly grassy, undulating steppe with wheat and sunflower fields near the built-up areas. It was good tank country, if only the panzers could break through the defensive belts and take full advantage of it.

▲ Three generations of partisans: a bemedalled veteran of World War I, his daughter and granddaughter. During the months before the opening of the Kursk battles, Moscow would begin to take a firmer grip on partisan operations as the numbers and the usefulness of such forces became more apparent.

The Red Air Force

As with the ground forces, the Red Air Force had made significant progress in preparing for the Battle of Kursk. Large numbers of Ilyushin Il-2 *Shturmovik* armoured ground-attack aircraft were deployed, along with the Lavochkin La 5FN and Yakovlev Yak 9 fighters. However, although the numerically inferior *Luftwaffe* was hampered by a lack of fuel, as an airborne force it still retained an edge, primarily by virtue of its "Freya" radar system, but also through the outstanding skill of its pilots. However, the *Wehrmacht* could no longer take air superiority for granted over the Eastern Front, even though Red Air Force losses suffered at its hands were enormous.

The First Day

The Battle of Kursk began with the Germans making heavy and sustained assaults in the north and south. But commanders on the ground soon realized that the defences in front of them were much more formidable than they had expected.

During the weeks of May and June Soviet partisan activity to the rear of Army Group Centre had been stepped up, as had the efforts of the Red Air Force. Hundreds of locomotives and thousands of items of rolling stock had been destroyed or disabled. Axis attempts to control the partisans appear to have achieved little, other than alienate further an already restive population. The tension and foreboding aroused in the troops moving up to the front on increasingly insecure railway lines was in no way alleviated by their

▼ The empty shell cases scattered by the ammunition feeders holding the next rounds testify to the work of this 76.2mm antitank gun, nicknamed the *ratsch bumm* by the Germans on account of the noises it made on firing and impact respectively. These weapons were highly regarded by the *Wehrmacht*, which pressed many captured pieces into service, since they were capable of destroying the T-34 at a time when it was the scourge of their own inadequately equipped antitank units.

▲ StuG IIIs and Sd Kfz 251 armoured personnel carriers of the *Leibstandarte* Division advance on the first day of Kursk. Commanded by SS-Brigadeführer Theodor Wisch, *Leibstandarte* smashed through the positions of the 151st Guards Rifle Regiment.

▼ SS grenadiers, possibly of the *Totenkopf* Division, aboard a Panzer III. Paul Hausser's II SS Panzer Corps was very powerful, having a strength of 356 tanks and 95 assault guns and being supported by a *Nebelwerfer* multiple rocket launcher brigade.

going into action. They could only sit in their trenches and consider the task confronting them.

After several postponements, Hitler announced, on 25 June, that Operation Citadel would begin in the early hours of 5 July. On 4 July, on the eve of the attack, he issued his order of the day to be read out to his forces and then destroyed.

"Soldiers! Today you begin a great offensive whose outcome can have decisive significance for the war. Your victory must even more than before reinforce throughout the world the fact that, in the final analysis, it is useless to render any resistance whatsoever against the German Army ... Until now it was Russian tanks, first and foremost, which helped them to achieve some success. The colossal attack, which this morning will strike the Soviet armies, must shatter them to their very foundation. And you must know that everything depends on the success of this engagement."

The Russians had been warned by "Lucy" that the offensive would begin between 3 and 6 July but the time was not given. Rokossovsky and Vatutin immediately put their fronts on full alert. Instructions were issued to watch for any German activity, particularly mine-clearance operations. Now both sides could only sit and wait for the colossal events that were about to unfold. The Red Army men and their opponents could almost feel the tension in the hot summer air.

▲ Although the value of armoured trains had diminished with the advent of air power, they were still capable of delivering a useful weight of fire. Later models used obsolete tank turrets in the interests of standardization and ammunition supply.

The tension was particularly noticeable in the forward outposts located in front of the first line of Soviet defences. The troops manning these positions, referred to in the Red Army as "combat security points", would be the tripwire that alerted the Russians to the fact that the Germans were on the move; theirs would be the red-rimmed eyes that saw the Germans break cover, and move through the dust and haze, firing as they came. These outposts were not expected to do more than gain enough time for the main defences to wake up and man their guns, after which they would fall back should they survive the initial contact. The Russians were, by this point in the war, well aware of the methods employed by the Germans at the opening of an offensive, as they followed the

successful formula that had reaped such spectacular rewards during the early years of the war. The Soviet commanders were waiting for the Germans to drive in their outposts with small units, often the reconnaissance battalions, locating and clearing the minefields with engineers as they advanced. When contact with the first line of Soviet defences was made, the Germans would halt their advance and move the bulk of their attacking formations into their "jump-off" positions. Whilst these men and vehicles were taking their places, the German artillery would open fire. Happily for the Russians, the *Wehrmacht* did not deviate from its usual pattern.

On 4 July the Russians were presented with evidence that the attack was imminent. A Slovene deserter from a German engineer platoon informed

▲ The Red Army's rapid but highly effective response to the armour of the German Tiger: the SU-152. The "animal hunter", as the SU-152 was nicknamed, was simply an ML-20 152mm gun-howitzer mounted in a heavily armoured superstructure, on a KV-1 chassis. The aerial indicates a formation commander's vehicle, as the use of radio was still in its infancy in the Soviet tank force.

▼ German artillery near the frontline at Kursk. During the early hours of 5 July Red Army artillery shelled known German artillery positions, causing death and destruction to German gunners preparing to support their offensive.

▲ **With an expression that reflects both apprehension and determination, a Red Army man stands guard over the field gun he may soon be operating against the Germans as dawn breaks over the Kursk salient.**

his Soviet interrogators that his unit had been ordered to clear lanes through the minefields and barbed wire in front of their lines. Furthermore, they had been issued with vodka and rations for five days, while the opening of the offensive had been set for 03:00 hours on 5 July. This information related to the southern flank of the salient. Late on the afternoon of 4 July the Germans made the move that confirmed that the storm was about to break. Several battalions of XLVIII Panzer Corps, to the south of the salient, began a reconnaissance in force, moving against the outposts of the Soviet 52nd Guards Rifle Division on Vatutin's Voronezh Front.

The heavy fighting that the Germans became embroiled in was an ominous portent of what was to come. Although the grenadiers of the *Grossdeutschland*, 11th Panzer and 3rd Panzer Divisions had, by 21:00 hours, managed to push back the Russian outposts, the mission had not been an easy one. The next phase, XLVIII Panzer Corps' assembly, now took place. The *Grossdeutschland*'s fusilier and grenadier regiments were supported by the division's panzer regiment and the Panthers of 10th Panzer Brigade. To the left and right of *Grossdeutschland*, the 3rd and 11th Panzer Divisions, respectively, gathered as silently as armoured troops can.

At 01:15 hours II SS Panzer Corps began its reconnaissance-in-force and, a little less than two hours later, had achieved its objectives. Again the assembly of tanks and men took place; however, it was hampered by a violent thunderstorm, the torrential rain turning the area's famous "Black Earth" into a muddy soup which clogged the tracks and wheels of many vehicles.

The junction of XLVIII Panzer Corps and II SS Panzer Corps was covered by the 167th Infantry Division. On the *Leibstandarte*'s right flank lay the tanks of *Das Reich* and to their right was the third division of Hausser's SS Panzer Corps, the *Totenkopf* Panzergrenadier Division. Further to the south-east, German reconnaissance had little effect due to the Soviet positions following the eastern bank of the River Northern Donets. Unfortunately for the Germans, during the reconnaissance phase on III Panzer Corps' front, an infantryman from the 168th Infantry Division was captured and revealed that the main attack was scheduled for dawn on the morning of 5 July. Dawn comes early – 03:00–04:00 hours – in Russia during the summer. Vatutin was now convinced that the great moment was at hand. Marshal A.M. Vasilevsky, Chief of the Red Army General Staff and STAVKA representative on the southern flank of the salient, gave permission to Vatutin to begin his counterpreparations and informed Zhukov, his counterpart to the north, of the situation.

German preparations

To the north of the salient, Model had not been idle. Mine-clearance and reconnaissance operations had been under way all along the front of the Ninth Army for much of the evening of 4 July. However, during the course of that evening Soviet combat patrols had struck lucky and, having observed and engaged a party of engineers, took a prisoner. Any lingering doubts that the Russians may have harboured as to the timing of Operation Citadel were completely dispelled by the "tongue" of Lance-Corporal Bruno Fermello of the 6th Infantry Division, who claimed that the attack was to begin at 03:00 hours on 5 July 1943. Swiftly this intelligence was passed on to Zhukov, who immediately ordered Rokossovsky to begin a pre-emptive bombardment and then informed Stalin in Moscow that battle was about to be joined. Stalin had already spoken to Vasilevsky and approved Zhukov's decision requiring him to keep in regular contact.

The artillery of the Voronezh Front opened fire at 01:10 hours and that of Central Front at 02:20 hours. Stalin telephoned Zhukov shortly after 02:20 hours for an update. The targets were pre-planned, being known or suspected German assembly points and artillery positions. The fortunes of the Russian gunners were mixed but undoubtedly their efforts caused disruption. When informed of the Russian countermeasures, OKH responded by postponing the jump-off time by two and a half hours for Army Group Centre and three hours for Army Group South. So before the offensive proper had begun, the Germans had been

▼ The contrast between the simple technology of this windmill, unchanged for centuries, and the mechanized warfare raging within a few miles, is stark. Buildings such as this were very obvious observation points and inevitably drew fire from the enemy eager to deprive them of any vantage point.

forced to alter their plans by the Soviets; it was a pattern that was to be repeated many times during the following days, an ominous omen for Hitler and his generals.

In addition to their artillery's efforts, the Russians undertook a massive air strike with the aim of hitting the *Luftwaffe* aircraft on the ground immediately prior to take-off, when they would be fully fuelled and armed but totally vulnerable. Flying at heights of 2133–3048m (7000–10,000ft) in tightly maintained formations, due to the inadequacy of their night-flying capabilities, the Soviet bombers lunged towards the *Luftwaffe*'s airfields in the early hours of the morning. The operation was to be undertaken by the forces of the Second and Seventeenth Air Armies. A total of 417 aircraft took part.

However, thanks to the recent installation of the "Freya" radar system, the Germans were given just sufficient warning of the Red Air Force's approach and were able to scramble enough fighter cover to intercept the Russian bomber force before it could do much damage. The Soviets claimed to have destroyed or damaged 60 enemy aircraft as a

▲ On careful inspection, the depth of this antitank ditch becomes very clear when compared with the height of the man towards the top of the picture. The length of the grass provides ideal, natural camouflage, hiding the trench until the last possible moment. Such simple devices took their toll of the more careless German tank drivers.

▼ The crew of this ML-20 152mm gun is seen completing application forms to become members of the Communist Party. Family members of soldiers killed in battle were only informed of their loss if the soldier had been a party member. This fact encouraged the less idealistic troops to sign on the dotted line before going into action.

► The crews of these PBHM Model 1938 mortars await the order to open fire. The Red Army placed great emphasis on the use of mortars, regarding them as equal in importance to their "big brothers", the artillery. Their simplicity of manufacture, maintenance and operation, and mobility were clear assets in the close-support role.

result of these raids on the airfields south of the salient. German claims, for the southern area, amount to 432 for the first day. It seems, from the Soviet General Staff Study of the Kursk operations, that the Red Air Force over the Central Front did not become active until the *Luftwaffe* appeared:

"During this initial period of the defensive operation, however, our air operations had an episodic rather than a planned character." Laconic words, but the airmen's orders stated that they should "combat enemy aircraft as they appeared over our territory". The instructions were followed to the letter, if not the spirit.

Following this action there can have been little doubt at OKH that the Russians were well aware of German intentions and that perhaps their optimistic outlook was not justified. But by this stage it was simply too late to reappraise the situation; for better or worse, Operation Citadel would not be postponed again.

▲ Clearly extemporized and definitely optimistic use of both the PTRD (left) and the PTRS (right) antitank rifles in the antiaircraft role. What the likelihood was of success for these gunners in shooting down anything faster than an observation balloon would be difficult to imagine!

Following the cessation of the Soviet artillery strike, the German artillery preparation began at 04:30 hours. It was to last for 80 minutes and the targets were within the first 4km (2.5 miles) of the Russian defences. The Soviet artillery, using over 900 weapons of all types and calibres, followed 5 minutes later with counterbattery fire that lasted for 30 minutes. *Luftwaffe* strikes paralleled those of the artillery. The hideous cacophony of exploding shells, whistling bombs and the banshee-like wail of diving Stukas must surely have stretched the already taught nerves of many of the recently

recruited Russian troops to breaking point. Then, at 05:30 hours, the first German ground forces advanced, the infantry closely supported by a limited number of tanks. The initial move was made by Freissner's XXIII Corps on the right flank of the Ninth Army. This attack was aimed at the junction of the Thirteenth and Forty-Eighth Armies and designed to draw the Soviets' attention from the main German effort farther to the west. The strength of the Soviet defences rapidly became apparent. Antipersonnel mines took a high toll of the men of the 78th, 216th and 38th Infantry Divisions. In the face of stiff opposition, even with close air and armoured support, little headway – no more than 1.5km (1.2 miles) – was made towards their objective, the town of Maloarkhangelsk.

Greater success rewarded the efforts of Model's main attack that was to be undertaken by elements of XLVII Panzer and XLI Panzer Corps. Model had only committed the 20th Panzer Division to the first wave of the attack and its Panzer III and IV tanks kept close to their accompanying engineers, who were to clear lanes through the lethal Russian minefields. By 09:00 hours the 20th Panzer Division had reached the village of Bobrik and clawed into the defensive positions of the

▲ Precise observation was an essential feature of accurate artillery fire. This was particularly true when the combat was close. These forward observation officers are using binoculars and a stereoscopic rangefinder to check the fall of shells as the signaller reports their findings by telephone. All are members of a Guards artillery unit.

► Pictured under camouflage netting – somewhat skimpy protection from the prowling bands of *Luftwaffe* ground-attack aircraft – the commander of a formation of KV-1s scans the countryside for signs of the advancing German panzers.

▲ The photographs on this page are a selection from a series which depicts the actions of the *Grossdeutschland* Panzergrenadier Division during the Battle of Kursk (note the divisional symbol of a German helmet on the rear of the vehicle above).

▼ Led by Lieutenant-General Walter Hoernlein, the *Grossdeutschland* was an élite unit. Equipped with its own panzer regiment, it boasted 132 tanks and 35 assault guns. It was part of Lieutenant-General Otto von Knobelsdorff's XLVIII Panzer Corps.

▲ In the early hours of 5 July, both Soviet and German artillery fire lit up the sky along the frontline. Caught in the glare of the shellfire, this evocative painting shows Red Army engineers carrying out the hazardous and delicate task of mine-laying in the rear of the first defensive belt. Note the DP light machine gun to the right.

Soviet 15th Rifle Division to a depth of some 5km (3 miles). By late morning the Tigers of Heavy Tank Battalion 505 had taken Butyrkin and threatened the flank of the Soviet 81st Rifle Division. Further penetrations, along the rail line running to the south in the direction of Ponyri, were achieved by *Jagdpanzer* (Tank Hunter) Battalion 653 operating *Ferdinands*. Yet more success had been gained by another *Ferdinand* unit which had taken control of Alexandrovka, but this force was cut off from its supporting infantry.

Firefight at Ponyri

With his Thirteenth Army under mounting pressure, Rokossovsky sent in two antitank brigades, an artillery brigade and the 21st Separate Mortar Brigade, equipped with 82mm and 120mm mortars from the front reserve. Pukhov, commanding Thirteenth Army, committed his reserve 27th Guards Tank Regiment, mobile obstacle detachments and combat engineers to hold German infantry pushing towards Ponyri. Rokossovsky provided air support, some 350 planes, to support Pukhov's men. In the words of the commander of the German 6th Infantry Division: "The Russians used aircraft in numbers such as we have never seen in the East."

During the afternoon the 15th Rifle Division was driven back to the line of ridges west of Ponyri. This withdrawal exposed the right flank of the Seventieth Army, the easternmost unit of which, the 132nd Rifle Division, was also pushed back. The advancing Germans were finally halted by minefields and artillery fire. Further attacks by *Ferdinands*, supported by Goliath remote-control demolition machines, broke into the defence zone around Maloarkhangelsk but were held by the Russian 129th Armoured Brigade. On this sector of the front alone, Soviet engineers, often working under heavy small-arms fire, succeeded in laying over 6000 new mines, creating further hazards for Model's tanks and infantry. A German's comments on the tactics of the Russian infantry are apposite:

"The Soviet infantry refused to panic in the face of the roaring Tiger and *Ferdinand* tanks ... Everything had been done to inoculate the troops against the notorious 'tank panic'. The result was inevitable." The quote continues:

"The Russian infantrymen allowed the tanks to rumble past their well-camouflaged foxholes and then came out to deal with the German grenadiers in their wake. Thus the battle continued to rage on in sectors that the forward tank commanders believed had already been won.

"Tanks and assault guns had to be brought back to relieve the grenadiers ... By evening the grenadiers were exhausted, and the tanks and assault guns were out of fuel."

Here and there groups of armoured vehicles had pushed deeper into the Russian lines but were isolated. Cut off from their supporting infantry, they found it necessary to pull back. By the end of 5 July Model's troops had advanced 8km (6 miles) into the Soviets' first belt of defences, west of Ponyri, on a front of almost 15km (12 miles).

However, the attackers had sustained 20 percent losses in their panzer units, approximately 200 out of the 300 tanks and assault guns committed, and nearly 20,000 men. At Ninth Army headquarters the outlook was cautiously optimistic; the first day had gone well but the Red Army was a tenacious defensive foe and its positions were as substantial as Model's reconnaissance had foretold. The battle of attrition that the Russians had anticipated was unfolding. As one commentator put it:

"Nowhere had the enemy been taken by surprise. Nowhere has he been soft. He had clearly

▲ German infantrymen positioning a *Granatwerfer* 34 (GrW 34) 81mm mortar. The GrW 34 was well regarded by the soldiers that used it, being sturdy, reliable and accurate. Normal assignment was six 81mm mortars per mortar platoon within each rifle company.

► A German flamethrower team rushes forward on the morning of 5 July. Flamethrowers were useful for dealing with enemy infantry in trenches and bunkers. The Germans also used tank flamethrowers.

▲ A happy group of German prisoners, mainly pilots and aircrew, stand around awaiting interrogation. Their apparent cheerfulness was doubtless caused by their conviction that their captivity would be brief and liberation would shortly arrive in the shape of the triumphant German panzers.

▼ The Red Army used two types of antitank rifle. Shown here is the more complicated PTRS, a weapon which utilized a clip-fed magazine instead of the bolt-action of the simpler PTRD. The calibre of both was 14.5mm. There was little difference in the performance of these two-man weapons.

◄ Colonel-General Hermann Hoth (front) commanded the Fourth Panzer Army. This aristocratic Prussian officer had some of the best divisions that Germany had at Kursk, including the *Grossdeutschland*.

▼ These Red Army men are prepared for antitank fighting. To the rear of the position is a PTRD antitank rifle. Only marginally effective against tanks, it was still useful against lightly armoured vehicles. The grenade to the right of the submachine gunner is an RPG-40 antitank grenade that was dropped on engine covers or through any open hatches, with devastating effect.

been expecting the attack and numerous statements by Russian prisoners of war have confirmed this."

Rokossovsky, basing his plans on those drawn up in the weeks before the fighting began, ordered a counterattack for the following day. The objective of the attack was simple: the restoration

▲ Tiger tanks of the 2nd SS Panzergrenadier Division *Das Reich* at Kursk. The division, commanded by SS-Gruppenführer Walter Kruger, was the strongest of the three divisions of II SS Panzer Corps, fielding 145 tanks and 34 assault guns. The strike force of this unit was the 2nd SS Panzer Regiment.

of the first defensive belt. The attack was to be carried out by XVII Guards and XVIII Guards Rifle Corps, supported by II Tank Corps' 3rd and 16th Tank Brigades. XIX Separate Tank Corps was to cover the Seventieth Army's endangered right flank and IX Tank Corps was to be brought up from the front reserve, north of Kursk, and take up positions from which it could support II Tank Corps. It was, given the strength of the German forces arrayed in front of them, an overly ambitious plan.

Day One: Army Group South

Army Group Kempf and Hoth's Fourth Panzer Army began their contributions to Operation Citadel three hours later than scheduled. The main objective of the Fourth Panzer Army was to seize bridgeheads over the River Psel, south of Oboyan, by the end of 6 July.

To achieve the objective, XLVIII Panzer Corps and II SS Panzer Corps made their attacks up two converging roads leading north through Pokrovka (not to be confused with Prokhorovka) and Oboyan towards Kursk itself. The immediate objective for XLVIII Panzer Corps was the village of Cherkasskoe, a major point in the first Soviet defensive belt on the southern bank of the River Pena. The centre of the thrust was to be the *Grossdeutschland* Panzergrenadier Division, flanked to the left by the 3rd Panzer Division and to the right by the 11th Panzer Division. The flanks of the panzer thrust were to be covered by the 332nd and 167th Infantry Divisions to left and right respectively.

The 3rd Panzer Division and 332nd Infantry Division were faced by the 71st Guards Rifle Division and, after intense fighting, punched through the Soviet first and second defensive belts, driving the Russian soldiers before them. Fortunately for the Russians, the Germans were moving northwards and this allowed the 71st Guards Rifle Division to establish defences facing eastwards from their original line. By nightfall the 3rd Panzer Division had reached the banks of the River Pena.

The *Grossdeutschland* Division had moved off at 05:00 hours, led by its own Tiger company, aiming directly for Cherkasskoe. Almost immediately the 10th Panzer Brigade, attached to the *Grossdeutschland*'s left flank and equipped with 200 Panthers, ran into an undiscovered minefield near an area of marshy ravines. The bogged and damaged vehicles gave the Russian artillery just the target the mines had been intended to provide, and the storm of shells, fired over open sights, caused heavy casualties, particularly to the German engineers. In the ensuing confusion some 36 Panthers were lost. This chaotic situation was almost beyond the resources of the *Grossdeutschland*'s engineers, who laboured frantically for almost 12 hours before the way was clear and the tanks could move forward to support the flagging infantry. Interestingly, when the tanks did move forward a *Grossdeutschland* artillery officer commented:

"Where are our tanks? ... they're stuck in the mud ... Suddenly tanks appear behind us, more and more of them: they have a very long gun, a completely new type. Oh yes, the new Panther! Once again, however, our enthusiasm is dampened straight away."

It was thanks to the furious attacks launched by 11th Panzer Division, cutting through the Soviet defences and reaching the village of Cherkasskoe, that the Panthers could extract themselves from the marsh.

Grossdeutschland's Tiger company, at the tip of the wedge, had forced its way through the Soviet lines, leaving the clearance of the trenches to the supporting grenadiers. Fighting all the way, the 67th Guards Rifle Division was driven from its positions. Despite being reinforced by antitank guns and self-propelled artillery, the guardsmen fell back to the relative safety of the 90th Guards Rifle Division's trenches along the River Pena. However, the ferocious tenacity of the Soviet troops and the strength of their defences had thrown Hoth's schedule into disarray and, by nightfall, XLVIII Panzer Corps had fallen short of its objectives.

Hausser's II SS Panzer Corps, having successfully negotiated the minefields, launched its 356 tanks and 195 assault guns along the main road towards Bykovka. The firepower of the SS divisions' integral artillery batteries was supplemented by the aircraft of VIII Air Corps and the weight of an entire *Nebelwerfer* brigade. The *Nebelwerfer* was a multi-barrelled rocket launcher capable of delivering six rockets with 2.5kg (5.5lb)

▲ **The artillery duel that began in the early hours of 5 July continued for hours. This battery of 76.2mm ZiS-3 divisional guns are of the 1942 type which was a development of the 1939 model with an extra muzzle-brake and a split trail. The maximum range of this gun was 13,300m (14,545yd). Further development of this excellent weapon continued into the 1970s.**

warhead. The three SS divisions were deployed in a parallel echelon to the right. Each division possessed its own Tiger formations which formed the tip of the armoured wedge. The opposition to the SS consisted of the 52nd Guards Rifle Division and 375th Rifle Division, both veteran formations; the positions that they occupied were amongst the strongest in the salient, as the Soviet leadership was well aware of the fighting prowess of the élite troops that would be facing them.

As the advance guard of the *Leibstandarte* pushed towards Bykovka, it encountered the 5th Guards Mortar Regiment which included several batteries of *Katyusha* multiple rocket launchers in its strength. In what was to become a common practice, the *Katyusha* crews dropped the angle of the launch ramps and fired straight over open sights at the advancing Germans. In many areas specially designed ramps had been built to provide just this facility. Bykovka fell to the *Leibstandarte* at 16:10 hours; with barely time to draw breath, it was ordered to keep going and break through the "second enemy lines ... and to establish a bridgehead across the Psel". However, having run into stiff resistance, the *Leibstandarte* halted for the night "to resume its attack in the morning". *Das Reich*, having met with easy successes during the early hours of the offensive, and having cut the Oboyan–Belgorod road, found its way barred by the 96th Tank Brigade. *Totenkopf* had driven the 155th Guards Rifle Regiment into the right flank of the 375th Rifle Division, but was unable to complete its destruction.

The effectiveness of the Soviets' defensive flexibility prevented the Germans from breaking through the Russian defensive positions north of Belgorod, causing problems for Hoth's forces in the days to come. However, by the end of the first day Hausser's men had advanced almost 20km (16 miles), broken into the second Soviet defensive belt and, in the process, sliced the 52nd Rifle Division in two. The southernmost German force to attack on 5 July was Army Detachment Kempf. The main task allocated to Kempf's troops was the protection of Hoth's right flank, and this role would prove to be one of vital importance.

In the wake of a short artillery barrage, the infantry and tanks belonging to Army Detachment Kempf rolled forward across the Northern Donets River before breaking out from their bridgehead at Mikhailovka near Belgorod. Facing them was the Seventh Guards Army. The Russians defended ferociously, so much so that Kempf was forced to redeploy the 6th Panzer Division.

At 11:00 hours the 19th Panzer Division broke into the Soviet positions across the River Northern Donets. During the course of the day, the 19th Panzer Division's panzergrenadiers drove the 228th Guards Rifle Regiment back and began to bring its tanks across the river. During the early afternoon the 6th and 7th Panzergrenadier Regiments of the 7th Panzer Division managed to crash through the defences of the Soviet 78th Guards Rifle Division and unleash their tanks, before hurling the Russians back along high ground for 6km (4.5 miles). By taking this high ground, the Germans dominated the area on the left of the river for more than 10km (8 miles). As night fell the bridgehead had been expanded to 1.5–2.5km deep and 7km wide (2–4 miles deep, 10 miles wide). This expansion gave Kempf the chance to employ the 6th Panzer Division, which was moved to act in concert with the other armoured formations.

The damage that had been inflicted on the Seventh Guards Army was serious. However, its sacrifices had not been in vain, as Army Detachment Kempf had fallen behind its schedule. The consequences for the armoured formations under Hoth and Hausser's command were to prove

▼ On the horizon sits a knocked-out *Sturmgeschütz* (StuG) III assault gun that had penetrated the second defensive belt, only to fall victim to a Soviet minefield. The Russians in the foreground illustrate the mix of weapons in use by the infantry during the Kursk battles. The machine gun is the Soviet version of the Maxim Model 1910, as used by the Imperial Army during World War I. The familiar two-wheeled Sokolov mounting is hidden by the foxhole.

more and more problematic as the gap between them and Kempf's troops that should have been covering their flank widened, and they were forced to use troops that should have been advancing in a defensive role to protect their increasingly vulnerable eastern flank. However, although slower progress had been made than the Germans anticipated in their planning, on the southern flank of the salient the outlook was not too bad, and greater success was anticipated during the following days.

Vatutin's responses, during the course of the day, had been to move his reserves to block the German axes of advance. Russian plans that were made for counterattacks were rendered obsolete almost before the ink was dry due to the speed of the German advance. Therefore the First Tank Army was instructed to hold a line east of the River Pena, supporting the infantry already in place there. The Fifth Guards Tank Army was moved up to positions in the rear of the 51st Guards Rifle Division; XXXI Tank Corps was held as a rapid-response force waiting to react to any threat that arose. Elsewhere on the line the 93rd

▲ T-34/76 tanks moving out from their camouflaged positions into the dust and smoke of battle. At the rear of the hull can be seen the spare, external fuel tanks. Their position on the vehicles proved to be a deadly liability as they were unarmoured. The smoke and dust of combat during the summer months severely restricted visibility from the inside of a closed-down tank.

◄ Draped in camouflage, men and equipment, this heavy gun moves into position. The majority of Soviet heavy artillery was tractor-drawn. The most common tractor was the Stalinets S-60, produced in the Soviet Union under licence from the American Caterpillar company. The gun's tube is protected by a *chekol* (dust cover), as the sandy soil could seriously impair its performance.

▲ The air battle that took place in the early hours of the Kursk offensive was the largest that was seen during World War II. Furthermore, it marked the coming of age of the Red Air Force in terms of men and machinery. Numerically the Red Air Force enjoyed a clear advantage; its success at Kursk provided the pilots with the moral fillip to have more confidence in their abilities.

Guards Rifle Division was moved to occupy defensive positions east of the Lipovyi Donets River, south-west of Prokhorovka, in order to prevent the troops of II SS Panzer Corps and Army Detachment Kempf linking up. The manner in which Vatutin would deploy and use his tanks – these vehicles numbering almost 1000 – aroused criticism from both Stalin and Zhukov.

However, Vasilevsky and Khrushchev, who were both on the spot at that time, supported Vatutin's performance. The lack of counterattacks notwithstanding, Vatutin's methods were to characterize armoured operations in the days that followed. To their front, the panzer troops would face tanks that engaged them in vicious – sometimes almost suicidal – defensive battles, while their eastern flank became ever longer and more exposed to increasingly powerful Soviet armoured attacks. So powerful were these Soviet attacks that they threatened to cut through, and isolate, the German spearhead.

Vatutin spent the entire night pouring much-needed reinforcements into the area. These forces included the 27th Antitank Brigade, with 72 guns. The power of the German onslaught against the Voronezh Front had taken the Russians completely by surprise. Consequently, much of their armoured force had been committed in an infantry support role. However, the nature of the German advance had exposed the *Wehrmacht*'s eastern flank, thereby offering a prime opportunity, one that the Russians could not afford to let slip through their fingers.

▼ Russian infantry counterattack during the afternoon of 5 July. Covering fire is provided by a 7.62mm Degataryev light machine gun, nicknamed the "record player" because of its top-mounted magazine. The dry, dusty conditions, well illustrated in this photograph, taxed the endurance of the men and efficiency of their equipment to the limit; during battle, water became as essential as ammunition.

Northern Deadlock

As the tanks and assault guns of Model's Ninth Army tried to batter their way through the Soviet defences in the north of the salient, Rokossovsky fed in reserves to stem the German tide, then launched a devastating counterattack.

Rokossovsky ordered his staff to prepare for a counterattack, which had the sole objective of restoring the first defensive belt. On the night of 5 July, he submitted a report to Josef Stalin:

"The Supreme Commander told me that the Front was being reinforced with Lieutenant-General S.T. Trofimenko's Twenty-Seventh Army, taken from the reserve. This was good news indeed, and I sent several staff officers out to meet the Army. However, our joy was short-lived and next morning we received new orders: in view of the threatening situation in the neighbourhood of Oboyan the Twenty-Seventh Army was to proceed to the Voronezh Front. GHQ went on to say that we could count only on our own forces, adding that we were assigned the additional task of defending Kursk in the

▼ Grimly determined to defend to the last round, these Red Army men await the German assault on the positions of the Central Front. The light machine gun is the Degatyarev DP squad automatic weapon – the "record player". The ammunition drum held 47 rounds and was capable of firing at a rate of 550 shots per minute.

event of an enemy breakthrough on the Voronezh Front to the south."

Stalin replied: "Your neighbour on the left is in a grave situation, and the enemy may strike at your rear from there." Consequently Rokossovsky was forced to turn for troops to the Sixtieth Army, commanded by General I.D. Chernyakhovsky, defending the "snout" of the salient, which provided a reserve formation. However, greater strength than this would be needed to achieve Rokossovsky's purpose, so to this end several units were set in motion.

XIX Separate Tank Corps was moved up to support the right flank of the Seventieth Army, and IX Corps from the Front Reserve north of Kursk was to support the Second Tank Army. XIX Separate Tank Corps was to join the attack when it arrived and III Tank Corps was to defend Ponyri Station. The divisions of XVII Guards and XVIII Guards Rifle Corps were to attack out of their positions in the second defence belt supported by III Tank and XVI Tank Corps of the Second Tank Army. Unfortunately only the 17th Guards Rifle Division and XVI Tank Corps were in their designated jump-off positions by the appointed time. Consequently less than half of the Second Tank Army's 465 tanks were available for the attack. Notwithstanding this shortfall, the fresh input of Russian armour raised the numbers – when added to those committed by the Germans – to over 1000 tanks and other armoured fighting vehicles.

The scene was now set for the mighty struggle that was to rage for four days along the ridges stretching between Ponyri and the heavily defended villages of Olkhovatka and Samodurovka.

▲ German Army artillery on the north of the salient. Many German artillery pieces were knocked out during the battle by effective Red Army counterbattery fire, thereby weakening *Wehrmacht* assaults.

▼ K.K. Rokossovsky, commander of the Central Front. The son of a railroad engineer, he served in the Imperial Army as a non-commissioned officer in World War I. In 1918 he joined the Red Army and served in the Civil War, rising through the ranks to various Far Eastern commands.

▲ The hot, arid conditions that prevailed throughout much of the summer of 1943 are highlighted by the dried-out vegetation and suntanned infantryman nearest to the camera. The defensive position is typical of those facing Model's troops as they tried to wrest control of the heights that faced them.

▼ The ZiS-3 76mm divisional gun proved its worth during the summer of 1943. It was frequently used as an antitank gun. One of its advantages was that it was small enough to be manhandled, as has happened here. The surrounding cereal crop was typical of the ungathered harvest in the battle zone.

It was clear to both Model and Rokossovsky that the line of ridges held by the Russians was the key to the northern route to Kursk. In this region the engineers of the Red Army, ably assisted by many hundreds of civilian labourers, had created one of the densest and most sophisticated defensive systems in the salient. The main topographical feature, dominating the ridge line, was Hill 274 close by the village of Olkhovatka, which itself had been turned into a veritable fortress. It was the Red Army that was to make the first move on the second day.

The guns of IV Artillery Penetration Corps opened fire at 03:50 hours on 6 July onto pre-registered targets. In order to confuse the German artillery observers, the Russians exploded canisters of dynamite, located well away from the actual artillery positions, simultaneously with the fire of real guns. Thirty minutes later Russian bombers were intercepted on their way to attack German tanks and infantry forming up in anticipation of the Soviet attack. A vicious air battle ensued. Soviet losses on 5 July were calculated at some 100 aircraft, and the Red Air Force claimed to have shot down 106 German planes, but these losses did not greatly reduce aerial activity on 6 July.

The 107th and 164th Tank Brigades of XVI Tank Corps attacked at 04:00 hours in the direction of Step' and Butyrki with some 100 T-34 and T-70 tanks. The Soviet 107th Tank Brigade attacked first, but German artillery fire cut the Russian infantry off from their tanks. After two hours of intensive fighting, tanks of the 107th Tank Brigade succeeded in driving the Germans back to the line Ponyri 1–Step'–Saborovka.

▲ Looking down over the approaches to a village on the line Samdurovka–Ponyri, a well-camouflaged Soviet artillery battery prepares to add its firepower to the Red Army's defensive effort, showing the daunting nature of the task facing Model's troops attacking such positions across open ground.

▼ A group of unidentified staff officers hurry across the railway line running south from Ponyri to Kursk. The gauge of track in the USSR was wider than that elsewhere in Europe and necessitated considerable work on the part of the *Wehrmacht*'s engineer corps to render it compatible with their gauge.

The next phase of the Soviet advance fell foul of a well-prepared German ambush. Model had moved up his 2nd Panzer Division, attached to which was Heavy Tank Battalion 505 equipped with Tigers. In a few minutes the 107th Tank Brigade lost 46 out of 50 tanks to 16 dug-in Tigers and Panzer IVs, and withdrew behind its infantry. The 164th Tank Brigade lost 23 tanks and also withdrew behind its infantry screen. Instead of the powerful counterattack Rokossovsky had envisaged, a piecemeal thrust had achieved little.

In his memoirs Rokossovsky describes the activities of XVII Guards Rifle Corps:

"... XVII Corps advanced two kilometres, where they were joined by elements of the 15th and 18th Divisions which had been fighting in encirclement for the second day. Holding out on various sectors were two battalions, seven companies, eleven platoons and a number of smaller groups headed by officers. Occupying advantageous positions, they did not falter when enveloped by enemy panzers. On the contrary, by striking from their rear these brave men forced them to slow down their advance. The Nazis threw large forces against them, but they stood firm, repelling panzer and infantry attacks and greatly helping our counterattacking troops, which reached them in time. Now these officers and men joined the advancing units and forged ahead." However, the activities of XVII Guards Rifle Corps were curtailed by their lack of armoured support, and they were forced onto the defensive.

The Russian withdrawals were followed closely by tanks of XLVII Panzer Corps advancing to the second defensive belt held by XVII Guards Rifle Corps' 70th and 75th Guards Rifle Divisions. Again to quote Rokossovsky:

▼ Surrounded by men of his artillery regiment, a political officer delivers an inspirational speech. Interestingly, the political officer is the only man wearing the previously proscribed shoulder boards (*pogoni*). All the tunics are of the pre-1943 type.

▲ Pictured immediately prior to take-off, this Ilyushin Il-2m3 shows very clearly the rear-gunner introduced with this model. The Red Air Force rarely tallied "kills", but the three stars on the tailplane indicate three victories, probably ground-attack targets. The writing on the fuselage indicates that this aircraft is part of a Guards formation.

► Colonel-General Walther Model commanded the German Ninth Army. He concentrated his Tigers and *Ferdinands* in small but powerful battalions whose task was literally to smash their way through the enemy's defences.

"An enemy attempt to break into the second line of defence on the heels of the retreating troops was repelled. In view of the enemy's superiority in tanks, especially in heavy ones, our troops were ordered to reinforce their lines with tanks dug in to carry on firing from stationary positions. It was permitted to use tanks for counterattacks only against infantry or light enemy armour, and then only after his battle formations had been disarrayed by fire.

"This order had been prompted by circumstances. I remembered only too well the time when our tankmen had hastily launched a head-on attack against Tigers. They had suffered substantial casualties and had been hurled back

▲ **Dramatically captured on film, a Tiger of Heavy Tank Battalion 505 "brews up". To the right of the picture a *Ferdinand* moves steadily forward towards the outskirts of Olkhovatka on 9 July 1943.**

behind the infantry lines. The situation had been saved by our artillery, which had stopped the enemy with well-aimed, direct fire."

The flexibility of the Red Army's artillery was an important feature of its defensive strength. One particular example is the movement of the 23rd Guards Mortar Brigade equipped with M-30 *Katyusha* rocket launchers. The M-30 units were rarely used in defence because of their low mobility, the necessity for extended fire preparations, and the impossibility of rapidly turning the launchers for a salvo in a new direction. The 23rd Guards Mortar Brigade carried out a shift to fire against a new German thrust in 45 minutes, an operation that should have taken between two and three hours, all the while under air and artillery attack. Direct fire from ramps and over open sights became an increasingly common phenomenon carried out mainly by the lighter, more manoeuvrable M-13 *Katyushas*.

From behind the German lines could be seen the dusty settlement of Olkhovatka, Hill 274 and the low ridges that stood on the road to Kursk. Pausing to regroup after their failure to penetrate the Russian second defensive belt in the wake of the Soviet withdrawal, the troops of XLVII Panzer Corps drank deeply from their canteens as the sun rose higher above the open fields. The assault was to be launched during the late morning and the spearheads of the panzer wedges were to be the Tigers of Heavy Tank Battalion 505. Overhead screamed ground-attack and fighter aircraft of both

▼ **One of the hundreds of 85mm Model 1939 antiaircraft guns deployed in the Kursk salient by the Red Army during the battle. In performance this gun compared favourably with the famous German 88mm. However, it seems to have rarely been deployed in the antitank role. Antiaircraft guns were often crewed by women.**

▲ **Panzer front! A 45mm Model 37 antitank gun makes ready to fire. This gun was a derivative of the German 37mm antitank piece. The Soviets had increased the calibre to take larger, high-explosive shells to enable it to be used as an infantry support weapon. A new version, the Model 1942, was introduced before Operation Citadel.**

▼ **The German *Nebelwerfer* multi-barrel rocket launcher was a fearsome weapon. Mobile *Nebelwerfer* batteries were able to lay down heavy and unexpected concentrations of fire. It was known as the "Screaming Meemie" or "Moaning Minnie" for the sound made by the incoming rockets. Maximum range was 5500m (6014yd).**

▲ **Carrying only their weapons, this antitank rifle squad dash forward. They are passing a pair of shattered Panzer IIIs, possibly knocked out by Soviet air strikes during the early hours of the fighting. The men have replaced their standard issue knee boots with puttees, which was a not uncommon practice by this stage of the war.**

▼ **Pictured here, awaiting orders, are two Red Army engineers. In front of them are some of the mobile antitank defences that proved to be highly effective during Operation Citadel. Constructed from girders and easily moved, these latter-day *chevaux-de-frise* were another useful part of the Soviet defensive belts.**

sides, rockets from *Nebelwerfers* and *Katyushas* adding their characteristic howling and, as a final note to this soundtrack from hell, the perpetual drumming of the artillery. Inside their gently simmering steel vehicles, Soviet and German tank crews waited. At last the order was given, "*Panzer marsch*!"

Supported on their flanks by the lighter tanks and assault guns, the Tigers rolled forward into an inferno of Russian fire coming from weapons of all calibres. The hamlet of Soborovka fell. Model ordered the 9th Panzer Division into the fray to reinforce this success, but his losses were mounting inexorably.

▲ The work of forward artillery observation officers was, by its very proximity to the enemy line, hazardous. The men here are under heavy German counterbattery fire but continue to report the fall of their own shot by landline.

▼ A KV-1 – the Red Army's main heavy tank at the time of the Operation Citadel – goes into action supported by infantry on the Central Front. A little over 200 KV-1s were used at Kursk. An interesting feature of the KV-1 was the ball-mounted 7.62mm machine gun in the rear of the turret.

▲ **The bolt-action of the single-shot PTRD antitank rifle is clearly shown in this photograph. With a calibre of 14.5mm, the PTRD packed a formidable punch and was much valued as a sniping weapon. Stability was provided by a metal bipod.**

Grinding slowly forwards, the Germans were becoming more and more enmeshed in the complex web of the Russian defences. As superbly camouflaged and sited Soviet antitank gun batteries caught their tanks, so the German infantry were shot down in their hundreds as the Russian machine guns took their toll. From behind the forward trenches, Russian mortar crews fired off hundreds of rounds to further dislocate the German attack. For the German troops on the ground, the main objective became one of survival, but nowhere was safe. Seeking cover in a depression could result in the loss of a limb or worse, as the Soviet engineers had foreseen this eventuality and liberally scattered antipersonnel mines in such, apparently, safe havens. Nor were the German rear positions secure; Soviet troops appeared, as if by magic, from hiding places where they had stayed patiently waiting as the tanks drove past them, only to emerge and wreak havoc. Snipers, too, carefully targeted officers and other important personnel such as mine-clearing parties as they moved forward, causing the Germans to divert men to mopping-up duties who could have been better employed elsewhere.

Time and again the Tigers reformed and pushed forward; time and again the Russians drove them back. The unharvested cereal crops, now crushed flat beneath the tank tracks and soldiers'

▼ **This scout unit, recognizable by its specialist camouflage suits, is capable of delivering a colossal weight of fire. The man in the foreground is armed with the PPSh Model 1942 with a curved box magazine that held 35 rounds. At full power, fire at a rate of 2000 rounds per minute could be delivered by the guns pictured here.**

boots, began to stain with the blood of thousands of men. Over this grim spectacle, the smoke from hundreds of burning vehicles darkened the blue summer skies. Finally exhaustion put an end to the merciless fighting and, as evening fell, both sides paused to count the cost.

Wherever possible, tank recovery units came forward to rescue damaged vehicles and repair them for the next round. Fresh supplies of ammunition were brought forward, as was fuel for the tanks. Casualties were evacuated to the rear and the sounds of shot and shell were replaced by the sighs and moans of the wounded of both sides as they lay, untended and thirst-wracked, amidst the carnage.

No way through for the panzers

To the east of the line General Josef Harpe's XLI Panzer Corps again tried to split the Thirteenth and Forty-Eighth Armies. The tank component of the Panzer Corps was the 18th Panzer Division, which was equipped with fewer than 100 tanks, the majority of which were poorly armed Panzer IIIs and IVs. The weight of the attack was to be delivered by the *Landser* of the 292nd and 86th Infantry Divisions. In their support, the Germans had deployed the "Grizzly Bears" of the 216th Panzer Battalion which would provide mobile heavy artillery support. Fighting desperately, the Germans pushed forward and gained ground in the village of Ponyri. The momentum of the German advance was checked by troops of the

▲ The bitter price of failure. German infantry lie dead before the barbed wire of the Russian defences outside Ponyri. These men are possibly from the 10th Panzergrenadier Division committed by Model during the night 10/11 July in a last, desperate attempt to breach the Soviet lines.

307th Rifle Division who tenaciously defended their positions in and around the station. The 307th held the second line of the positions allotted to XXIX Rifle Corps.

The final area, which was attacked by the Germans, was the settlement of Maloarkhangelsk to the extreme east of the northern shoulder. The forces engaged here were again mainly infantry, the 216th Infantry Division and the 78th Assault Division, supported by the 72 StuG IIIs of the 185th and 189th Assault Gun Detachments. Despite these German efforts, the solidity of the Soviet defences and the resolute stolidity of the troops manning them again bested the Germans.

Finally, by 18:30 hours the Soviet XIX Tank Corps was ready to go into the attack. The delay resulted from the time the corps had taken negotiating the infantry positions and cautiously feeling its way through friendly minefields. The general direction of the attack was towards Podolian'. The 150 tanks of XIX Tank Corps struck directly at the tip of the German 20th and 2nd Panzer Divisions in the Bobrik–Samodurovka sector. Once again, however, dug-in tanks

supplemented by heavy artillery fire and air support met the Soviet armour. The casualties that ensued forced the Russians to retire.

Although the Russians had contained the German advance, they had paid a high price in men and materiel. But the Germans had suffered a bloody day as well; by the time XLVII Panzer Corps had called a halt, the Tigers of the 505th Battalion had been severely mauled, many beyond repair. The Germans were allowed little respite that night as the presence of so many Soviet troops within the German lines – where such could be said to have existed – necessitated extensive patrolling to ensure some chance of sleep for the men who would be taking up the cudgels again the following day. Throughout the hours of darkness, German engineers laboured frantically to clear routes across the Soviet minefields for their reserves to cautiously navigate. All the while Russian engineers worked to sow more mines, repair bunkers and trenches, and shift mobile antitank obstacles. Those men that could snatched precious minutes of sleep as their commanders prepared fresh orders for the coming struggle.

Rokossovsky could draw consolation for the losses in his ground forces, however, as the situation overhead was slowly shifting in the Soviets' favour. The intensity of the aerial combat was such that the *Luftwaffe* was forced to call on fresh units from other parts of the front to meet the Soviet air armada. The technical superiority

▲ The lack of foliage indicates that this image predates the Kursk battles. However, the SU-76s pictured here were widely used during Operation Citadel. Although originally intended to provide direct, mobile fire support for the infantry, the SU-76 played a very valuable part as a tank destroyer.

▼ A Red Army 45mm Model 1932 antitank gun is towed to the frontline by a six-horse team. The location is possibly Kursk itself. The limber was generally used to carry two crew members and ammunition; this one seems rather overloaded.

and skill of the German pilots that had for so long rendered the Red Air force impotent was gradually falling victim to a battle of attrition from which the largest force would emerge triumphant. Soviet fighter squadrons were proving that it was possible for them to suppress the Messerschmitts and Focke-Wulfs for long enough to enable their ground-attack and bomber aircraft to do their work. From this day forward, the Red Air Force, in this sector of the salient, would become increasingly dominant. Soviet claims for 6 July are 113 enemy aircraft for 90 of their own.

On the other side of the line, Model had cause for concern: the Soviet defences were as strong as, if not stronger than, predicted. Although the Ninth Army had made progress, it was minimal, and at the cost of some 25,000 men killed or wounded and about 150 tanks and assault guns. Aerial reconnaissance reported strong Russian columns moving westward, south of Maloarkhangelsk, towards Olkovatka and Ponyri. Obviously the Soviets were reinforcing as fast as they could.

The pattern of the fighting on the northern shoulder of the Kursk salient had been set. The Germans had to advance to achieve any sort of success; the Russians, having paid the bloody price of lessons in ill-prepared counterattacks, would defend. Numbers and tenacity would deliver victory to whichever protagonist was well supplied with both.

▲ Exhausted Red Army infantrymen take a well-deserved nap en route to the front. As the war progressed, more and more lorries, many provided by the USA, would carry the Soviet troops into battle, thus saving them tiring foot marches. The junior officer just visible to the left of the picture keeps watch over his men.

▼ Russian cavalry ride through the dust towards the frontline. Despite the increasingly mechanized nature of warfare, both Axis and Soviet forces used horses on a grand scale. Much of the Axis artillery was horse-drawn, and the Red Army used cavalry in great numbers.

Target Oboyan

Hoth launched his Fourth Panzer Army against the defences of the Voronezh Front, and at first success seemed at hand. But Soviet tenacity and strong defences began to deplete the strength of the attacking panzer divisions.

The drive on Oboyan did not resume until the mid-morning of 6 July. Oboyan was the headquarters of Vatutin's Voronezh Front, and the site of an all-important crossing bridging the River Psel. As such, it had to be held.

Hoth deployed the 3rd Panzer, 11th Panzer and *Grossdeutschland* Divisions for the attack, which was launched after a 90-minute period of artillery preparation. The *Luftwaffe* flew some 200 ground-attack missions and, in a short space of time, the Soviet forward positions had been overrun. The 67th Guards Rifle Division was pushed back until it was fighting with its back against the 52nd Guards Rifle Division that was facing II SS Panzer Corps farther to the east. However, by the late afternoon, the Russian Guardsmen were withdrawn to positions in and behind the second Soviet defensive belt.

▼ Infantry of the *Das Reich* Division on the advance across the grassy steppe south of Oboyan. The lead soldier is shouldering an MG 42 machine gun, which had a cyclic rate of fire of over 1000 rounds per minute.

▲ **Panzer IVs of II SS Panzer Corps during the early phase of the Kursk offensive. These tanks, equipped with armoured skirts and additional turret armour, are obviously some way from the frontline judging by their wide spacing, open hatches, empty skies and undisturbed terrain.**

The depth of the second Soviet defensive belt and the tenacity of the men holding it thwarted eight attacks by elements of Knobelsdorff's XLVIII Panzer Corps. Consequently, having failed to force their way up the Oboyan road, the Germans refocused their efforts.

A slow and bloody advance

Reconnaissance units of the 3rd Panzer Division probed towards the River Pena near Rakovo. Unfortunately, the shallowness of the river belied the swampy terrain nearby and the abrupt, muddy banks made the area unfavourable for tanks. Following an assessment of the situation, it was decided to redirect the tanks of the 3rd and 11th Panzer Divisions and *Grossdeutschland* along a more suitable axis of advance. The route chosen ran north-eastwards, past Alekseevka, Lukhanino and Syrtsevo, following the Tomarovka–Oboyan road.

Pushing forward vigorously from Cherkasskoe, the leading troops of 11th Panzer and *Grossdeutschland* came into contact with the Soviet 90th Guards Rifle Division and III Mechanized Corps along the River Lukhanino. Russian reinforcements, including the 35th Antitank Regiment, were moved into place as the German attacks increased in ferocity. A German writer described the situation in the following terms:

"On the left flank, the attacks by the 3rd Panzer Division against Zavydovka were as unsuccessful as those of *Grossdeutschland* against Alekseevka and Lukhanino. The entire area had been infested with mines, and tanks operating with

▼ **Wearing the recently introduced Model 1943 *gymnastiorka* (blouse) with stand-up collar and shoulder boards, the Guards artillery officer pictured here keeps watch for the advancing Germans. The *pilotka* forage cap was designed during World War I for wearing under the steel helmet, as seen here.**

▲ **A photograph of men and machines of II SS Panzer Corps taken considerably closer to the action. The men in the foreground are riding in an Sd Kfz 251 armoured personnel carrier, while the tank at right is a Panzer III.**

▼ **A Panzer IV medium support tank of II SS Panzer Corps at Kursk, possibly of the *Totenkopf* Division. The short-barrelled 75mm gun had excellent penetration capabilities, though this tank has no additional armour.**

all the advantages of high ground supported the Russian defence along the whole line. Our assault troops suffered considerable casualties, and the 3rd Panzer Division had to beat off counterattacks. In spite of several massive bombing attacks by the *Luftwaffe* against battery positions, the Russian defences did not decrease to any extent."

The *Grossdeutschland* Division was up against the dug-in 1st and 3rd Mechanized Brigades of Major-General S.M. Krivoshein's III Mechanized Corps, reinforced by a regiment of the 90th Guards Rifle Division and the remains of the 67th Guards Rifle Division. The Russian tanks numbered 100 or so; however, they were only part of the defensive belt, a clear picture of which can be gained from the extract from the *Grossdeutschland*'s history:

▲ These T-34s are gathering prior to counterattacking II SS Panzer Corps. The log on the tank nearest to the camera is an unditching beam for placing under the tracks should the going be too soft for them to grip. The metal drums along the sides are for

▼ An excellent photograph of infantry and halftracks of II SS Panzer Corps at Kursk. Hausser's corps only had three divisions but boasted 451 tanks on 4 July. It is an indication of the severity of the fighting during the battle that on 9 July this had been

" ...the panzers reported that the advance was proceeding smoothly and that the area south of Dubrova (on the Lukhanino River) could be taken. However, a heavy tank battle developed in the broad cornfields and flat terrain there against the Bolsheviks grimly defending their second line of resistance. Earth bunkers, deep positions with built-in flamethrowers, and especially well dug-in T-34s excellently camouflaged made the advance extremely difficult. German losses mounted, especially among the panzers. The infantry fought their way grimly through the indepth defence

◀ Cavalry scouts who, apart from their sub-machine guns and wrist watch, could date from the wars of the nineteenth century, look for the Germans. Both men are wearing camouflage trousers over their breeches and carry Cossack-pattern sabres which lack a hand guard. The sabres are carried in the traditional Russian manner, with the edge upwards.

▼ This photograph shows the most up-to-date Soviet specialist antitank gun, the 57mm Model 1943, fielded during the Battle of Kursk. Interestingly, the performance of this piece was enhanced by its ability to fire tungsten-cored ammunition, which had much more effect than the standard steel round against enemy tanks.

▲ **Equipped with entrenching tool, breadbag and their trademark rolled greatcoat, Russian infantry jog forward in the wake of a T-34 carrying a squad of tank *desant* men. The speed of the tank is apparent from the dust kicked up by its tracks. Overhead circles an unidentified aircraft. Given the open terrain, it is to be hoped that it is a Soviet aircraft.**

▼ **The strain of battle is clearly etched on the face of this panzergrenadier of the *Grossdeutschland* Division, whose infantry often had to fight without tank support as the vehicles got stuck in mud and minefields.**

zone, trying to clear the way for the panzers. Finally that evening the brave panzergrenadiers of I Battalion under Major Remer were able to advance by Dubrova and take Hill 247.2 where they dug in ... it appeared that the breakthrough had not yet succeeded, instead the attackers were still sitting in the midst of the enemy defence zone.

"Numerous Panthers had already been put out of action: the panzer regiment was forced to abandon many of its tanks on account of hits or track damage inflicted by mines and leave them ... for repairs."

The Soviets claim that by 17:00 hours the Germans lost 74 tanks in the River Pena fighting:

"All attempts by the Germans to continue the offensive in a northern direction were thwarted by the stubborn resistance by units of Colonel V.G. Chernov's 90th Rifle Division, and by First Tank Army's VI Tank and III Mechanized Corps, which had occupied prepared defences in the second line.

"In the Lukhanino, Syrtsevo, Hill 247.2 sector, the enemy undertook eight attacks during the course of the day; simultaneously throwing in up to 250 tanks and infantry ... In the region of Hill 247.2 separate groups of tanks succeeded in penetrating into our defences and filtered through the combat formation of Colonel A.K. Babadzhonian's 3rd Mechanized Brigade. While separating the infantry from the tanks, the brigade's soldiers did not waver and, by means at hand, they destroyed the penetrating machines."

▲ A sight to gladden the heart of any hard-pressed Soviet infantrymen: a line of T-34s rolling across the steppe. With a top speed of 51km/h (32mph), when operating in dry conditions the dust thrown up meant that charging into action necessitated tanks spreading out to see where they were going.

Panzers forward

Once again the Germans had been held by defence in depth, and the judicious use of reserves; again they had fallen short of the River Psel. However, the German position was a good one, although the Soviets were proving to be an even tougher nut to crack than had been anticipated.

Rested and refuelled in the early hours of 6 July, Hausser's II SS Panzer Corps was once again ready to attack. Late in the morning, after an artillery barrage, with the *Leibstandarte Adolf Hitler* on the left, and *Das Reich* on the right, the panzers advanced up the Belgorod–Oboyan road. Smashing through the 51st Rifle Division, the leading Tigers came up against the T-34s of V Guards Tank Corps south of Iakovlevo. As one German commentator put it:

"On separate slopes, some 1000m [1094yd] apart the forces faced one another like figures on a chess board, trying to influence fate, move by move, in their own favour. All the Tigers fired. The combat escalated into an ecstasy of roaring engines. The humans who directed and serviced them had to be calm; very calm, they aimed rapidly, they loaded rapidly, they gave orders quickly. They rolled ahead a few metres, pulled right, manoeuvred to escape the enemy crosshairs and bring the enemy into their own fire. We counted the torches of every tank which would never again fire on German soldiers. After one hour, 12 T-34s were in flames. The other 30 curved wildly back and forth, firing as rapidly as their barrels would deliver. They aimed well but our armour was very strong."

Despite their bravery, the Guard tanks were thrust aside and withdrew to the east and the south-east with the remains of two Guards Rifles divisions. Elements of III Mechanized Corps' 1st Guards Tank Brigade and 51st Guards Rifle

► A squad of Russian infantry pass the disembowelled remains of a Panther which has clearly been abandoned for some time. Although a highly effective tank, the initial production-run of Panthers, as used at Kursk, was still plagued by mechanical problems. The German Balkan cross marking can be made out at the front of the side armour.

▼ Yakovlev fighters peel away from escorting a bomber group. The Red Air Force marked their aircraft clearly with large red stars outlined in white. The numbers on the fuselage indicate the machine's number in a particular squadron.

◄ In a scene reminiscent of World War I, Russian infantry advance across the open steppe. Their weapons are held in the regulation position. Despite the technology involved, the infantry of both sides still fought and died in large numbers at Kursk because they had to occupy and hold the ground after the tanks had pushed on.

Division held out in Pokrovka and Bol'shie Maiachki on the left flank of II SS Panzer Corps.

Now Hausser found himself in an interesting position. Having penetrated the second Soviet defensive belt, the route to Prokhorovka was open. However, his orders were clear: to proceed north to Oboyan. Furthermore, his flanks were becoming more and more exposed, as the infantry tasked with protecting those areas had not yet arrived. Therefore Hausser chose to cover his flanks and not advance towards Prokhorovka.

In the event, Hausser's decision was justified as, in the early evening, the Soviet II Tank Corps launched an attack across the Lipovyi Donets River against the corps' right flank, which coincided with another by 96th Tank Brigade farther south, aimed at cutting into the SS rear echelons. The attack by the Guards tanks was halted by the ground-attack aircraft of the *Luftwaffe*, but it had underlined how vulnerable Hausser's flanks were. SS Panzergrenadier Division *Totenkopf* was detailed to

▼ Leading specially trained antitank dogs towards the front, and the dogs' inevitable doom. One can only wonder at the thoughts of the handlers as they led their charges towards their fate.

▲ In the heat and dust of a Russian summer it was more comfortable for tank crews to drive, in non-combat zones, with all the hatches open. Russian tanks were notorious for their lack of crew consideration at the basic design stage. The twin turret hatches show this to be a T-34/76 Model 1943.

protect the corps' eastern flank, having made little forward progress during the course of the day.

To the south of the German line, Army Detachment Kempf was making good progress, crashing out of its bridgehead over the River Northern Donets. Leading the way were the tanks of the 7th and 19th Panzer Divisions, that were joined late in the afternoon by the 6th Panzer Division. The 19th Panzer Division took Belovskoe but was halted by the last available reserves of the 81st Guards Rifle Division near Iastrebovo.

The 7th Panzer Division was engaged in desperate fighting with the recently arrived 73rd Guards Rifle Division, which was supported by two tank regiments, a self-propelled artillery regiment and the 72-gun 31st Antitank Brigade. With the arrival of the 6th Panzer Division the Russians were driven back to a low ridge running from Gremiachii to Batratskaia Dacha, where they consolidated their positions.

Kempf's dilemma

Once again the tanks had broken into the Russian defences and pushed them back, but now it was Kempf's turn to face a dilemma similar to that of Hausser: protect his flanks or drive northwards. Again the hunt was up for infantry to protect the panzers' march. By nightfall, a total of 30 percent of Manstein's armour was being used as flank guards.

However, there was cause for optimism at Army Group South's headquarters. The lead elements of XLVIII Panzer Corps had established a link with those of II SS Panzer Corps near Iakovlevo, establishing a clear threat to Oboyan. Despite grievous losses and a creaking schedule, the Germans were still advancing.

◀ **The radio team of a scouting formation communicates the intelligence it has gathered. During the Kursk operations, scout troops often worked closely with partisan groups and civilians, making use of their local knowledge to add to the Germans' difficulties.**

Vatutin was now confronted by a gaping hole in his forces' front, and consequently by nightfall he had committed much of Central Front's reserves. That evening he requested four tank corps and two aviation corps.

Vasilevsky, STAVKA representative at the Voronezh Front, added his own comments to Vatutin's request:

▼ **A mixed formation of Soviet armour advances in support of an infantry attack. The lead vehicle is a T-34/76 Model 1941, which can be identified by the large, one-piece turret hatch. The second vehicle is a Model 1943. The spongy nature of the ground is typical of the damper areas in the salient.**

"I consider it expedient ... to reinforce the front with two tank corps, sending one of them to the Prokhorovka region and the other to the Korocha region ... In addition, I consider it necessary to move Rotmistrov's [Fifth Guards Tank Army] to the Oskol River and to the region south of Staryi Oskol."

Stalin replied to Vatutin by telephone. He agreed to release the two tank corps, and further ordered him to:

"exhaust the enemy at prepared positions and prevent his penetrations until our active operations begin on the Western, Briansk and other fronts."

The commander of Steppe Front, General I.S. Konev, was ordered to bring forward V Tank Corps. Major-General A.F. Popov's II Tank Corps was set in motion, and the two corps moved towards Prokhorovka and Kovocha.

▲ The Red Army had, during the early months of the war, sent lorry-borne infantry into battle in support of their armoured formations. The results of such a transportation method was frequently disastrous. The use of tank *desant* troops was another method of providing tanks with close support, albeit uncomfortable for the infantry.

▼ STAVKA was continually moving reinforcements to threatened areas of the front. The camouflage was a precautionary measure though, in this case, possibly a token gesture. The gun, a 122mm Model 1930 howitzer, is being towed by a caterpillar tractor, a vehicle much favoured by the Red Army for its cross-country capabilities.

Vatutin's change of plan

Vatutin revised his plans with the aim of holding the Germans with his present forces and then destroying them with the two new tank corps when they arrived. The air force of the Voronezh Front was to be used against the Oboyan axis and that of the South-Western Front against Army Detachment Kempf.

XXXI Tank Corps would advance towards the right flank of II SS Panzer Corps. II Tank Corps and V Tank Corps would threaten the SS left flank, while VI Tank Corps and III Mechanized Corps would halt XLVIII Panzer Corps' progress up the Oboyan road.

The Air Battle

Though the Battle of Kursk is rightly considered a tank engagement, the struggle in the skies was no less important. The* Luftwaffe *gave the panzer divisions excellent aerial support, but the Red Air Force was to prove the eventual master in the air.

The *Luftwaffe* commitment at the beginning of Operation Citadel was 1800 aircraft. This figure represented some two-thirds of the machines deployed on the entire Eastern Front. The bulk of this force was concentrated to support the southern pincer under VIII Air Corps commanded by General Otto Dessloch. A squadron commander during World War I, Dessloch had vast experience, having led various *Luftwaffe* units prior to the Kursk operation. Under Dessloch's leadership, VIII Air Corps controlled the flying units of 4th Air Fleet, 1st Hungarian Air Division and I FlaK (antiaircraft artillery) Corps, disposing a total of 1100 aircraft. Included amongst these flying formations were seven units of dive-bombers, the infamous Ju 87D Stuka.

The Stukas were expected to carry out their classic role, established during four years of war, as flying artillery plunging out of the skies to bomb and strafe the enemy immediately ahead of the panzer wedges. The near-vertical dive that preceded bomb release was accompanied by a howling wail, as the pilot aimed his aircraft at the target, a wail that froze the blood of the men on the ground, convincing them that they as individuals had been specially chosen for death.

▼ By 1943 Soviet aircraft such as the Lavochkin La-5 could match these Focke-Wulf Fw 190s in terms of speed. In addition, Soviet fighters tended to have better performance at low altitudes.

Operation Citadel was the last time the Stuka would be employed in this manner, as its performance no longer matched the demands of the Eastern Front. When their dive-bomber role was rescinded, all the remaining Stukas were transferred to low-level ground-attack duties, and it was during the Kursk operation that Stuka "tank busters" were employed on a wide scale for the first time. A 37mm antitank gun was fitted under each wing, and this weight of fire in the hands of an expert such as Flight-Lieutenant Hans-Ulrich Rudel was to wreak havoc in the Soviet tank fleets. It is claimed that Rudel destroyed 12 tanks on the first day of Citadel alone.

Another first for the *Luftwaffe* at Kursk was the employment of *Schlactsgeschwaders* (ground-attack wings) utilizing Focke-Wulf Fw 190 A-4s and Henschel Hs 129 B-2/R2s in large numbers. The Henschel Hs 129 had been designed specifically as a "tank buster". In its nose were two 7.92mm machine guns and two 20mm cannons, but its real power was in its main armament, a single 30mm Mark 101 or 103 cannon housed in a gondola beneath the fuselage. When brought to bear on the thin engine housing at the rear of a tank, unarmoured lorries or the timber-built Soviet bunkers, this weight of fire was usually fatal. The Fw 190s operated closely with the Hs 129s, dropping SD1 and SD2 fragmentation bombs to disrupt the Soviet infantry attack lines.

▲ "Scramble!" Soviet pilots, weighed down by their parachutes, run for their Lavochkin La-5s. The La-5 had an air speed of 648km/h (403mph), which was faster than the Messerschmitts and Focke-Wulfs that it faced. Armament consisted of two 20mm fixed, forward-firing cannons in the upper part of the forward fuselage.

▼ The Bf 109 was an excellent fighter and, in the hands of an ace pilot, could outfight any Soviet aircraft. However, by mid-1943 the *Luftwaffe* was stretched thin in the East, while the Red Air Force was growing in size.

▲ A flight of Pe-2s proceeds steadily towards its target. The range of the Pe-2, with a bomb load of 1000kg (2205lb), was 1500km (932 miles), which gave it an unlimited operational capacity over the Kursk salient. The 7.62mm machine gun located in the belly is clearly visible. The nose glazing was intended to increase the accuracy of bomb runs.

The slow speed of the ground-attack aircraft such as the Hs 129 and the Stuka necessitated close fighter cooperation to allow their crews to concentrate on the job in hand, and this was to be provided by the Messerschmitt Bf 109 G-6 and Focke-Wulf Fw 190 A-5s. The armament of the Fw 190 – four 20mm cannon in the wings and two 7.92mm machine guns in the forward fuselage – coupled with a speed of 605km/h (382mph), made it a fighter to be reckoned with. The weaponry and performance of the Bf 109 was similar. Heavier bombing operations were to be conducted by other tried and trusted aircraft, such as the Heinkel He III and the Junkers Ju 88.

The *Luftwaffe* supported the northern pincer with Colonel-General Ritter von Greim's 6th Air Fleet, which consisted of the 1st Air Division, the 12th FlaK Division and the 10th FlaK Brigade. The mixed bag of antitank fighter and bomber aircraft numbered 730. Amongst these were three Stuka groups. The guns of the FlaK units were highly effective weapons, particularly the 88mm. However, such was the effectiveness of the 88 against Soviet tanks that many FlaK batteries were assigned to the *Wehrmacht* to bolster the antitank gun formations which had less effective weapons. The consequence was that the protection available to Axis airfields was severely curtailed.

◀ This *Shturmovik*'s rear-gunner carefully checks each cartridge in an ammunition belt. The 12.7mm machine gun was a clear asset, as the Il-2 series had a maximum speed of only 415km/h (258mph), due to their armour plating, and consequently were at the mercy of roving Axis fighters.

The *Luftwaffe* that now geared up for Operation Citadel was not the one that had dominated the Russian skies for almost two years. Commander of the *Luftwaffe*, Hermann Göring, had promised that no bombs would fall on the Reich. By early 1943 the emptiness of his words was proven daily by the Anglo-American bomber offensive that damaged Germany's industrial output and chiselled away at the people's morale. To counter this, Göring had withdrawn many fighter squadrons from the Eastern Front and diverted aircraft output to the West, with the consequence that the Eastern Front fought with diminished assets. To further compound this difficult situation, the Western air war was given priority in the allocation of fuel, so that the fuel allowance for the Battle of Kursk was 30 percent below its actual requirement.

However, the experience of the aircrews, the efficiency of the ground crews and the superiority of the machines were all factors that the ordinary German soldier took for granted; after all, had not the *Wehrmacht* enjoyed almost total air superiority over the Red Air force since the first hours of Operation Barbarossa? What the *Landser* in their trenches were unaware of was that the Red Air Force was now not, as it had been for so long, mere target practice for the Red Baron's protégés, but a real force to be reckoned with, and one to be taken very seriously indeed.

The Red Air Force

On the eve of 22 June 1941 the Red Air Force (RAF) on the western frontier of the USSR had numbered 2770 aircraft. During the opening days of Operation Barbarossa, astronomic claims were made by the *Luftwaffe* for the numbers of Soviet aircraft destroyed: 1811 by the end of day one, of which 1489 were caught in neat rows on the ground. As one anonymous Russian pilot was brave enough to advise the Party Central Committee in writing in June 1941:

"our camps adjoining the frontier are set out as if for inspection with white tents in rows, clearly visible from the air."

▼ These flights of Pe-2s are returning, apparently without fighter escort, from a mission over the Kursk salient to a base in the rear. Although they had ceiling of 8800m (28,870ft), these aircraft appear to be flying considerably lower than that.

To compound this "target highlighting", aircraft were being delivered to frontline squadrons in factory finish, often-reflective silver, with little or no attempt being made to disguise them. On Stalin's orders, work was put in hand to devise camouflage schemes. Unfortunately, it was too little, too late. Also, the aerodromes used by the RAF were generally located much nearer to the fighting line than their counterparts in the *Luftwaffe*, and losses were suffered due to the effects of German artillery fire on bases that had been targeted before 22 June.

Furthermore, training had been a very unimaginative process and following the textbook was the standard by which young Soviet pilots were judged. Maintaining formation in the teeth of enemy ground and air fire was encouraged, as was the practice of using large, unwieldy bomber formations, sending wave upon wave into a maelstrom of FlaK, with the inevitable result that they were blown from the sky in vast numbers.

Aircraft design in the USSR had not progressed as a rapidly as in Germany, and the RAF was equipped with many hundreds of obsolescent machines that were no match for the experienced and well-equipped *Luftwaffe*. One of the consequences of this situation was that Soviet pilots reverted to the desperate expedient of ramming their enemies in mid-air! Interestingly, the Russian leadership did not discourage such acts as long as the exchange was one obsolete Russian machine for a modern German one. The survival rate of Russian pilots who engaged in this risky form of combat, known as *taran*, seems to have been quite good – as long as they bailed out at a sensible altitude. Amongst *Luftwaffe* personnel, the rumour quickly spread that Soviet aircraft were manufactured with special armoured propellers in order to facilitate such actions.

In line with the Red Army and Navy, from December 1941, the honorific title of Guards was awarded to formations of the RAF that had distinguished themselves in action. Each man was issued with a small red and white enamel badge, with the inscription "Guards", that was to be worn on the right breast pocket. This emblem was also

▼ These women of the 47th Squadron are dressed in both the new and old styles of Red Air Force uniform. The officer on the right is wearing the new, 1943-style blouse, or *gymnastiorka*, and shoulder boards. The others retain the pre-war, more proletarian style of uniform. The enamelled badge worn on the right breast indicates that this squadron was part of a Guards formation.

painted on the fuselage of aircraft and the turrets of tanks. To symbolize this recognition of élite status, an elaborate ceremony took place. The proclamation from the People's Commissariat for Defence was read aloud to the assembled unit, with officers and men kneeling while their commander received and kissed the new colours. They then repeated the oath word for word after him:

"In the terrible years of the Great Patriotic War, I swear to you my country and to you my Party to fight to the last drop of blood and my last breath – and to conquer. Such is the Guard's creed. Forward to victory! Glory to the Party of Lenin."

Guards units (of whichever branch of the armed forces) were usually issued with the latest equipment and were often larger in size than conventional formations. They were expected to serve as shock spearheads and it was anticipated they would set an example to others in overcoming the once-dreaded *Wehrmacht* and *Luftwaffe*.

But even such desperate measures as *taran*, no matter how well publicized in the Soviet media or how richly the pilots were rewarded, posthumously or not, could disguise the fact that the RAF lagged far behind the *Luftwaffe* in terms of training, experience and machines. The skies over Russia were to be a happy hunting ground for the Axis for almost the next two years, even though Soviet

▲ With their aircraft warming up in the background, the crew of this Ilyushin Il-2 prepare for yet another ground-attack mission. The Il-2 was better known as the *Shturmovik*. The *Shturmovik* was responsible for the destruction of hundreds of Axis armoured and unarmoured vehicles during the summer of 1943, and was a classic ground-attack aircraft.

aircraft production rose steeply as relocated factories returned to production. Unlike the Red Army's tank armada, the RAF suffered from a plethora of designs that inevitably diffused production. But as combat experience taught the Red Army, so the RAF learnt as well.

By 1943 the RAF was receiving fighter aircraft such as the Lavochkin La-5FN, which matched the German Fw 190 A-4 and Bf 109 G-4 for speed. The Yakovlev design team came up with the Yak-9 fighter, which was available for use at Kursk and performed equally well. Furthermore, Britain and the USA, under the Lend-Lease scheme, had provided large numbers of aircraft. Of particular note was the Bell P-39 Airacobra (4000 were sent to the Russians) as flown by the second highest-scoring Soviet fighter ace, Alexander Pokryshkin, who was credited with 59 victories.

▲ A variant on the Tupolev SB-2 series was the SB-2bis which had uprated, different engines and greater fuel capacity than the original SB-2. Defensive armament consisted of twin 7.62mm machine guns in the nose and one 7.62mm machine gun in the dorsal and belly turrets.

▼ The Petyakov Pe-2 was built in a host of varieties, but the majority of the 11,427 constructed were designated as attack bombers. With a crew of three, it could carry an internal and external bomb load of 1600kg (3527lb). Two 7.62mm fixed, forward-firing machine guns were located in the nose.

The P-39 was nicknamed *britchik* (little shaver) by the RAF and proved to be an ideal fighter-*Shturmovik* (literally ground-attack) aircraft because of its 37mm cannon firing through the propeller hub. This propeller hub cannon position was later emulated in Soviet designs like the LaGG-3, and eventually on the Yak-9T.

Of all the Soviet aircraft operating over the Kursk salient during Operation Citadel, one stands out: the Il-2 *Shturmovik* "Special Purposes Ground Attack" plane. Combining the ability to carry a terrifying weapons package with an armoured fuselage to protect it from light ground fire, the Il-2 was a truly formidable machine that struck fear into the hearts of the Führer's panzer forces. When the decision to defend Kursk in depth was made, care was taken to plan the role of the RAF with a much higher level of thoroughness than had been the case prior to previous operations.

By May 1943, the RAF was three times as large as it had been but a year before, with over 8000 aircraft. During the weeks preceding Operation Citadel the RAF conducted night raids by planes of the ADD (*Aviatsiya dal'nevo deistviya* – Long

▲ Yak fighters prepare to take off in the early morning. Judging by the lightness of the camouflage, enemy air attack was deemed unlikely. Apart from its fighter capabilities, the Yak series of machines could carry an extremely useful external bomb and rocket load of up to 200kg (441lb).

► The skilled, hard work of Soviet ground crews is often overshadowed by the glamour that is attached to the pilots. However, without the careful, painstaking efforts of the men on the ground, the pilots would have been unable to function. The careful packing of ammunition belts was an essential feature of this crucial work.

▲ **A Tupolev SB-2 being manhandled by its crew and their helpers. The SB-2 design dated from the mid–1930s, when it had been designated a light bomber. The internal bomb load was 600kg (1323lb). The ability of the SB-2 to operate from rough-ground airfields was a distinct advantage.**

Range Air Arm) flying Il-4 and Lend-Lease North American B-25 Mitchell bombers against the most important rail centres serving the Germans in Russia. On 3 May, over 100 ADD bombers attacked the rail junction at Minsk, followed by raids on Gomel, Briansk and Orsha. On these occasions partisan groups were directed to sabotage lines outside of the towns, causing the trains to stack up and thus present an ideal target for the RAF bombers to attack.

When the German troops and their equipment finally reached their frontline assembly points, they were battered nightly by formations of *Nahmaschinen* ("Sewing machines", the German nickname, on account of its engine's sound) of U-2 bombers. One of the U-2 formations was the 46th Guards Women's Night-Bomber Regiment, which was an all-female regiment. The RAF had a total of three all-female regiments by 1945.

Luftwaffe bases were also kept under constant surveillance. Between 6 and 8 May, a concerted series of strikes on 17 airfields was made by 112 day-bombers, 156 *Shturmoviks* and 166 fighters. Six Soviet air armies contributed to this operation, extending over five army fronts, in which a leading part was played by the Sixteenth and Second Air Armies on the Central and Voronezh Fronts.

Intermittent intruder raids against forward *Luftwaffe* airfields were kept up by these two air armies throughout the next two months. Both were commanded by men whose experience had been acquired in the Battle of Stalingrad: General S.I. Rudenko retaining command of the Sixteenth Air Army; and General S.A. Krasovski replacing General Smirnov in the command of the Second Air Army after handing over the Seventeenth Air Army on the South-Western Front to General V.A. Sudets. To their immediate rear lay Konev's Reserve (later re-titled Steppe) Front, where five armies were supported by General S.K. Gorynov's Fifth Air Army, reconstituted after its move from the North Caucasus, where most of its air regiments had been transferred to K.A. Vershnin's Fourth Air Army or the Black Sea Fleet Air Force.

Rudenko and Krasovski were also reinforced by air corps from the GKO (*Gosudaarstvenny Komitet Obovony* – State Committee for Defence) Air Reserve, the Sixteenth Air Army receiving Yumashev's VI Fighter Corps, Karavitski's III Bomber Corps and Antoshkin's VI Composite Air Corps, while the Second Air Army was bolstered by Podgorny's IV Fighter Corps, Polbin's I Bomber Corps and Ryazanov's I *Shturmovik* Corps. Together with the flanking Seventeenth Air Army and some supporting ADD corps, a total of 2500–3000 Soviet aircraft had been prepared, and they were ready and waiting for the moment when the German offensive would at last begin.

In one respect, however, the Soviets were unprepared. The most threatening thrust was expected from the north, but *Luftflotte* 6, with bases in the Orel-Briansk region, had only 730 aircraft. However, the Red Air Force held a clear numerical superiority, possessing twice as many fighters as the *Luftwaffe* – largely due to Zhukov's insistence that fighter strength should be substantially increased to meet the German offensive – and with many times the German number of ground-attack aircraft. Only in its day bombers was the Red Air Force inferior to the *Luftwaffe*. The Soviet air operations were to rely heavily on the newer, better armed and better engined Ilyushas (Il-2s) for their success.

As at Stalingrad, overall coordination of air operation was the responsibility of Air Marshal Novikov, subordinate to Zhukov as Stalin's deputy, assisted by his First Deputy, General A.V. Vorozheikin, and his newly appointed Chief of Air

▲ The Mikoyan-Gurevich MiG-3 was an aircraft of very high performance, but one that was difficult to fly. Although originally designed as a high-altitude fighter armed with one 12.7mm and one 7.62mm fixed, forward-firing machine guns in the upper part of the forward fuselage, the MiG-3 could also carry external bomb and rocket loads for ground-attack missions.

▼ A pilot and fitter of an unidentified unit discuss the finer points of aircraft tuning during the Kursk battles. The machine is a MiG-3. Capable of speeds of up to 640km/h (398mph) and with a range of 1195km (742 miles), the MiG-3 was very useful in the fighter-bomber role, and could carry 200kg (440lb) of rockets and bombs.

▲ ***Shturmovik* prepares to take off from a forward airfield during the last days of the Kursk fighting. This is the Il-2M with a 12.7mm rear-facing machine gun in the heavily armoured cockpit area, in addition to the two 23mm forward-firing cannon in the leading edges of the wings. Rockets and bombs weighing up to 1000kg (2205lb) completed the formidable range of munitions carried by this remarkable aircraft.**

Staff, General Khudyakov. A network of secondary command and control centres was set up inside the salient, and deputy air commanders were posted to the headquarters of those ground armies primarily involved in meeting the first onslaught of the German offensive. Rudenko's deputy, Major-General Kosykh, was stationed with the headquarters of Pukhov's Thirteenth Army confronting Model, with first priority in summoning air support and allocating strikes in the interests of Pukhov's army.

Large numbers of auxiliary and emergency airstrips were prepared and existing airfields enlarged, one-third of these as decoy or dummy fields to deceive the *Luftwaffe*. On the whole, Soviet tactical fields were farther back than those prepared by the *Luftwaffe*, and while German *Staffeln* flew into airfields which were situated 18–20km (11–12 miles) behind the frontline on 4 July, with some advanced fighter strips only 5km (3 miles) from the front, the Soviet fighters were based 25–49km (15.5–30.6 miles) behind the front, while *Shturmoviks* were stationed 60–70km (37–43.5 miles) and bombers 120–130km (74.5–81 miles) to the rear of the frontline.

Although this was in accordance with the planned Soviet defence, it also showed a clear respect for the *Luftwaffe*'s talent in hitting forward airfields unexpectedly and hard, and it was preferred to maintain patrols of 18–30 fighters over the front, rather than run the risk of losing fighters waiting on standby on frontal airstrips. Final preparations included the designation and timing of rendezvous for fighter escorts, arrangements for cooperative support between neighbouring air armies, the allocation of call-signs and the readying of repair and recovery services.

In general, the subdued level of *Luftwaffe* activity immediately prior to the breaking of Citadel enabled a good deal of preparatory work to be done, although, as events proved, not enough to prevent breakdowns in effective air control under pressure. In the waiting air regiments, the political officers tuned the fighting spirit of their aircrews. When one pilot received a letter from relatives in recently reoccupied territory recounting the atrocities committed by the SS, the *politruk* read it aloud to the assembled unit and exhorted everyone to avenge themselves in the coming battle. Many aircraft carried slogans painted on the side of the fuselage in which the words "vengeance" and "damned fascists" figured more frequently than expressions of patriotic zeal.

On 5 July the day dawned bright and warm. On the dusty runways of Belgorod, Kharkov, Poltava and Dnepropetrovsk the Ju 88 and He 111 bombers of VIII Air Corps lined up for take-off as the first waves of the Citadel air offensive, when the wireless monitoring service reported a considerable increase in Soviet air traffic, and soon afterwards the "Freya" radar at Kharkov detected the approach of large air formations from the east. These formations contained 132 *Shturmoviks* and 285 fighters of the Second and Seventeenth Air Armies, detailed to destroy the German bombers on the ground when their fighter escorts were not yet airborne. But this pre-emptive strike was not to succeed. The Soviet regiments were intercepted by the Bf 109 Gs of *Jagdgeschwader* (hunting formations) 3 "Udet" and JG 52 scrambled from Kharkov East and Mikoyanovka, which claimed 120 air victories in the opening air battle.

In the northern sector, the Germans reported that Soviet fighter reaction to 1st Airborne Division operations began only in the late afternoon, and the Fw 190 fighters of JG 51 and JG 54 had claimed 115 Soviet aircraft by nightfall. The committal of fighters to the abortive pre-emptive strike in the early morning left the RAF unable to contest *Luftwaffe* air supremacy on the southern flank of the salient, and in the north, Soviet replies to the *Luftwaffe* attacks were tardy and ineffectual. The two fighter corps designated to give frontline cover, Yumashev's VI Fighter Corps over the Central Front and Klimov's V Fighter Corps over the Voronezh Front, were unable to cope. Without adequate air cover, the Soviet ground forces lost confidence and the *Wehrmacht* began to make headway. Novikov had to give his attention first to the failings of his fighters and, as a result of his investigations, Yumashev and Klimov were both replaced, VI Fighter Corps being taken over by Major-General Yerlykin and V Fighter Corps by Major-General Galunov.

Nor were the Soviet attacks on German armour initially successful. Despite new antitank bombs, their RS-82 rockets and more formidable 37mm cannon, the Il-2 *Shturmoviks* failed to get through and stop the panzers rolling forward. Flying in small groups, the Il-2s and Pe-2s often lacked fighter escort or they were abandoned when the very first sign of trouble appeared.

On Khudyakov's orders, the *Shturmoviks* began to fly in much larger formations of regimental size to make escort easier, and to enable the Il-2s to break through and suppress ground fire by sheer weight of numbers and the persistence of attack. Flying in *pelang* formation – staggered line abreast – the Il-2s no longer made hasty passes at low level under favourable conditions, but carried out calculated dive approaches from under 1000m

▼ The shattered remains of this Stuka ground-attack aircraft symbolize the failure of the *Luftwaffe* to maintain its air superiority over the Eastern Front. Underpowered and underarmed, the Stuka, when deprived of fighter cover, was a vulnerable target for the increasingly confident Soviet fighter pilots.

▲ **The model of *Shturmovik* shown here is the Il-2M3, which carried the 37mm antitank cannon in its wings. In addition, and also wing-mounted, the Il-2 series carried two 7.62mm machine guns. The Red Air Force officers are discussing bullet holes in a parachute that belonged to one of their comrades, whose life it saved.**

(3280ft) at angles of 30–40 degrees, releasing their bombs and rockets when 200–300m (656–984ft) from their target, and making repeated passes with cannon and machine guns.

At the end of the second day, in the north of the salient, the RAF had overcome its problems and was able to contain the German fighters, if not the bombers. But from 7 July the Sixteenth Air Army got into its stride and began to wear down the *Luftwaffe*. By 8 July Khudyakov was able to report on the improvement in *Shturmovik* potency, and the *Luftwaffe*'s power to control air space over the battle areas declined. The *Luftwaffe* was running out of replacements to maintain its squadrons at full strength, and the RAF began to range more freely over the German lines.

◀ **The despondency of this captured *Luftwaffe* man is evident. The Axis had taken air superiority for granted for so long that the improved performance of the Red Air Force over the Kursk salient was a deeply traumatic experience for German pilots.**

Although the Germans could still mount effective ground-support missions, in specific areas if not along the entire combat zone, their superiority was being eroded at an alarming rate. By the end of effective ground-offensive operations in the northern sector, the power of the *Luftwaffe* was much reduced.

The picture to the south was much the same. Soviet weight of numbers and the increasingly efficient use of machines whittled away at the numerically inferior Germans, and by 11 July the *Luftwaffe* was only able to achieve success in narrow areas such as supporting the thrust of II SS Panzer Corps towards Prokhorovka. As Rotmistrov described the scene over the battlefield of Prokhorovka from his command post:

"At the same time, furious aerial combats developed over the battlefield. Soviet as well as German airmen tried to help their ground forces to win the battle. The bombers, ground-support aircraft and fighters seemed to be permanently suspended in the sky over Prokhorovka. One aerial combat followed another. Soon the whole sky was shrouded by the thick smoke of the burning wrecks."

If Prokhorovka was, as Konev described it, "the swansong of the German armour", then Operation Citadel would mark the coming of age of the Red Air Force. For the first time since the outbreak of war, the RAF had met the *Luftwaffe* on almost equal terms, and although there was a long way to go before they reached the final victory, the Soviet air fleets had clipped the wings of Hitler's *Luftwaffe* and had gained control of their own skies once more.

▲ Appraising the results. These Soviet aircraft are pictured flying over a heavily bombed area "somewhere in the Kursk theatre of operations". It was over this ground that the Red Air Force, for the first time, wrested air superiority from the *Luftwaffe*. Once gained, this achievement was not surrendered.

▼ Although a decade old in 1943, the Polikarpov I-16 was still widely used as a frontline fighter-bomber by the Red Air Force. Its speed of 489km/h (304mph) put the I-16 at a distinct disadvantage when faced by the faster, more manoeuvrable German fighters. Losses of this type over the Kursk battlefields were very heavy and it was subsequently withdrawn from operational service.

Slaughter at Ponyri

In the north of the salient the Germans launched an all-out attack to seize the village of Ponyri, which was the hub of road and rail links with Kursk itself, in an attempt to penetrate the Central Front's second defensive belt.

The objective for the Germans operating on the northern shoulder of the Kursk salient was very clear. They had to break through the Central Front's second defensive belt around the village of Ponyri and to the north of Olkhovatka, some 10km (6 miles) to the west. The tactical significance of Ponyri was obvious to all concerned: it controlled the road and rail links with Kursk from the north. In the words of the Soviet General Staff study of the battle of Kursk:

"The most intense fighting on 7 July took place for Ponyri, which the defending 307th Rifle Division had controlled with a strong defensive centre."

It was a position from which it was clear that:

" ...by defending it, it was possible for our forces to deliver flank attacks against the enemy groupings advancing along the Maloarkhangel'sk

▼ Go, Go, Go! Red Army men breaking from the cover of a ruined building. The junior officer, with his PPSh submachine gun, is about to give covering fire. This scene allegedly took place in "a village to the east of Ponyri" during the afternoon of 10 July. The privates are all wearing the popular *pilotka* side cap, and the officer wears a *furashka* or peaked cap.

and Ol'khovatka axes. Understanding the significance of this centre, the Germans decided to capture it all costs on 7 July so that they could freely advance to the south."

Units of the German 292nd Infantry Division had captured the railway embankment and established a foothold on the northern outskirts of the village on the first day. However, despite receiving reinforcements on 6 July, the Germans had made little progress in the teeth of determined opposition. Bitter experience had taught the Soviet commanders that long-range firefights against the 88mm guns of the Tiger were futile. Consequently, all Soviet armour on the line was ordered to dig in and leave only their turrets showing and "conduct only a positional [in place] struggle against infantry and light tanks."

A torrent of steel

As the sun rose, so came the *Wehrmacht*. Supported by tanks of the 18th Panzer Division, the men of the 292nd Infantry Division launched fierce, headlong attacks on the lines held by the 307th Rifle Division. On each occasion, small gains were made, but their losses mounted. Intricately woven barbed-wire entanglements, liberally seeded with mines, tore bloody gaps in the ranks of the German infantry. Yet more mines tore the tracks from the Panzer IIIs and VIs as their crews strove to make headway amidst the steel torrent of rockets, antitank shells and bullets that the Soviet forces unleashed.

As the morning drew on, the sky was blackened with the oily smoke from dozens of burning tanks. Overhead, the *Shturmoviks* and Stukas performed a deadly aerial ballet, a *danse macabre*, that spelt death for the anonymous men and vehicles beneath them. Screaming through the smoke of battle, with split seconds to pick a target, it would be difficult to guarantee hitting definite enemy targets. It is open to speculation how many men and tanks fell victim to friendly fire when the operational area was so restricted.

Finally, at 10:00 hours, a dust-coated group of German infantry, red-eyed with exhaustion and stress and supported by 50 tanks, broke into the southern outskirts of Ponyri. But this success was short-lived. Like spectres from the crumbling ruins, Major-General M.A. Enshin's men of the

▲ A remarkable image of a *Katyusha* formation at the moment of firing. The simplicity of these weapons, coupled with the awesome weight of shot that they could deliver, made them one of the Red Army's most formidable tools. These are firing the 132mm rocket with an 18kg (40lb) warhead.

▼ Behind the Soviet defence lines and armies in the Kursk salient lay the forces of Army General I.S. Konev's massive Steppe Front, which provided reinforcements and extra depth to the Red Army's defences.

307th Rifle Division rose and drove back the Germans. Step by bloody step, building by shattered building, the Germans retreated, past the torn, fiery shells of their tanks until they reached their start line, and relative safety.

At midday Hoth received cheering news. To the east of Ponyri, the 1st May State Farm had fallen to a battle group of a dozen tanks and two battalions of infantry that had pressed on into the suburbs of Ponyri itself. To the west the 9th Panzer Division had driven back the 6th Guards Rifle Division to occupy part of the forest.

◀ Grim-faced tank *desant* men await the order to attack. The commander of the T-34 Model 1943 stands surveying the situation. Just visible on the side of the turret is part of a unit marking or patriotic slogan. A broad white band across the top of the turret identified Soviet tanks to the air forces of both sides during the Kursk fighting. Use of the national symbol, the red star, was, at this stage of the war, rare.

▼ The soldier on the left is a Guards private named Kuznetsov. Here, Kuznetsov is seen having his application for membership of the Communist Party checked by his unit's political officer. Happily Kuznetsov survived the action he was about to participate in and was awarded a medal for bravery.

▲ A Tiger crew takes a well-earned break during the attack on Ponyri. Judging by the shell mark on the turret, this vehicle has been in action. The Tiger was an excellent tank, but was available in only limited numbers. The Ninth Army, for example, had a total of only 31 Tiger tanks at the beginning of the battle.

▼ An infantry squad moves cautiously past an abandoned StuG III Ausf G. This StuG variant was armed with a 105mm *Sturmhaubitze* 42. For close defence, an MG 34 with 600 rounds was mounted on the top of the superstructure. The thinness of the armoured side skirts is apparent.

▲ These five grizzled partisans are reportedly the "oldest members of the Orel region partisan organization." The men are all well-armed with the later-model PPSh. Their varied clothing is a mixture of civilian and military items. The fur caps all appear to be decorated with a strip of red cloth to indicate their political leaning.

Refusing to be concerned with these threats to both flanks, Enshin fed in the 1023rd Rifle Regiment to hold the German tide. Further Soviet forces were committed during the course of the afternoon: tanks of the 129th Tank Brigade, batteries from the 13th Antitank Brigade, and the 1442nd Self-Propelled Artillery Regiment.

The see-saw battle for Ponyri raged throughout that summer's afternoon, burning buildings and vehicles only adding to the discomfort of the men sweating to operate their increasingly hot weapons.

◀ The nervousness of these German prisoners is obvious from their body language, particularly the senior NCO on the right. Prisoners of war, as can be seen here, frequently had their boots removed to prevent them from escaping. The central figure is wearing the Model 1942 reed-green summer field uniform.

Fresh water was at a premium, as was ammunition supply to the men on both sides who endured in the rubble. Often urine was the only available source of coolant for the barrels of guns that poured out their torrent of death. As the afternoon lapsed into evening, the Germans counted themselves lucky to have wrested half of the village from its defenders. As a German later wrote:

"Ponyri, a strung-out village, and Hill 253.5 were the Stalingrad of the Kursk salient. The most fiercely contested points were the tractor station, the railway station, the school and the water tower."

However savage the battle for Ponyri, that for Olkhovatka was no less important, certainly in General Model's eyes. The high ground here fell away to the south, Kursk itself being some 150m (133yd) below Olkovatka and within its sight. To take these commanding ridges, Model, having decided to reduce the pressure on Ponyri, launched the 2nd Panzer Division with the Tigers of the 505th Panzer Detachment and the 20th Panzer Division on the right against the Soviet lines between Samodurovka and Olkhovatka. This position, the second defensive belt of the Soviet Thirteenth Army, had been reinforced during the previous day and night. Once more the *Luftwaffe* and artillery hammered the Soviet defenders as the panzers massed. However, powerful as the attack was, it was attended only by local success.The Soviets described the action thus:

"A large group of tanks penetrated into and captured Teploe. However, the neighbouring 70th and 175th Divisions firmly held on to their positions and closed the penetration by introducing their reserves into combat in the

▼ Two very smartly turned out female snipers. Both are armed with Mosin-Nagant 91/30 rifles with PU sniper sights. The camouflage suits are worn over the 1943-pattern *gymnastiorka* (blouse). Snipers were frequently recruited from the members of civilian rifle clubs. In the fluid conditions of the Kursk fighting, Russian snipers were greatly feared by their German targets.

▲ Rifle-armed Soviet infantry dash through an overgrown garden. The usually carefully tended plots in Russian villages grew wild when their owners were evacuated from threatened districts. Visibility in such areas was limited by the heights to which the plants grew. It was usual for infantry attacks to be covered by machine-gun teams.

▼ Captured on film charging into the attack. Although many Soviet photographs are clearly posed, Russian combat camera men took as many risks as their counterparts in other armies and suffered high casualties as a result. The general release of many images of war was officially suppressed in the interests of security.

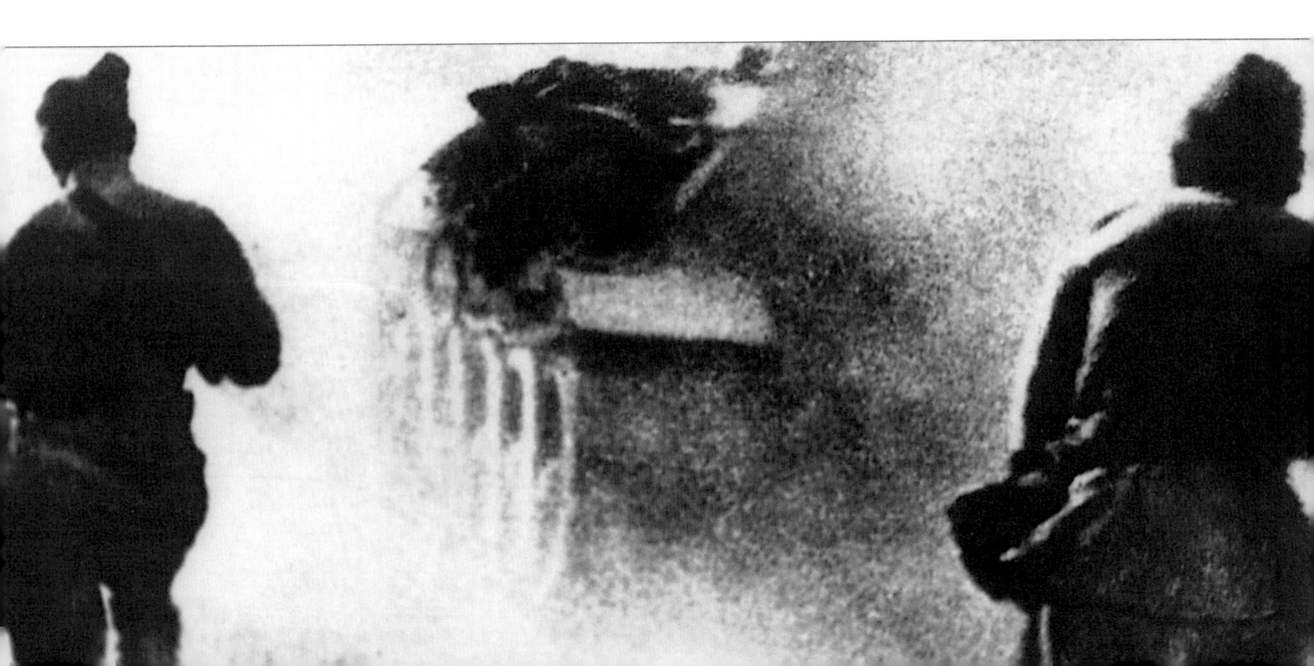

direction of Samodurovka, cutting off the tanks and infantry which had infiltrated from the main enemy forces. German tanks in the Teploe region repeatedly attempted to link up with their forces near Samodurovka, but they were unable to do so and were destroyed by our antitank units."

Cut off from their *Waffenbruder* (brothers in arms), German tanks and infantry tried to break out from this encirclement. Russian infantry engineers with Molotov cocktails, grenades and mines played a deadly game, hunting down their foes as the shadows grew longer.

The fighting died down. The Ninth Army had advanced, but at a heavy cost in men and machines. But Model still held an ace up his sleeve: the 101 tanks of 4th Panzer Division, a fresh unit commanded by General Dietrich von Saucken, with which he hoped to break through the Russian lines. The blow was to fall on Samodurovka.

However, it was Rokossovsky, not Model, whose men attacked first. At dawn on 8 July the men of 307th Rifle Division poured across the debris that had once been Ponyri station. The 51st and 103rd Tank Brigades simultaneously struck at the 1st May State Farm, which they took after three hours of fighting. The Soviets claimed to have knocked out "16 Tigers and 24 medium tanks in the attack." Their force numbered 140 tanks.

▲ The Model 1937 45mm antitank gun was a light, manoeuvreable weapon that doubled as an infantry support gun. Consequently it was an ideal piece to use in rough or built-up terrain, such as that pictured here. The thin armoured shield provided the crew with a modicum of protection from small-arms fire.

Taking advantage of every scrap of cover, be it metal, stone or human debris, and fighting like men possessed, the Russian infantry gradually drove back their foes. In the brutal, close-quarter street fighting, men hacked and slashed at one another with sharpened entrenching tools, knives and anything that came to hand. Having regained part of the town, the Russians faced renewed German counterattacks, but despite these, they conceded barely a metre.

Both Model and Lieutenant-General N.P. Pukhov, commander of the Thirteenth Army, fed in reserves. During the next 48 hours the paratroopers of the élite Soviet 3rd and 4th Guards Airborne Divisions and the fresh German 10th Panzergrenadier Division and 31st Infantry Division were poured into the maelstrom. On 9 July the German 508th Grenadier Regiment, supported by six *Ferdinands*, were employed to attack Hill 253.3. The Germans trusted in the

▲ **Encapsulated in this small area are all the factors that made fighting in ruined zones so testing. The Russians are all armed with PPSh submachine guns, weapons that were ideal for conditions where the rate of fire was more important than accuracy. In Ponyri the street fighting was so vicious that it was dubbed the "Stalingrad of Kursk".**

▼ **Just visible, left of centre, is a sign in German indicating that the building housed a command post. The low-level visibility has been caused by the dust raised by collapsing masonry, a very real hazard when fighting in built-up areas. The number of incidents of casualties caused by friendly fire in conditions such as these was very high.**

heavy armour of the *Ferdinands* to carry them through the Russian lines and create a gap that the supporting infantry could exploit. Hill 253.2 was carried by the Germans, but they lacked the strength to build on this achievement.

During the early hours of 11 July, Model played his last card, the 10th Panzergrenadier Division, which launched a series of desperate attacks into the wreckage of Ponyri. Although the Germans now held most of the town, it was impossible to move forward as their losses had been too great. To the west the Soviet XVII Guards Rifle Corps took the full force of the German attack. Wave after wave of German tanks in groups of 60–100, closely supported by infantry, moved

► *Gefallen*: "killed in action". These German corpses in Ponyri bear mute testament to the fighting in and around the "Stalingrad of Kursk". The building in the background is possibly the school, one of the Germans' main objectives. The SU-76 has sustained damage to its right track guard and the glacis plate has an unpleasant stain.

▼ This squad machine-gun team is caught on camera moving through Ponyri railway station during the see-saw fighting of 9–12 July. By 12 July, the Germans held the main street of the village. However, they were unable to effect a breakthrough, due to the strength of the Russian defences.

▲ **A Red Army platoon rushes to launch a counterattack on an unidentified village. The mixture of thatch and shingle roofing is typical of village buildings in this part of the Soviet Union. Most of the men appear to be counterattacking armed with rifles.**

against the ridge north of Olkhovatka, Samodurovka and Hill 257. A German eyewitness reported the course of the battle:

"The grenadiers of 20th Panzer Division fought a ... furious battle on 8 July near the village of Samodurovka under a scorching sun. Within an hour, all the officers of 5th Company, 112th Panzergrenadier Regiment, had been killed or wounded. Nevertheless the grenadiers swept through cornfields, capturing trenches and excavating new ones. The battalions melted away."

Within sound of this ferocious encounter, the 4th Panzer Division broke through the defensive belt at the junction of the 175th and 70th Guards Rifle Divisions and took Teploe.

"The battalion had already lost 100 men. But the divisional commander did not want to give the Russians time to gather their wits. The 3rd and 35th Panzer Regiments were lined up on the edge of the village [Teploe]. Armoured troop-carrying vehicles joined them. Dive-bombers shrieked overhead towards Russian positions.

"Now!

"On the opposite slope were the 3rd Antitank Artillery Brigade. Moreover, T-34s had been dug in. Their flank was covered by a Soviet rifle battalion with antitank rifles, simple but highly effective weapons against tanks at short range ...

"After a few hundred yards, the German grenadiers lay pinned to the ground. It was impossible to get through the Soviet fire of a few hundred guns concentrated on a very narrow sector. Only the tanks moved forward into the wall of fire.

"The Soviet artillerymen let them come within 500, then 400 yards. At that range even the Tigers were set on fire by the heavy Russian antitank guns.

"But then three Mark IVs overran the first Soviet gun position. The Grenadiers followed. They seized the high ground. They were thrown back by an immediate Russian counterattack.

"For three days the battle raged in the field in front of Teploe. The 33rd Panzergrenadier Regiment stormed the ground. They were dislodged again.

"The neighbouring 6th Infantry Division similarly only got to the slope of the hotly contested Hill 274 at Olkhovatka."

From the Russian perspective, Hill 257 was the key to XVII Guards Rifle Corps' defensive sector.

" ...the enemy again shifted to the offensive and attempted to penetrate our defence on a front from Ponyri to Samodurovka. The Germans

► **The pilot of a Mikoyan-Gurevich MiG-3 of an unidentified Red Air Force squadron checks grid references pre-take-off. At this time, the Red Air Force was more lavish in its use of markings than the Red Army. The pilot's sidearm is the standard Soviet issue Nagant 7.62mm model of 1895.**

▼ **Panzer IV tanks storm forward during Colonel-General Walther Model's all-out assault on Olkhovatka. He massed the tanks and assault guns of the 2nd, 4th and 20th Panzer Divisions, supported by fighter-bombers and infantry, in an attempt to shatter the Soviet line. However, once again the Germans failed to pierce enemy defences, though at a terrible cost to the Red Army. Citadel's northern pincer was slowly but surely grinding to a bloody halt.**

attacked four times here, but each time encountered all types of organized fire.

"The fiercest battles took place on Hill 257.0 ... Three times in groups of 60–100 tank, each simultaneously from the north-east and the north, the enemy attacked the hill; German infantry, despite fire from defending units, attempted to advance behind tanks to the hill. By 17:00 hours the enemy had successfully occupied it, this further advance was stopped. The enemy was completely unsuccessful in the remaining front sectors of XVII Guards Rifle Corps.

"Thus on 8 July, after fierce battles along this axis, German forces were unable to achieve significant success. The final attempt to penetrate Olkhovatka failed."

A latter-day Verdun

A Soviet officer's report in this area is revealing:

"The enemy has occupied Kashara, Kutyurka, Pogorelovtsy and Samodurovka and, preparing for a second frontal attack, is moving up 200 tanks and motorized infantry in the direction of Teploe.

"The 1st and 7th Batteries have perished, but they have not withdrawn a step. Forty tanks have been destroyed. There have been 70 percent losses in the first battalion of the antitank rifles.

"The 2nd and 3rd Batteries and the second battalion of antitank rifles have prepared to meet the enemy. I have communications with them. There will be a struggle. We will either stand or perish. I need all types of ammunition. I have committed all my reserves. I await your orders."

The concerns expressed here are tinged with a determination to hold the line, whatever the cost, and hold it the Russians did.

Lack of real success on 8 July forced Model to waste precious time the following morning regrouping his forces for an all-out assault on Olkhovatka. Once again the Germans would push forward, past the charred human and mechanical evidence of their earlier failures in an attempt to achieve their goal.

Numbering almost 300, the massed tanks and assault guns of the 2nd, 4th and 20th Panzer Divisions prepared to make a last bid to break through the Russian defensive belt. The men of the 6th Infantry Division who were to provide the support for the armour listened as waves of Stuka dive-bombers delivered tonnes of high explosives onto the Soviet defence lines on the lower slopes of Hill 274. Thousands of German shells and mortar rounds churned up the ground into a latter-day Verdun.

Under the weight of explosives that hammered at the Russian positions, it seemed to the German infantry that nothing could survive to block their way. As the last shell exploded and the Stukas withdrew, the momentary silence was broken by the roaring of panzer engines exploding into life and metallic grinding as hundreds of tank tracks signalled that, once again, the Germans were attacking. The Russian artillerymen stood to, staring at the lines of "Hitlerite Bandits" moving towards them.

▼ A heavily camouflaged convoy of artillery heads for new positions. The guns are being towed by American-supplied US-6 Studebaker 2.54-tonne (2.5-ton) lorries. The Red Army's artillery was almost fully motorized, thanks to Lend-Lease vehicles such as these.

▲ **Wrapped in their greatcoats against the evening chill, an artillery crew waits patiently to move forward. The tractor unit is based on an American design of pre-1920 vintage. The huge scale of the traffic movements within the Russian defensive areas involved a colossal feat of logistics.**

Within minutes the first German infantry relived the experiences of their fathers on the Western Front in World War I, learning that artillery fire makes a poor wirecutter. Everywhere men were falling to Russian mines and bullets, yet they pushed on. Through the afternoon, the men of the German 6th Infantry Division hurled themselves at the Soviet defences, lunging into the labyrinth of trenches, barbed wire and infantry.

Model's regrouping had given the Soviets time to bring up reserves, the 162nd Infantry Division. It was against these fresh troops that the Germans failed. It was apparent that Operation Citadel's northern pincer was not sharp enough to cut through the Red Army. Zhukov and Stalin were sure that on 12 July, troops of the Briansk and Western Fronts should move against the Orel Bulge.

A Soviet report noted: "On 11 July the enemy went on to the defence along the entire front and began to gather his threadbare panzer divisions in the immediate rear for their subsequent transfer against Briansk Front Forces."

The German Ninth Army had totally failed in its attempt to breach the Soviet lines. Now all Germany's hopes lay with Manstein and Army Group South.

▼ **The use of captured weapons is as old as warfare itself. The squad of Soviet infantry is advancing into a typical central Russian village, which has a mixture of crops and houses. The supporting weapon is a captured German MG 34, which was capable of firing 800 rounds per minute.**

Crisis in the Salient

In the south, Hausser's II SS Panzer Corps and Knobelsdorff's XLVIII Panzer Corps reached the last defensive belt of Vatutin's Voronezh Front. Unless they were stopped, they would break through and give Adolf Hitler victory.

Vatutin's plan to contain the seemingly inexorable march of Hoth's tanks was built on the foundation that placed First Tank Army's XXXI Tank Corps on the right flank of Hausser's II SS Panzer Corps, and II and V Guards Tank Corps on Hausser's left flank. In this position, the SS panzers would be trapped between two fires. To the west, XLVIII Panzer Corps' progress along the Oboyan road was to be curtailed by VI Tank and III Mechanized Corps.

Driving as hard as they could to the support of the Voronezh Front were II and X Tank Corps and Fifth Guards Tank Army. It was vital that Vatutin's forces held the Germans until such time as these reserves came up. The time of the reserves' arrival would be crucial to the success, or not, of Vatutin's operations. If the hard-pressed men of Voronezh Front broke, then they would expose those coming up to all the hazards of fighting an encounter battle, straight from the march, surrounded and

▼ Patience, sharp eyes and single-minded concentration were essential assets for any scout formations. The scouts were the forerunners of the present-day Russian Special Forces, the *Spesnatz*. During the Kursk fighting, specialist troops, such as this man, often fought behind the German front-lines, attacking supply columns and ammunition dumps.

impeded by the detritus of those retreating in the face of the men of the swastika. Indeed, the longer the Voronezh Front presented the Germans with a cohesive defence, then the greater the opportunity for the reserves to arrive, refuel, rest and deploy their tanks for the imminent titanic struggle.

XLVIII Panzer Corps' objectives

Lieutenant-General I.M. Chistiakov's Sixth Guards Army and the mobile corps of Lieutenant-General M.E. Katukov's First Tank Army were in strong defensive positions along the Rivers Pena and Lukhanino and south-east of Pokrovka. These forces had been supplemented with all Vatutin's remaining armour, antitank and fighter aviation units.

Following often vigorous conversations with STAVKA, Vatutin had received reluctant permission to dig in his tanks, as had been done by Rokossovsky in the north, rather than fritter them away in attacking the Germans' longer-range weapons. With over 600 armoured fighting vehicles, Katukov's Tank Army and Chistiakov's Guardsmen were aware that their mettle would soon be put to the test. In fact, that testing process began more swiftly than Vatutin had anticipated.

The day of 7 July started with a series of German attacks along the whole of the Fourth Panzer Army's front. As dawn broke in the east, so XLVIII Panzer Corps rolled forwards. The task facing Knobelsdorff's men was twofold: to continue their march on Oboyan, and to clear and protect the left flank of II SS Panzer Corps. A third task would rapidly emerge: that as it progressed

▲ One of the heaviest weapons in the Soviet arsenal, the 203mm B-4 Model 1931 howitzer. The projectile weighed 100kg (220lb) and one can be seen being loaded by crane in the centre of the picture. The B-4 was towed into position by a tractor unit, its tracked carriage proving an immense advantage in muddy or rough conditions.

▼ Under fire these Soviet engineers work at laying mines behind their barbed wire defences. The alteration of safe zones through the minefields was carried out at all times of the day and often behind German lines. The heroic story of these brave men remains, to this day, very much unknown.

▲ **Major-General Senchilov is seen here distributing medals to a group of Guards non-commissioned officers. Rank was indicated by stripes, stars and embroidery on the recently reintroduced shoulder straps. The tunics are of the pre-1943 type. The rakish angle at which the forage caps are worn is typical.**

northwards, the left flank of XLVIII Panzer Corps would in its turn be exposed.

When the *Luftwaffe* and the artillery had done their work, the tanks of the *Grossdeutschland* and 11th Panzer Divisions cut their way into First Army's defensive positions astride the Oboyan road. A total of 300 tanks, including nearly 40 Panthers, were on the move between Sirtsev and Iakovlevo. Dubrova fell, despite heroic resistance from the Soviet forces. The next target was Syrtsevo, as Soviet records state:

"During the repeated attacks, by introducing fresh forces, the enemy penetrated the defensive front and began to spread in a northern and north-

▼ **Like soldiers all over the world, Red Army men enjoyed their periods of rest and relaxation. Here, a concert party entertains an unidentified Guards formation to a selection of popular melodies. The accordion is a popular instrument in Russia. As the propaganda emphasis moved closer to promoting patriotism than political clichés, the political officers became responsible for organizing entertainment such as this.**

▲ **In a scene that, but for the 1940-pattern helmet, could be directly from the trenches of World War I, Soviet troops eat their dinner. The defensive belts in the salient were built along World War I lines, with duckboards and timber *revetments*. Here, entire silver birch trunks have been used to reinforce the sides of the trench.**

westward direction. The brigades [1st and 3rd Mechanized] withdrew in bitter fighting. A platoon of the 3rd Battery, 35th Antitank Artillery Regiment, occupied firing positions at a fork in the road at Hill 254.5. A group of enemy tanks, including Tigers, advanced on the artillery's positions. Permitting the tanks to approach within 200–300 metres, the artillery opened accurate fire and over the course of several minutes set fire to five heavy Tiger tanks. The remaining tanks turned back."

Elements of the 11th Panzer Division thrust to the north of Syrtsevo, and *Grossdeutschland* to the north-east; both were hilly areas. It fell to the tanks of *Grossdeutschland* to make a frontal attack on the

▼ **Intimations of mortality? Yet another applicant for the Communist Party of the Soviet Union fills in the forms before going into action. In this case it is a *Yefreitor*, lance-corporal. On his wrist he appears to be wearing a compass.**

▲ **Snipers Nomokonov and Kanatov are the best in their division." So reads the original caption to this photograph. The patience and attention to detail demanded a particular mentality and sniping was a highly regarded skill in the Red Army. It was a sniper who killed the commander of 6th Panzer Division, General von Hunersdorff, on 14 July on the River Northern Donets.**

town itself. The official history of the *Grossdeutschland* provides a vivid picture of what happened next.

"Unfortunately for the attackers, at this point the Panthers suffered enormous losses in tanks knocked out and the fully deployed Strachwitz panzer group drove into a minefield which had not been identified, frustrating all further movement. An advance by I Battalion Panzergrenadier Regiment *Grossdeutschland* was thus stopped for the time being. The panzers and panzergrenadiers tried to maintain their positions under very heavy fire, and the lack of mobility of the tanks cost them further losses ... finally the remaining tanks of I Battalion, as well as the few remaining Panthers, succeeded in crossing the minefield, in the course of which they became involved in a sharp tank-versus-tank engagement late in the morning.

"Meanwhile, farther to the north II Battalion Panzergrenadier Regiment *Grossdeutschland* launched an attack in the direction of Sirtsev but progress was slow ... Very heavy attacks by enemy close-support aircraft disrupted these movements considerably; in some places the fighting entailed very heavy losses. The advance proved to be slow and laborious; heavy close-quarters fighting broke out over every single position."

A similar picture is drawn by the Soviet account of the fighting.

"North of Syrtsevo, in the area of Hill 230.1, the tankists of Colonel M.T. Leonov's 112th Tank Brigade stood heroically in their defensive positions. Heavy battles raged here until late evening during which the Hitlerites lost 15 tanks, including 6 Tigers. The brigade also suffered heavy losses, losing 15 tanks."

Sirtsev fell to the Germans, and the Russian formations fell back towards Syrtsevo, Gremiuchii and Verkhopen'e.

The Chief of Staff of XLVIII Panzer Corps, writing after the war, describes the Soviet withdrawal:

"The fleeing masses were caught by German artillery fire and suffered very heavy casualties; our tanks gained momentum and wheeled to the north-east."

The timely arrival of reserves propped up the sagging Russian lines as, in the late afternoon, tanks of the 112th Tank Brigade at last began to arrive. At nightfall, some 60 tanks of the 112th went into the attack against the *Grossdeutschland*'s armoured reconnaissance and assault gun battalions. The Germans claim to have destroyed 35 Soviet tanks, while the Russians were responsible for destroying " ... 21 enemy tanks including 6 Tigers."

▲ StuG III assault guns of II SS Panzer Corps on the road to Prokhorovka. At Kursk these vehicles provided valuable direct-fire support for infantry attacks, and with their long-barrelled 75mm guns could also fight tanks.

▼ Troops of the *Grossdeutschland* Division, probably of the Antitank Battalion, prepare a 50mm *Panzerabwehrkanone* (Pak) antitank gun for action. It could knock out a T-34 up to a range of 500m (547yd).

The *Grossdeutschland* had pushed these units ahead as the result of an error by some panzergrenadiers, who mistakenly reported their location, as General F.W. von Mellenthin wrote:

"The grenadiers were under the illusion that they were in Nowosselowka [Novoselovka] and could not believe that they were only in Gremutschy [Gremiuchii]. Thus the report of the so-called success of the grenadiers was proved wrong; things like that happen in every war and particularly in Russia."

Soviet realignments took place. Katukov, to support Krivoshein when his defences gave way, had ordered Major-General A.L. Getman's VI Tank Corps to shift into new positions facing eastwards across the River Pena to the south of Verkhopen'e. This was to be followed by a counterattack to cover the withdrawal of III Mechanized Corps; this attack went in at nightfall. As darkness descended, Hoth's men also made adjustments to their positions as the fighting drew to an end. The panzergrenadiers of *Grossdeutschland*, under heavy fire from the Russians on the east bank, cleared the last vestiges of Soviet resistance from the west bank of the River Pena.

▲ Clearly an anachronism by 1943, but a sight that would have stirred the hearts of ordinary Soviet fighting men, a *tachanka*. Basically a light country carriage with a Maxim machine gun mounted on the back, the *tachanka* had gained a legendary reputation during the Russian Civil War and it was to continue in service with the Red Army during World War II.

◄ Two T-34/76s await their turn to join the fight. On the turret of the tank farthest from the camera is the vehicle's formation marking. The marking is diamond-shaped, which was the Red Army's map symbol for a tank. The symbol was stencilled on in white or yellow paint. However, the numbering system identifying brigade, battalion, company or corps was at this time not standardized.

►A Soviet machine-gun team rushes to a new position, towing their Maxim gun behind them. As well as the familiar Sokolov wheeled mounting, the Maxim could also be fired from a tripod. However, the water-cooled, armour-shielded Maxim was an awkward gun to move and consequently the wheeled mounting was preferred.

▼ A *Katyusha* rocket-launcher which, judging by the crew clinging on, is moving quite rapidly. The smoke thrown up by a battery of these weapons provided an ideal target marker for German artillery or *Luftwaffe* countermeasures. Above the windscreen is a thin piece of armour plate which was fitted to protect the glass from the heat of the rocket's propellant.

Rest that night was difficult for the men of both armies, as a German soldier noted:

"The sky was fire-red, heavy artillery shells shook the earth, rocket batteries fired at the last identified targets. Soon the Soviet 'crows' were in the air dropping large numbers of bombs on the fires and other targets."

Just as they had caught the Russians the previous day, now it was the turn of the Germans to be pre-empted. Over 40 Russian tanks of III Mechanized Corps sallied out from Syrtsevo in an attempt to stop the Germans. Unfortunately, they almost immediately drove into the sights of the Tiger company of *Grossdeutschland* and lost 10 tanks in quick succession. *Grossdeutschland*'s history describes the subsequent operations:

▲ A section of machine gunners towing their guns past a burnt-out Soviet truck on the road to Prokhorovka in the days before the battle. The open nature of the ground is obvious from the background beyond the dust track that serves as a road.

" ...I Battalion Panzergrenadier Division GD together with the tanks advanced on Syrtsevo from the east. The attackers broke into the village at about 12.30 [14:30 hours Moscow time] in the face of heavy antitank fire from the west bank, after which they mopped up the remaining Soviet defenders in Syrtsevo. The 3rd Panzer Regiment assisted in this attack from the west."

The Soviet account draws a similar picture:

"Up until 13:00 hours, the 10th Mechanized Brigade, the remains of the 1st Mechanized Brigade and the 112th Tank Brigade held off the German attack by a force of up to 2 infantry regiments and 70 tanks, while suffering heavy losses from aviation and artillery fire. In the light of his great losses, at 13:00 hours VI Tank Corps' commander gave permission to his brigade to withdraw across the River Pena [from Syrtsevo] and dig in."

◄ A pause during their march to the front. Soviet infantrymen break ranks to drink from a drum of boiled water carried by a pack-horse, visible to the rear of the picture. The action of sun and dust on the men's clothing is plain to see, its khaki hue has been lost and faded almost to white.

North along the River Pena, *Grossdeutschland*'s panzergrenadiers were recorded by their historians as being:

" ...involved in heavy fighting with fresh Soviet tank reserves at the eastern end of Verkhopen'e ... That evening, after refuelling, the Gottberg Panzer Battalion (II Battalion) was pulled out of Syrtsevo and likewise sent in the direction of Verkhopen'e ... Extending for a kilometre along the Pena in a north-south direction, it was a tough nut to crack. The effect of enemy fire from the west bank of the Pena on the mass of panzergrenadiers attacking from the south and east was especially uncomfortable and disruptive."

The significance of this apparently tiny settlement lay in the load-bearing capacity of its bridge across the River Pena, which the Soviets were determined to hold. The official history continues:

"The 200th Tank Brigade did not succeed in entrenching itself along its designated lines and suffered considerable losses from enemy air attacks. During the course of the day the brigade held off 12 enemy attacks, but, by the day's end, withdrew behind the River Pena, where it set about digging in its tanks."

Invigorated by the achievements of his men during 7 and 8 July, Knobelsdorff felt that he was in reach of the River Psel, and indeed it looked as if XLVIII Panzer Corps was poised to burst the central sector of Vatutin's defences. But what of Knobelsdorff's right flank, II SS Panzer Corps?

The men of Hausser's II SS Panzer Corps had, during the first two days of the offensive, been drawn towards Prokhorovka by following the Soviets' least line of defence. It was to be in this direction that the SS headed again on the morning of 7 July. *Totenkopf* pushed into the valley of the River Lipovyi Donets on II SS Panzer Corps' left flank, whilst the *Leibstandarte*'s two panzergrenadier regiments attacked Pokrovka and Bol'shie Maiachki. Thus reads the Soviet account:

"In the Pogrelovka and Mikhailovka region the enemy attacked the 1st Guards Tank Brigade. Up to 100 enemy aircraft bombed it from the skies. All enemy attempts to penetrate into the brigade's defences failed. Simultaneously, the Hitlerite command threw up to 30 tanks and an infantry battalion against Pokrovka and captured it. This

▼ A motorized reconnaissance troop moves towards the front. The vehicles are M3A1 White scout cars provided by the USA under the Lend-Lease agreement. Imported vehicles were usually left in the paint scheme provided by the country of origin, in this case American olive-drab. The weapon is a Browning .30-calibre medium machine gun, again of American manufacture.

created a threat to the brigade's left flank. Lieutenant-Colonel A.F. Burdov's 49th Tank Brigade was rushed to the Pokrovka region to restore the situation. He drove the enemy from Pokrovka, but during the subsequent battles, he fell back to the north and the enemy again occupied Pokrovka."

Leibstandarte's 1st SS Panzer Regiment and *Das Reich*'s 2nd SS Panzer Regiment advanced up the Prokhorovka road, driving parts of V Guards Tank Corps ahead of them, through and past Teterevino. The momentum of the SS tanks was slowed by the need to detach two panzergrernadier regiments to deal with Soviet forces on their flanks.

Further detachments of panzergrenadiers were dispatched to expand the wafer-thin flank screen provided by the *Totenkopf*. However, hard fighting at the tip of the *Panzerkeil* (armoured wedge) meant that the flanks were crucial and had to be held inviolate. The records show that the *Leibstandarte* claimed Soviet losses in their sector for 7 July to be 41 (later raised to 75) tanks, 12 aircraft, 23 artillery pieces, 13 deserters and 244 prisoners. II SS Panzer Corps gathered the tanks of the *Leibstandarte* and *Das Reich* Divisions during the evening in preparation for the operations the following day:

▲ Scout infantrymen occupy a recently captured German foxhole. The sacks carried on the men's backs contain the bulk of their equipment and food, as well as all their personal possessions. In the summer heat, corpses deteriorated very rapidly, a strong inducement to bury them quickly.

"After assembling its attack forces by 06:00 hours with the main point of concentration on the right wing of its sector as far as the road from Belgorod to Obajan [Oboyan], the LAH [*Leibstandarte*] is to move left of DR [*Das Reich*] and is to establish contact with XLVIII Panzer Corps north of Nowososselowka [Novososlevka]. Elements should also be moved out of the Lutschiki area, turned from the west to the south, and be deployed to capture Bol Majatschki [Bol'shie Maiachki]. The completion of the preparations should be reported to the Corps. The start of the attack will be given by order."

Leibstandarte's panzergrenadiers took Bol'shie Maiachki, whilst its panzer regiment moved against the Soviet 242nd Tank Brigade nearby. *Totenkopf*'s two panzergrenadier regiments succeeded in pushing the 237th Tank Brigade from Gresnoe up to the River Psel.

► It is sometimes forgotten that the rivers threading through the Russian landscape provided a vital element in any defensive lines due to the absence of significantly high ground. In the early morning mist, a small Russian unit carries out a security mission on a waterway in the Kursk area. The slow punting method of propulsion was preferred to the noise of an outboard motor.

The Russians, however, had plans of their own. *Totenkopf* and *Das Reich* advanced straight into the path of Major-General V.G. Burkov's X Tank Corps, fielding 185 tanks and self-propelled guns. Burkov's force was meant to have formed part of a Soviet spoiling attack against the right flank of II SS Panzer Corps, timed to coincide with a similar blow at the left flank of XLVIII Panzer Corps. X Tank Corps launched a series of piecemeal attacks during the course of the morning, but all were bloodily rebuffed.

▼ A well-entrenched Soviet antiaircraft gun, an 85mm Model 1939, is prepared for action. The almost cloudless sky is ideal for air operations at any altitude. The conditions are equally good for the ground forces. The gunners are wearing the Model 1936 helmet and the pre-1943 tunics. Soviet artillery pieces were generally left in their factory-finish khaki paint scheme.

II Tank Corps of General A.F. Popov arrived in the late afternoon, too late to support Burkov, and suffered a similar bloody repulse. The 100 tanks of V Guards Tank Corps were badly mauled in and around Kalinin and Iasnaia Poliana. But it was Burdeiny's II Guards Tank Corps that was to take the most vicious pounding.

The Soviet tanks, emerging from the woods where they had spent the night, were spotted by a flight of Henschel Hs 129s, led by Hauptmann Meyer. Meyer called up four squadrons of Henschels and, with their 30mm antitank guns, proceeded to riddle the thinly armoured engine covers of the T-34s. Within an hour, some 50 Soviet tanks were in flames, a blazing monument to the first occasion in history when an armoured attack was defeated by airpower alone. Fw 190s peppered the Russian infantry with antipersonnel bombs to complete this vista from hell. Vatutin's hope of carving a wide swathe through the rear of Hausser's advance was burning on the steppe.

▲ **More reserves, for the slaughter house that Operation Citadel had developed into, march towards the front. Soviet officers usually rode on horseback, and their task was to marshal the troops and deliver orders by riding to and fro. The regimental commander had the luxury of a staff car.**

II SS Panzer Corps claimed to have destroyed no less than 121 Soviet tanks on 8 July. The SS forged ahead, linking up with XLVIII Panzer Corps at Sukho-Solotino. However, Hausser was forced to use *Das Reich* as the right flank guard until such time as III Panzer Corps should arrive and offer assistance.

Army Detachment Kempf was engaged in a fight to protect its own flank as the Soviets launched violent counterattacks on the 106th and 320th Infantry Divisions near Maslova Pristan. This action tied down the 7th Panzer Division, which the 106th should have been able to release from flank guard.

However, early on 7 July, elements of the 7th Panzer Division went into the attack. With the 45 Tigers of 503rd Heavy Panzer Detachment to the fore, the 6th Panzer Division and those parts of the 7th Panzer Division which were free to do so advanced towards the vital road junction of Miasoedovo. That evening, the Soviets committed two divisions of XXXV Guards Rifle Corps to support the collapsing defences which were east of Belgorod.

On the left flank of III Panzer Corps, the 19th Panzer Division took Blizhniaia Igumenka in the rear of the 81th Guards Rifle Division, but failed to cross the River Northern Donets. Worryingly for Kempf, the 168th Infantry Division was making poor inroads against the Soviet defences east of the River Northern Donets and Belgorod.

On 8 July, with the Tigers in the lead, 6th Panzer Division pushed on 8km (4.9 miles) and

◄ **A heavily camouflaged artillery piece drives past a group of fascinated locals near to Kursk itself. The very cheerful gunner seated to the right of the photograph is mounted on a tracked prime mover. The Red Army had pioneered the use of halftracked vehicles during the Russo-Polish War of 1920.**

took the next key road junction at Melikhovo, east of the River Lipovyi Donets. But both the 19th and 7th Panzer Divisions had failed to keep up. Although III Panzer Corps was clear through the first Soviet defensive belt east of the River Northern Donets, it could not break through the line of the River Lipovyi Donets and into the rear of the Russians, east of Belgorod.

The countermeasures which were adopted by Lieutenant-General M.S. Shumilov, commanding the Seventh Guards Army, were extremely effective, and they served to reinforce defensive areas whilst simultaneously continuing to attack Army Detachment Kempf's right flank.

Throughout 7 and 8 July, Vatutin's men had held, but this had been achieved at a price. Nearly all of the Voronezh Front's reserves had been committed, as well as units drawn up from elsewhere. At a meeting which took place during the evening of 7 July, with the front of the Sixth Guards Army in ribbons, Khrushchev addressed his assembled commanders. He expressed himself in the following terms, and it was clear that he would brook no failure:

"The next two or three days will be terrible. Either we will hold out or the Germans will take Kursk. They are staking everything on this one card. For them it is a matter life or death. We must see to it that they break their necks."

▲ In a hastily prepared position, an antitank gun crew awaits the commander's order to play its part in the battle.

This bald statement was as true, if not more so 24 hours later, but by then the tanks from Steppe Front were even closer than they had been before.

▼ Dressed in the pre-1943 tunics a group of replacement infantrymen are briefed on their new position by another soldier. The simplicity of the equipment carried by Red Army men of all branches of service is evident from this photograph.

SS Spearhead

As the German northern pincer ground to a halt, all hopes of victory at Kursk rested with the forces of Army Group South. In II SS Panzer Corps Manstein had an élite force that was capable of giving the Führer his victory.

During the night 8/9 July, STAVKA speeded up the assembly of strategic reserves by ordering Rotmistrov's Fifth Guards Tank Army of three mobile corps, totalling 593 tanks and 37 self-propelled guns, to accelerate his march towards the region of Prokhovka, and subordinating him to Vatutin's Voronezh Front. At the same time, General A.S. Zhadov's Fifth Guards Army was transferred to Voronezh Front control, and ordered to deploy its two Guards rifle corps along the River Psel from Oboyan to Prokhorovka. It would take several days to position Zhadov's 80,000 men.

Simultaneously, Vatutin was orchestrating further movement within the Voronezh Front to consolidate the defences along the Oboyan road. The result of this rejigging gave Katukov's Fourth Tank Army another two tank corps: Burkov's X and Major-General A.G. Kravchenko's V Guards. New tanks would be provided on the march and it was anticipated that both corps would be in position early on 10 July, providing additional support for the First Tank Army's Oboyan road defences, or for an attack on Knobelsdorff's XLVIII Panzer Corps' left flank along the River Pena. As well as the tanks, infantry, antitank and artillery regiments from various, more secure locations and STAVKA reserves were put at Katukov's disposal.

On the German side of the line, Hoth had not been idle. It was decided to clear the threat to XLVIII Panzer Corps' left flank once and for all.

▼ Two grenadiers of the *Totenkopf* Division prepare for another assault at Kursk. As well as a panzer regiment, the division had two panzergrenadier regiments, an artillery regiment, and antiaircraft and antitank units.

▲ II SS Panzer Corps was equipped with the *Ferdinand* tank destroyer. This metal monster was armed with the 88mm Pak 43/2 L/71 gun, which could knock out any Soviet tank with ease. However, its lack of any secondary armament put it at a distinct disadvantage against Soviet antitank infantry.

To this end, the *Grossdeutschland*, 3rd Panzer Division and 332nd Infantry Division would deal with the Russians to their west, while some elements of the *Grossdeutschland* and 11th Panzer Division would continue to drive against Oboyan. The bulk of *Grossdeutschland*, having dealt with the flank problem, would then proceed north again. However, Knobelsdorff had underestimated the resilience of the Russian troops which had been positioned on his left flank.

II SS Panzer Corps would attack north with the *Totenkopf* and *Leibstandarte* Divisions, while the *Das Reich* and 167th Infantry Divisions covered their eastern flank along the River Lipovyi-Donets to Prokhorovka. The thrust on Kursk would rest on the shoulders of Hausser's 283 tank and assault gun crews. Manstein himself allocated all available close air support to bolster the force of the Waffen-SS attack.

► The commander of Army Group South, Field Marshal Erich von Manstein. Writing in his memoirs after the war, he described Army Group South's work at Kursk thus: "Difficult enough and made only slow progress."

▲ T-34 tanks and infantry of Rotmistrov's Fifth Guards Tank Army make their way towards the Prokhorovka region. Made up of V Guards Mechanized Corps and XXIX Tank Corps, its 170 tanks and 21 self-propelled guns would prove crucial in defeating the southern wing of the German offensive.

The objective of XLVIII Panzer Corps on 9 July was Novoselovka, which was defended by Krivoshein's III Mechanized Corps and Baksov's 67th Guards Rifle Division. Verkhopen'e fell during the morning, its defenders going down under a welter of German armour, aircraft and artillery fire. As *Grossdeutschland*'s history states:

"At about the same time, about 07:00 hours, the panzergrenadiers again set out against Verkhopen'e with II and III Battalions in an effort to finally take possession of the town in spite of heavy flanking fire from the west. Battle Group von Strachwitz supported the advance from the southern tip of Verkhopen'e with about 19 Panzer IVs [long], 10 Tigers and about 10 of the surviving Panthers. At the same time, in a massed attack, Stuka wings dropped their bombs on recognized targets in the town and on the west bank of the River Pena in order to soften up the objective. Finally, at about 08:35 hours, the commander of II Battalion, Panzergrenadier Regiment *Grossdeutschland*, reported that he was in the last houses in the northern part of Verkhopen'e, which meant as much as the capture of the hotly contested town. The strong flanking fire from the west continued, an indication that our left neighbour had been unable to keep up with our advance; he was still farther to the south-west and was heavily engaged with enemy tank concentrations."

Stuka dive-bomber support

Elsewhere progress was equally good. The official history continues:

"The morning of 9 July saw the Panzer Fusilier Regiment *Grossdeutschland* advancing beneath a cloudy sky past Verkhopen'e to the east towards Novoselovka and Point 240.4 [just west of Novoselovka]. There, however, it was halted by a very strong defence of antitank guns and tanks. At about the same time – about 06:00 hours [08:00 hours Moscow time] – the Armoured Reconnaissance Battalion, bolstered by the Assault Gun Battalion *Grossdeutschland*, was carrying out the division order for an advance towards Point 260.8 along the road to Oboyan.

"The attack was preceded by Stuka attacks on what appeared to be enemy armoured spearheads and troop concentrations farther to the north. Waves of dive-bombers dropped their loads with precision on the Russian tanks. A tall pillar of flame erupted each time a crew was sent to 'commissar and Red Army heaven'. Under cover of this really outstanding air support the battle group of Armoured Reconnaissance Battalion *Grossdeutschland* approached Point 260.8. Observations revealed that to the east the 11th Panzer Division, which was still partially equipped with the Panzer III, was preparing to attack along the road to the north ...

"With the good progress of the panzer fusiliers in the direction of Novoselovka and the reinforced Armoured Reconnaissance Battalion towards Point 260.8, the Strachwitz Panzer Group was pulled out of the area south of Verkhopen'e as quickly as possible and sent to the north-east. It soon reached Point 240.8. The Strachwitz Panzer Group then drove through the Armoured Reconnaissance

Battalion Battle Group in the direction of Point 240.4. Our tanks soon ran into the enemy tank concentration [86th Tank Brigade], however, which were sighted from a distance of 2500–3000 metres [2734–3280yd]. A major tank-versus-tank battle developed, with the Stukas providing continuous support. Hill 243 was reached after heavy fighting and the panzers halted there initially. On the horizon were burning and smoking enemy tanks. Unfortunately three of 6th Company's tanks had been knocked out as well ... In the further course of the engagement Hauptmann von Wietersheim succeeded in carrying the attack as far as the antitank defences at the village of Novoselovka and reached the hill."

"Extremely heavy fighting"

But the situation for the 3rd Panzer Division was far from good, as the report continues:

"However, the difficult situation of the 3rd Panzer Division on the left forced the division command to change its plans. The Panzer Fusilier Regiment *Grossdeutschland* held farther north and north-east of Novoselovka and south of Point 244.8. The 1st and 2nd Battalions and the regimental command of the Panzergrenadier Regiment *Grossdeutschland* were now committed west and north-west of Novoselovka and screened the front to the north and north-east. Panzer Group Strachwitz had to turn almost 90 degrees in order to leave its former location on the road to Oboyan and head for points 251.4 and 247.0 [north-west of Verkhopen'e]. Its orders were to make a frontal attack on the enemy tanks in that area which were holding up 3rd [Panzer] Division's advance. The reinforced Armoured Reconnaissance Battalion followed this movement while screening the flanks to the south-west."

Grossdeutschland's turn through a right angle to face west was noted in its divisional history:

"These movements, the result of the difficult situation in which the 3rd Panzer Division found itself, brought the division's units to Point 244.8 on the road to Oboyan, which was obviously the deepest penetration into the Kursk pocket by *Grossdeutschland*. It was possible only at the cost of extremely heavy fighting and in some cases considerable losses."

Grossdeutschland was to spend the following days embroiled in a ferocious battle with the Soviet VI Tank Corps, which meant that although the *Grossdeutschland* Division would emerge victorious, XLVIII Panzer Corps was deprived of the extra strength it needed to break through to Oboyan. Vatutin was acutely aware of the choice presented to him. Rapidly forces were moved to the western flank of the Voronezh Front to ensure the *Grossdeutschland* and 3rd Panzer Division, along with their supporting infantry, would not have the opportunity to rejoin the drive on Oboyan, let alone Kursk. By the morning of 10 July, *Grossdeutschland* and 10th Panzer Brigade were reduced to some 87 tanks and assault guns, including 30 Panthers. Nevertheless, they and the 3rd Panzer Division launched themselves at the junction of the Soviets' VI Tank and III Mechanized Corps. The 11th Panzer Division alone would now undertake the march on Oboyan. A classified Soviet account describes the clash:

"Isolated and broken-up tank groups of the 200th and 112th Tank Brigades were encircled in the region north of Berezovka, where, during the

▼ One of the thousands of Soviet tank crew members who fought at Kursk. This man is taking ammunition on board for the tank's main gun. Note the machine-gun ammunition magazines scattered on the hull.

course of the day, they fought with enemy tanks and infantry. Only at night were they able to link up with the main force of VI Tank Corps. As a result of the combat on 10 July, VI Tank Corps suffered heavy losses and counted in its ranks only 35 tanks and 10 antitank guns. Having withdrawn to the line Novoselovka to Noven'koe, the corps halved its defensive front [20–10km/12.4–6.2 miles] and again restored its smashed defences."

This success, however, did not move XLVIII Panzer Corps towards Oboyan, as General Getman, commander of VI Tank Corps, wrote:

"Nevertheless, the Corps continued to resist the enemy. Having littered the field of battle with hundreds of his burned and destroyed tanks and guns and thousands of bodies, the enemy succeeded in pushing our lines back several kilometres. His attempt to seize fully the village of Noven'koe and advance further in a northern direction failed. Meeting organized fire resistance, he ceased his attacks at nightfall."

Mellenthin's summary of the day rather contradicted this. The 11th Panzer Division's progress towards Oboyan had been slow, pushing into, but not breaking, the Soviet defences, and all the while extending its right flank to relieve units of the *Leibstandarte*.

Late on 11 July, Knobelsdorff put into practice his plan for a thrust on Oboyan by *Grossdeutschland* and the 11th Panzer Division:

"With 11th Panzer Division waiting for *Grossdeutschland* to take up its place on the left the Germans could see far into the valley of the River Psel, the last natural barrier this side of Kursk. With field glasses the towers of Oboyan could be made out in the fine haze. Oboyan was the objective.

"It seemed within arm's reach. Barely 12 miles away. No distance at all under normal circumstances for a fast formation. Would XLVIII Panzer Corps make this last leap?

"According to Hoth's carefully worked out timetable, the following should now have happened: XLVIII Panzer Corps to strike towards Oboyan and seize the crossings over the Psel. Its bulk to wheel eastward and before thrusting on Kursk – to defeat, jointly with Hausser's SS Panzer Corps, the enemy strategic armoured forces approaching across the strip of land of Prokhorovka. That was Hoth's plan."

Although this was Hoth's plan for XLVIII Panzer Corps, Vatutin had other ideas. He simply ordered Katukov's VI Tank Corps and the battered remnants of his tank army to:

"prevent the enemy from penetrating northward of the Kruglik-Ol'khovatka line, and with your main forces, attack from the line Alexandrovka–Noven'koe in general south-eastern direction in cooperation with the Sixth Guards Army with the mission of seizing Iakovlevo and Pokrovka and, jointly with the Sixth Guards and Fifth Guards Tank Armies, encircle the penetrating [enemy] mobile group and subsequently exploit success to the south and south-west."

With his tanks, Katukov was to counterattack the left flank of XLVIII Panzer Corps.

II SS Panzer Corps

The main advance of II SS Panzer Corps on 9 July was to be undertaken by the *Leibstandarte* and *Totenkopf*. *Totenkopf*, now completely detached from its flank cover activities, had been moved across the rear of *Das Reich* and *Leibstandarte*. Attacking in line abreast, it drove back Krivoshein's crippled III Mechanized Corps and Chernienko's XXXI Tank Corps to Kochetovka.

To the north of the *Leibstandarte*, *Totenkopf* reached the banks of the River Psel and captured the village of Krasni Oktiabr. The fall of Krasni Oktiabr signified the breaching of the last defensive barrier in front of Kursk: the River Psel was bridged and the Germans had the opportunity to wheel northwards into the Soviet rear. The *Leibstandarte*, having linked up with the 11th Panzer Division, crossed the River Solotinka, but the division was held on the outskirts of Kochetovka by the Soviet X Tank Corps.

The relative ease with which the *Leibstandarte* and *Totenkopf* cut through the Soviet lines was at odds with the bitter fighting that *Das Reich* was engaged in on the eastern flank along the Prokhorovka road. The success of the *Leibstandarte* and *Totenkopf* was in stark contrast with the lack of progress by III Panzer Corps to the south. The 6th Panzer Division had regrouped near Melikhovo and reconnoitred to the north. Meanwhile, the 7th Panzer and 19th Panzer Divisions held their ground east of the River Northern Donets. Kempf sought vainly for infantry to release his precious tanks to march on Korocha and intercept Rotmistrov's Fifth Guards Tank Army and secure the eastern flank of Hoth's thrust. This was something that Kempf had so far been unable to do. Concerned for his flanks, alert to the need to open up the rear of the Soviet defences facing Army Detachment Kempf, Hoth had learnt from aerial reconnaissance that large armoured forces were moving towards the front from the north-east. In Hoth's own words:

"It is better first to dispose of the enemy who is to be expected at Prokhorovka before the thrust northwards to Kursk is set in motion."

The order to shift the axis of advance for II SS Panzer Corps was issued late in the evening of 9 July. It has subsequently become known as the Prokhorovka Order. The essential parts are sections two and three, and they indicate exactly what the German forces were expected to achieve:

▼ Troops of II SS Panzer Corps on the Kursk battlefield, 9 July 1943. On that day the Waffen-SS divisions breached the last defensive barrier in front of Kursk. The price in heavy casualties and knocked-out tanks was vindicated: victory appeared at hand.

1. Enemy forces prepared for defence are equipped with antitank weapons and tanks and are standing in a line from the western edge of the forest at Swch. Komsomolets to the railway line at Ivanovskii Vyselok.

2. II SS Panzer Corps is to move out on 10 July 1943 with the *Leibstandarte* to the right and SS Panzergrenadier Division *Totenkopf* to the left on both sides of the River Psel and head north-east. Attack objective: Prokhorovka/East – Hill 252.4 [2.5km/1.5 miles north-east of there] – Beregovoe – Hill 243.5 [2km/1.2 miles north-west of Koritnoe] – Kartashevka.

3. The reinforced LSSAH [*Leibstandarte*] is to move out at 06:00 hours on 10 July 1943 after the barrage by the entire Artillery Regiment/LSSAH and Werfer-regiment 55. After the *Luftwaffe*'s preparation, the LSSAH is to move along the road from Teterevino to Prokhorovka, capture the latter town, and hold it. First attack objective: Prokhorovka and Hill 252.4. SS Panzergrenadier Division *Das Reich* is to set out with LSSAH and to capture the high ground 2km [1.2 miles] south-east of Iwanowskij Wysselok. SS Panzergrenadier Division *Totenkopf* is to move forward from the Kliuchi bridgehead to the north-east."

During the short hours of darkness that typified a summer's night on the Russian steppe, both the Red Army and the *Wehrmacht* adjusted their positions. But far away on the sun-soaked beaches of the Mediterranean island of Sicily, events were shaping that would profoundly influence German operations on the Eastern Front. The Western Allies had opened a new front on Hitler's vulnerable southern flank by invading Sicily on 10 July. With American and British troops pouring onto Italian beaches, the very foundations of the Axis were under threat. Hitler's nightmare, a repetition of what had occurred in during World War I, was quickly becoming a reality: war on two fronts had finally come to pass. The Führer now had to reconsider where his

▼ The mighty Tiger proved a great success at Kursk, and the skill of the panzer crews resulted in staggering victories. The 1st SS Panzer Regiment, for example, destroyed 90 enemy tanks in three hours on one day.

▲ **Panzer IIIs of the *Totenkopf* Division advance towards the frontline. The division started the battle with 63 Panzer IIIs; by 10 July, this figure had fallen to 48. Note the swastika flag draped on the back of the right-hand tank for aerial recognition purposes.**

priorities lay, as he knew that his limited strategic reserves would be stretched almost to their breaking points.

Hitler received better news from Army Group South during the course of 10 July. Hausser's II SS Corps regrouped with considerable difficulty during the night 9/10 July. Indeed, such were the problems it faced that the attack was launched in an uncharacteristically piecemeal fashion, employing the forces immediately to hand. Shortly before dawn, the panzergrenadiers of the *Totenkopf* struck across the River Psel and attempted to storm Hill 226.6. The failure of this attack forced him to postpone his twin attack south of the river, and the efforts of the SS were delayed until 10:45 hours. However, this time the River Psel was crossed and a bridgehead secured on its northern bank east of Kliuchi, and the northern slopes of Hill 226.6 were taken.

Meanwhile, the *Leibstandarte* was making greater progress, advancing up the Prokhorovka road. Fighting all the way and warding off almost continual attacks by T-34s, the *Leibstandarte* 's panzergrenadiers had, by the early afternoon, taken the Komsomolets State Farm and were engaged in vicious fighting for Hill 241.6. Although defended by summer thunderstorms and emplaced Russian tanks, Hill 241.6 was taken just after night fell. The *Leibstandarte*'s claim for the day's fighting was 53 Soviet tanks and 23 antitank guns.

The advance of *Das Reich* was, in comparison, lacklustre. Operating south of the Prokhorovka road across the railway line towards Storozhevka 1, it met heavy resistance. After a gruelling battle of attrition, *Das Reich* had gained but part of the small village of Ivanovskii Vyselok. Once again, *Das Reich*'s performance had been blunted by its need to protect its right flank, a situation that was imposed by the regrouping of elements of the 167th Infantry Division, which freed more of *Das Reich*'s panzergrenadiers. Hausser's men had made slow progress, but they had nonetheless pushed ahead far enough for Hitler to order that Operation Citadel be continued.

From Vatutin's point of view, the German advance came at a most inopportune moment, just as his forces were carrying out their complex regrouping. The greater part of Major-General V.G. Bukov's X Tank Corps had withdrawn to join First Tank Army on the Oboyan road, leaving behind its 11th Motorized Rifle Brigade, which resisted *Totenkopf*'s advance throughout the day.

The three tank brigades – 26th, 169th and 99th – of General A.F. Popov's II Tank Corps had replaced Bukov's men across the Prokhorovka road and, at dawn on 10 July, launched themselves against the leading elements of *Leibstandarte* and *Das Reich*, engaging both divisions in the hot contest for Komsomolets State Farm and Hill 241.6. But, despite their best efforts, Popov's tanks were driven back. However, by nightfall reinforcements in the shape of the Fifth Guards Army began to reach Prokhorovka, the first being

▲ **Throughout the battle II SS Panzer Corps operated with close air support, mainly cannon-armed Stuka dive-bombers. Such close cooperation meant that it was imperative for panzer crews and German infantry to designate themselves as being friendly forces, hence the swastika flag.**

the élite 9th Guards Division, commanded by Colonel A.M. Sazonov. These troops, although weary and in need of rest, took up their defensive positions east of Prokhorovka.

More and more of Zhadov's Fifth Guards Army streamed through and around Prokhorovka during 10 July. By the end of the day, the 95th and 97th Guards Rifle Divisions had occupied the defences along the River Psel, reinforcing the battered remains of the 51st and 52nd Rifle Divisions in preparation for the next phase of Hausser's onslaught. These dispositions led in turn to the 183rd Rifle Division marching off to relieve V Guards Tank Corps forces that in their turn moved to bolster the First Tank Army farther to the west. As Kravchenko's tanks moved out, so Burdeiny's II Guards Tank Corps disengaged from its flank attack missions, on the right of II SS Panzer Corps, for re-equipping in preparation for its future role in support of the Fifth Guards Tank Army.

With all the skill and poise of a seasoned juggler, Vatutin had succeeded in regrouping his armoured forces and their supporting troops whilst contending with non-stop German attacks. What would the outcome have been for his carefully laid plans had the *Panzerkeils* of the SS broken through the sorely pressed Russian lines? The effect on vast convoys of vehicles and men struck in the flank by the long-range artillery of the Tigers can only be imagined. However, Vatutin's faith in his methods and men was paying off. Now he had the time to carry out the most significant placement in his complex jigsaw, that of the Fifth Guards Tank Army of General P. A. Rotmistrov's. This powerful force, having driven 100km (65 miles) by road, began to occupy assembly areas in the Fifth Guards Army's rear.

On 10 July Rotmistrov met with Vatutin and Chief of the General Staff A.M. Vasilevky in Oboyan. It is well worth quoting Rotmistrov's account of the conversation:

"The front commander invited me closer to the map, and pointing with a pencil at the Prokhorovka region, said:

" 'Having failed to penetrate to Kursk through Oboyan, clearly the Hitlerites have decided to shift the axis of their main blow farther east along the rail line to Prokhorovka. There, the forces of II Panzer Corps have assembled, which must attack along the Prokhorovka axis in cooperation with XLVIII Panzer Corps and tank formations of Group Kempf.'

"N.F. Vatutin glanced at A.M. Vasilevsky and then, turning to me, he continued: 'Thus Pavel Alekseevich, we have decided to oppose the SS tank divisions with your tank guardsmen – to deliver a counterstroke against the enemy with Fifth Guards Tank Army, reinforced by a further two tank corps.'

" 'Incidentally,' said A.M. Vasilevsky, 'the German tank divisions possess heavy Tiger tanks and *Ferdinand* self-propelled guns. Katukov's tank army has suffered considerably from them. Do you know anything about this equipment and how do you feel about fighting with them?'

" 'We know, Comrade Marshal. We received tactical-technical information about them from the Steppe Front staff. We have also thought about means for combating them.'

" 'Interesting!' added Vatutin and, nodding to me, said, 'continue.'

" 'The fact is that the Tigers and *Ferdinands* not only have strong frontal armour, but also a powerful 88mm with direct fire range. In that regard they are superior to our tanks, which are armed with 76mm guns. Successful struggle with them is possible only in circumstances of close-in combat, with exploitation of the T-34's greater manoeuvrability, and by flanking fire against the side armour of the heavy German machines.'

" 'In other words, engage in hand-to-hand fighting and board them,' said the Front commander, and again he turned to conversation about the forthcoming counterstroke, in which the First Tank Army, Sixth, Seventh and Fifth Guards Armies were to take part."

Rotmistrov's army was strengthened with the addition of II Tank and II Guards Tank Corps; the 1529th Self-propelled, 522nd, and 148th Howitzer and 148th, 93rd Gun Artillery Regiments; and the 16th and 80th Guards Mortar Regiments. With these powerful forces gathering, Vatutin's order was passed on to Rotmistrov's troops:

"On the morning of 12 July, together with the First Tank Army and Fifth Guards Army, launch a decisive offensive to destroy the enemy south-west of Prokhorovka and, by the end of the day, reach the line Krasnaia Dubrova [north-east of Syrtsevo] to Iakovlevo."

The jumping-off positions for the Fifth Guards Tank Army was a 15km (12-mile) wide swathe of open ground that spread west and south-west of

▼ At Kursk even the "supermen" of the Waffen-SS were halted by the tenacity of the Soviet defenders. II SS Panzer Corps suffered horrendous casualties as its offensive unfolded. The *Leibstandarte*, for example, had 181 killed and 906 wounded in two days.

521

Prokhorovka from north of the River Psel south across the road and rail link to Storozhevoe. On this ground of his choosing, Rotmistrov would commit a total of 500 tanks and self-propelled guns in his initial attack.

Then, on 11 July at 05:00 hours, the SS struck its first blow, and the *Leibstandarte*'s panzers lunged forward along both sides of the Prokhorovka road. The *Luftwaffe*, which once more achieved a threadbare, local air superiority, unleashed wave upon wave of bombers to blaze a path into the Soviet defences. Driving the elements of the already depleted Soviet II Tank Corps before it, the *Leibstandarte* Division was subjected to flank attacks and artillery fire. German reinforcements were pushed forward as the sun rose, but then the *Leibstandarte* crashed straight into the 9th Guards Airborne Division. The 26th and 28th Guards Airborne Regiments were to feel the full weight of Hitler's crack guards.

An important point in the Soviet defences was Hill 252.2. The area was subjected to a torrent of bombs, rockets and shells as the Germans attempted to soften up the target. A battalion of panzergrenadiers, supported by Tigers and assault guns, moved towards the high ground. Finally, after three hours of intense combat, the *Leibstandarte* took the crest of the hill and pushed on to capture the Oktiabr'skii State Farm.

From the Soviet account of the Guards Airborne Division, the following extract describes the main events of the day:

"On the morning of 11 July, when the formations of the Fifth Guards Army had still not firmly occupied their positions, having completed their regrouping, the enemy renewed their offensive.

"It was an overcast day. A fresh breeze disturbed the boundless sea of ripened grain between Prokhorovka, Prelestnoe and Pravorot.

"Up to a battalion of infantry, supported by 40 tanks and self-propelled guns, among them heavy Tigers and Panthers, and by hundreds of Ju 87 and Ju 88 aircraft, attacked the junction of the 9th Guards Airborne and 95th Guards Rifle Divisions. The main attack was against the 3rd Battalion, 26th Guards Airborne Regiment, which was defending Oktiabr'skii State Farm. A short but powerful artillery preparation and strong bomber strikes preceded the enemy infantry and tank attack. Armoured transporters carrying motorized infantry followed the tanks and self-propelled guns."

◄ Equipped with side skirts and additional turret armour, a Panzer IV tank halts while its commander and crew scan the horizon for the enemy. The vehicle is probably a Panzer IV Ausf H model, which first rolled off the production lines in April 1943.

A storm of steel

The commander of the 3rd Battalion, Guards Major D.I. Boriskin, reported on the situation to his regimental commander, Guards Lieutenant-Colonel G.M. Kashpersky, and ordered the commanders of his rifle companies to open massive fire as the tanks and infantry neared their positions.

"Oktiabr'skii State Farm, Hill 252.2, and Lutovo [village] shuddered from exploding bombs, shells and mines. The soldiers attentively observed the approaching enemy from the foxholes they had dug the night before.

"When only several hundred metres remained to the edge of the state farm, infantry poured out of the armoured transporters. Submachine gunners opened fire on the run, and concealing themselves behind the tanks, they began the assault. The distorted faces of the Fascists bore witness to the fact that their warlike ardour was roused by a fairly large dose of schnapps.

" 'Fire!' ordered the battery commander. A squall of 3rd Battalion fire met the Fascists. The long bursts of I.V. Khoroshikh's and P. N. Lyznikov's heavy machine guns struck the infantry in the flanks and were echoed by the Guardsmen's light machine guns and submachine guns. Divisional artillery and supporting battalions of the RGK [Reserve of the High Command] 3rd Artillery Penetration Division laid down an immovable defensive fire in front of Oktiabr'skii State Farm. The battalion and regimental artillery of Guards Lieutenants I.H. Samykin and A.F Shestakov delivered fire over open sights.

"The infantry were separated from the tanks, and facing a hurricane of fire from the state farm, they withdrew to the reverse slopes of Hill 215.4.

▲ **A Waffen-SS grenadier leaves the safety of a ditch to advance once again. It was unfortunate for the Germans that on 9 July torrential rain slowed the momentum of their attack. However, by this time the Soviets were launching counterattacks against the front and flanks of the panzer spearheads.**

The Fascists attacked the 3rd Battalion two more times before 14:00 hours. However, these were only reconnaissances in force."

An unequal struggle

The report continues: "At 14:00 hours up to 100 enemy tanks and up to a regiment of infantry riding in armoured transporters attacked Oktiabr'skii State Farm and Hill 252.2. Around 40 tanks and up to a regiment of motorized infantry attacked the neighbouring 287th Guards Rifle Regiment of the 95th Guards Rifle Division. Discovering the junction between the 95th Guards and 9th Airborne Divisions, the Fascists tried to drive a wedge between them. One hundred and forty tanks were attacking along a front of 3km [1.8 miles] in the sector from Oamki Farm to Andreevka. A powerful fire raid and bombing strikes by 50 dive-bombers preceded the assault. Once again fierce battle raged, but the effort was unequal. The enemy possessed absolute numerical superiority and displayed special obstinacy at the junction of the 26th and 287th Regiments ...

"Having pressed back the 26th and 287th Regiments, up to 40 enemy tanks concentrated against Prelestnoe and the southern edge of Petrovka and up to 60 tanks – across Hill 252.2 and along the rail line – towards Prokhorovka. The 26th Regiment withdrew to the positions of the 23rd Guards Airborne Regiment, on the south-western slopes of Hill 252.4 [1km/0.6 miles west of Prokhorovka]."

Another version of the situation was recorded in the *Leibstandarte*'s history:

"The line captured by this point (17:00 hours on 11 July) ran from Storozhevoe, the western and eastern edges of the forest north of there [held by the 1st Regiment], along the road as far as a point 500 metres north-west of Hill 252.2 [held by the 2nd Regiment], the hill just west of Swch. Oktjabrskij [held by the panzer group], to the eastern edge of Hill 252.2 [held by the Reconnaissance Battalion]. That line's position was reported to the corps, and it was not crossed again that day. The reason for stopping was the positions of adjacent units on both sides. They were so far behind the division's advance that we were outflanked on two sides. A frontal attack on Prokhorovka would have resulted in very heavy losses because of the strong enemy antitank and defensive artillery on the south-eastern edge of Prokhorovka and at the commanding position on Hill 252.4 north-west of the Psel [should read Prokhorovka]. This situation was reported to the commanding general at about 17:00 hours at the divisional headquarters in North Lutschki. A suggestion was made to him to concentrate all the artillery available to corps and to focus on the *Totenkopf* Division's attack on Hill 226.2 on 12. 7. 43. Only after the capture of this hill should the attack by Panzergrenadier Division *Das Reich* and Panzergrenadier Division *Leibstandarte* on Prokhorovka be continued. After conferring with the Chief of the General Staff, Colonel Ostendorf, Lieutenant-General Hausser declared himself in agreement with this plan."

"General, they are not our tanks"

Despite their exposed position, the progress of the *Leibstandarte* had been good. A wedge had been driven into the Russian lines in front of Prokhorovka and II Tank Corps' defences were in disarray. In company with STAVKA representative Marshal Vasilevsky, Rotmistrov inspected the area, as he later recorded:

"Sufficient daylight still remained and the marshal proposed an inspection of the jumping-off positions which I had selected for XXIX and XVIII Tank Corps. Our route passed through Prokhorovka to Belenikhino, and the quick-moving Willies [Willys jeep], bobbing up and down over the potholes, skirted round vehicles with ammunition and fuel, which were heading to the front. Transports with wounded slowly went past us. Here and there destroyed trucks and transports stood by the roadside ...

"There, along the northern edge of the forest, were the jumping-off positions of XXIX Tank Corps. XVIII Tank Corps would attack to the right, I explained to A.M. Vasilevsky ...

"The agricultural installations of Komsomolets State Farm could be seen two kilometres distant to the right.

"Suddenly, Vasilevsky ordered the driver to stop. The vehicle turned off the road and abruptly halted amid the dust-covered roadside brush. We opened the doors and went several steps to the side. The rumble of tank engines could be clearly heard. Then the very same tanks came into sight ...

"Instantly, I raised my binoculars. Indeed, tens of tanks in combat formation, firing from the march from their short-barrelled guns, were crossing the field and stirring up the ripened grain ...

" 'Comrade General, they are not our tanks, they are German ...'

" 'So, the enemy has penetrated somewhere. He wants to pre-empt us and seize Prokhorovka.'

" 'We cannot permit that,' I said to A.M. Vasilevsky, and by radio I gave the command to General Kirichenko to move without delay two tank brigades to meet the German tanks and halt their advance ...

"Thus the situation suddenly became complicated. The jumping-off positions that we had earlier selected for the counterstroke were in the hands of the Hitlerites."

Again, II SS Panzer Corps recorded the heavy losses suffered by their opponents: 99 tanks and 29 assault guns destroyed. But the SS had not escaped unscathed. The armoured strength of the *Leibstandarte* fell to 60 tanks, 10 assault guns and 20 self-propelled tank destroyers. The tanks included 4 Panzer IIs, 5 Panzer IIIs, 47 Panzer IVs, and 4 Tigers with, possibly, 10 captured T-34s. During the evening Hausser issued his orders for the following day, according the *Leibstandarte* the honour of the most important task:

▼ A Stuka ground crew at work. The Stuka crews were much admired by the army. The War Diary of the 3rd Panzer Division noted the Stukas "attacking the Russian tanks uninterruptedly and with wonderful precision."

"The reinforced 1st Panzergrenadier Regiment with the Panzer Battalion subordinated to it is to set out at 04:50 hours and capture Storozhevoe and Jamki. It is to establish a position adjacent to the 1st Battalion, 2nd SS Panzergrenadier Regiment, at the road beside Hill 252.2.

"The reinforced 2nd Panzergrenadier Regiment, the Panzer Group and the reinforced reconnaissance battalion are to stand ready to move in conjunction with elements of the *Totenkopf* Division, as soon as that division has neutralized the enemy attacks on our flank along the River Psel, and to capture Prokhorovka and Hill 252.4.

"The Artillery Regiment *Leibstandarte* is to send an Artillery Liaison Command to the *Totenkopf* Division in order to support the attack by that division on hill 226.6."

On the right flank of this operation, the *Das Reich* Division was responsible for taking Storozhovoe 1 and Vinogradovka, and then opening up the southern route which led to the crucial target of Prokhorovka.

Army Detachment Kempf's III Panzer Corps was to provide all possible support and, ideally, to join up with II SS Panzer Corps in Prokhorovka. Failing that, Kempf was to syphon off as much of the Soviet armour as possible from Hausser's front and flanks. The final part of the German plan involved XLVIII Panzer Corps taking the vital crossing points on the River Psel, south of Oboyan. When Prokhorovka was taken and the River Psel crossed, the two panzer corps would then push on across the steppe to Oboyan and Kursk, with III Panzer Corps covering the eastern flank. Vatutin and Rotmistrov deployed their forces rapidly to prevent this eventuality. To the west, spoiling attacks were to made against XLVIII Panzer Corps. The orders which Rotmistrov's issued to Vatutin were clear and utterly single-minded:

"At 10:00 hours on 12 July, deliver a counterstroke in the direction of Komsomolets State Farm and Pokrovka and, in cooperation with Fifth Guards Army and First Tank Army, destroy the enemy in the Kochetovka, Pokrovka, and Gresnoe regions and do not permit him to withdraw in a southern direction." Infantry support for Rotmistrov's tanks was to be provided by the 9th Guards Airborne Division.

Alarmed by the German attack on 11 July, Rotmistrov advanced the start of his attack, scheduling it to begin at 08:30 hours, Moscow time, which was two hours ahead of Berlin. Deprived of Popov's tanks as a result of their losses on 11 July, he decided on taking the following course of action:

"To strike a blow with the forces of XVIII, XXIX and II Guards *Tatsinskaia* [an honorific title] Tank Corps in the sector to the right – Beregovoe, Andreevka and Iasnaia Poliana; to the left – Pravorot', Belenikhino, Marker 232.0 and, by the end of the day, reach the line Krasnaia

▼ Typical scene at Kursk: a panzer tank, accompanying infantry and smoke and flames. By 12 July the initiative in the south had passed to Rotmistrov and his hundreds of T-34s and self-propelled guns.

Dubrova to Iakovlevo. The V Guards *Zimovnikovskii* [honorific title] Mechanized Corps, located in army second echelon, received the mission of being prepared to exploit the success of XXIX Tank Corps and II Guards *Tatsinskaia* Tank Corps in the general direction of Luchki and Pogorelovka. The tank corps had to occupy jumping-off positions from Prelestnoe through Storozhevoe to Mal. Iablononovo by 24:00 hours on 11 July and be ready to attack by 03:00 hours on 12 July."

Last stand at Prokhorovka

The jumping-off points were now right in the very suburbs of Prokhorovka itself. Rotmistrov's centre, astride the Prokhorovka road, was XXIX Tank Corps. XXIX Tank Corps consisted of the 31st, 32nd and 25th Tank Brigades, and the 1446th Self-propelled Artillery Regiment, and had a total of 191 tanks and self-propelled guns. Their task would be undertaken with the help of the 1529th Self-propelled Artillery Regiment's self-propelled guns, which numbered 21.

These troops would lead the Russian attack on the German lines between the Oktiabr'skii State Farm and Storozhevoe, and their efforts would be supported by the 28th Guards Airborne Regiment and 53rd Motorized Brigade. II Guards Tank Corps had 120 tanks, divided between the 4th, 25th and 26th Tank Brigades, and these were to strike at *Das Reich*'s positions from west of Vinogradovka along the railway line to Belenikhino, with support from the remains of II Tank Corps.

To Popov's rear lay the 53rd Guards Tank Regiment with 21 KV-1 tanks. A further 228 tanks and self-propelled guns of General B.M. Skvortsov's V Guards Mechanized Corps waited in the wings as a reserve force. A final, small armoured reserve, which was commanded by General K.G. Trufanov, occupied positions near Pravorot. Vatutin was tasked with providing supplementary artillery support, and his supporting force would include the 17th Artillery Brigade and 26th Antiaircraft Artillery Division, as well as five other mortar or artillery regiments.

In all, Rotmistrov was to open the attack with some 430 tanks and self-propelled guns, followed by another 70. Roughly half of these tanks were lightly armed and armoured T-70s. In order to counter the long range of the German tank guns, Rotmistrov specified to his tankers that they were to close with the Germans at high speed before swamping them, particularly the Tigers, by sheer weight of numbers.

By 02:00 hours on 12 July, Rotmistrov's forces were in place. It was a magnificent achievement, splendidly supported by the efforts of STAVKA. The days of movement had taken their toll on the men, but the effective number of tanks was due to their replacement and non-stop maintenance en route. There appeared to be very little left for the Russians to do but wait – praying was not part of the Soviet soldier's creed.

▲ A tired panzergrenadier stocks up with grenades for yet another day's fighting. The *Stielgranate* had a time delay of 4.5 seconds, giving the thrower time to take cover before the fragmentation warhead exploded.

Tanks Burning Like Torches

Operation Citadel, Hitler's last great offensive on the Eastern Front, was decided around the village of Prokhorovka on 12 July 1943 when hundreds of tanks clashed in the greatest armoured battle in the history of warfare.

The tank battles that took place along the southern pincer of the Kursk salient on 12 July were to mark the beginning of the end for Hitler's ambitious Operation Citadel.

In the main, the attention of historians chronicling the Battle of Kursk has focused on the bloody fields to the south-west of Prokhorovka, where Hitler's black-garbed guardsmen locked horns with Stalin's élite tankers. But events to the south-east and west of this armoured carnage should not be overlooked, as they too proved to be key factors in the overall equation. What took place on 12 July should be viewed as a whole, and not as a single, climactic tank battle.

Manstein and Hoth were attempting to weave three strands into a single thread that would give them the strength to wear down the Soviet defensive belts and finally burst through to Kursk and victory. The Russian commanders were equally

▼ A Soviet ROKS-2 flamethrower team in action. This model was intended to be used almost like a rifle; it featured a butt and was fired from the shoulder. The propellant was stored in the cylinder beneath the rectangular fuel tank. The weapon's shape made its operator less of an obvious target than other, more orthodox, flamethrower designs.

alive to the threats that hung over them. Vatutin's instructions for 12 July placed the main emphasis on the attacks of Katukov's First Tank, Chistakov's Sixth Guards, Rotmistrov's Fifth Guards Tank and Zhadov's Fifth Guards Armies against the most immediate German threat: Hausser's II SS Panzer Corps and Knobelsdorff's XLVIII Panzer Corps.

Orders for an attack into the right flank of Army Detachment Kempf east of Razumnoe were given to Seventh Guards Army's XL Rifle Corps. This attack was intended to prevent III Panzer Corps from making progress in its drive to link up with Hausser's men.However, the Russians were taken by surprise during the night of 11/12 July by a daring operation undertaken by elements of Kempf's 6th Panzer Division.

"All hell was let loose"

Headed by a captured T-34, a small group of tanks and halftrack troop carriers were sent forward to capture Rzhavets and the vital crossing points on the River Northern Donets. Under strict orders not to open fire or speak German, this battle group drove into Soviet territory a little after nightfall on 11 July. In the words of a German account:

"They moved past manned and well-established emplacements of antitank guns and multiple rockets. The moon shed a dim light. The Russians did not budge. Sleepily they were leaning in their positions along the road. They were used to such columns. All day long Soviet formations had been rumbling past them. Bäke [the German commander] overtook an enemy infantry column. Fortunately no Soviet soldier thought of hitching a ride on the tanks."

Despite the loss of the lead T-34, the column pushed on to reach Rzhavets. But now fighting broke out:

" ...all hell was let loose. The ghost journey was over. The Russians fired flares. Machine-gun fire rattled wildly from all sides.

"Bäke's tanks and armoured infantry carriers raced into the village. Antitank gun positions were overrun. Engineers captured a troop of multiple mortars.

"From the direction of the river came several dull thuds. The bridge! Bäke thought in alarm.

"A moment later his tank stood at the bridge over the Donets. The bridge had been blown. The combat group had missed the turn in the village which led to it.

"However, engineers and grenadiers managed to reach the far bank by a foot bridge. And the surprise among the Russians was such that the Germans succeeded in forming a bridgehead. At

▲ Turned against its own, this captured German *Nebelwerfer* (literally smokethrower) is speedily reloaded by its Soviet crew in an operation that will take approximately 90 seconds. Each high-explosive rocket weighed some 34kg (75lb). The angle of the tubes would suggest that the target is an armoured vehicle approaching over the crest of the ridge. The white star indicates an earlier "kill", possibly by this unorthodox method of firing.

▼ A typical village in the Prokhorovka area. The lives of the population were soon to be turned upside down by one of the greatest battles of all time. When the inhabitants eventually returned, it would be to a lunar landscape littered with the detritus of human savagery and mechanical destruction.

▲ **Major-General G.V. Baklanov, pictured right, receives instructions to move his troops to join the Voronezh Front on 8 July. Baklanov commanded the 13th Guards Rifle Division, part of the Fifth Guards Army.**

daybreak Bäke's vanguard detachment of the 6th Panzer Division was firmly established on the northern bank of the Donets."

The bridge was repaired swiftly and III Panzer Corps began to cross. Vatutin received word of the fall of Rzhavets at 04:00 hours on 12 July and realized the implications for his plans. In quick succession, Rotmistrov was alerted, and he in turn contacted Trufanov and issued him with the orders to use his reserve formation to:

" ...destroy the enemy in Rydvika, Rzhavets region and reach the line Shakhovo–Shchelovkovo by the end of the first day."

Trufanov's force included some 60 T-34 and 30 T-70 tanks. Communications were established with the Soviet forces already engaged in the area, and the leading elements of Trufanov's group went into action late on 12 July. Further Soviet attacks had forced Hunersdorff to withdraw the greater part of the 6th Panzer Division back across the River Northern Donets and contained the modest bridgehead held by the 19th Panzer Division.

The prompt, decisive reaction of Vatutin and Rotmistrov had restored the Soviet line along the River Northern Donets and had also prevented III Panzer Corps from driving on to Prokhorovka on 12 July. But even as Trufanov's men went south, events were shaping nearer to Rotmistrov's HQ that would demand his concentrated attention.

▼ **A Red Army Guards tank colonel gives a crew instructions. The tank formation to the left of the picture shows a pair of T-34s at rest. Navigation in underdeveloped areas such as these could pose great problems for tank units, and accurate communications were vital, particularly if enemy minefields were to be avoided.**

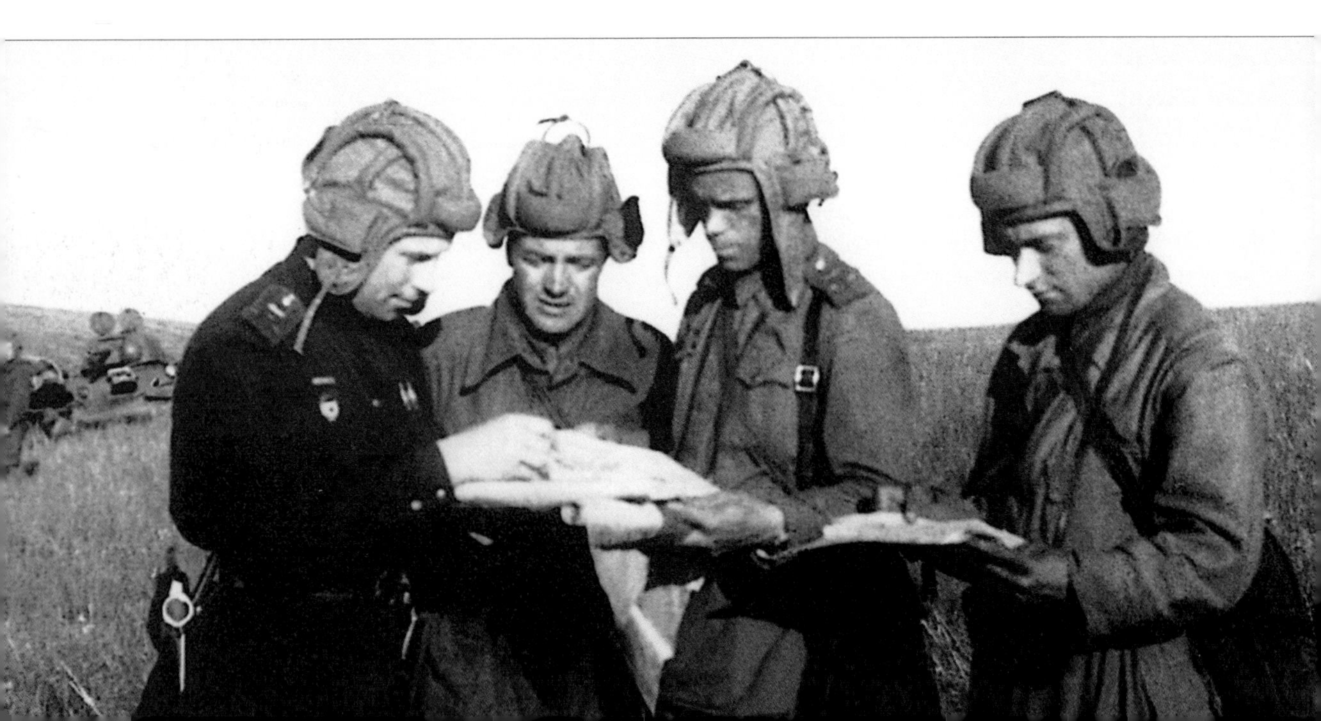

▲ **Lieutenant-General A.F. Popov's II Tank Corps moved from the South-Western Front on 8 July to join the Fifth Guards Tank Army on 11 July. The original caption reads, "Lt-Gen A.F. Popov speaking into the radio with a tank crew in action."**

The battle that became known as Prokhorovka took place in a constricted arena. From the German lines the northern boundary was the winding River Psel. To the south-east unharvested fields of rye and wheat rolled gently away and 4.8km (3 miles) further east lay Prokhorovka itself, with its skyline dominated by a tall grain silo. Only four miles from the River Psel was the southern extremity of the battleground, the railway cutting of the Kursk–Belgorod line, beyond which the ground was marked by hills and cut by ravines, a terrain which was totally unsuitable for any kind of tank-to-tank combat.

As the sun rose over the steppe, it began to dry out the ground, which had been dampened by the night's showers. A cool east wind blew clouds across the dull sky as the panzergrenadiers of the *Leibstandarte* drove into the first rays of the sun. They had one immediate objective: to capture Stovozhevoe. It was 06:50 hours. At just after 08:00 hours, 67 tanks of the *Leibstandarte* began to roll forward in support of their infantry. Suddenly, in the words of an SS panzer officer who was positioned in the van of the advance:

"A purple wall of smoke rose into the air, produced by smoke shells. It meant: tank warning!

"The same signals were to be seen all along the crest of the slope. The threatening violent danger signals also appeared farther to the right at the railway embankment.

" The small valley extended to our left, and as we drove down the forward slope we spotted the first T-34s, which were apparently attempting to outflank us from the left.

"We halted on the slope and opened fire, hitting several of the enemy. A number of Russian tanks were left burning. For a good gunner 800 metres [874yd] was the ideal range.

▼ **"P.T. Brud's gun team who destroyed seven tanks, one a Tiger. Junior Sergeant M.T. Finogim and Privates D.M. Chernoff and P.V. Zhitkilkh." Thus reads the original caption extolling the heroism of these men. The Red Army propaganda machine took many such opportunities to boost civilian morale by demonstrating the good use which was made of the weapons they produced.**

▲ Immobilized, this Panther Model D has become yet another Russian trophy. It appears to have fallen victim to the mechanical problems that beset the Panthers at Kursk. Judging by the tow wire and broken track, this Panther was abandoned while being recovered. The Model D had a flap in the glacis plate for the machine gun and a drum-type commander's cupola.

"As we waited to see if further enemy tanks were going to appear, I looked around, as was my habit. What I saw left me speechless. From beyond the shallow rise about 150–200 metres [164–218yd] in front of me appeared 15, then 30, then 40 tanks. Finally there were too many to count. The T-34s were rolling towards us at high speed, carrying mounted infantry."

These were the tanks of the Soviet XXIX Tank Corps' 31st and 32nd Tank Brigades. At the same moment, the left flank of the *Leibstandarte*'s panzer formation was hit by at least 60 Soviet tanks which it engaged at 600–1000m (646–9144yd). For the next three hours, a deadly battle raged, as related by an SS NCO:

"They attacked us in the morning. They were around us, on top of us, and between us. We fought man to man, jumping out of our foxholes to lob our magnetic hollow-charge grenades at the enemy tanks, leaping on our *Schützenpanzerwagens* [APCs] to take on any enemy vehicle or man we spotted. It was hell! At 09:00 hours [11:00 hours Moscow time] the battlefield was once again firmly in our hands. Our panzers had helped us mightily. My company alone had destroyed 15 Russian tanks."

All along the front of II SS Panzer Corps, the same scene was re-enacted again and again. As another SS soldier recounted:

" ...over the hill to the left of the embankment came three ... five ... ten ... But what was the use of counting? Racing at full speed and firing from all barrels, T-34 after T-34 rolled over the hill, right into the middle of our infantry positions We opened fire with our five guns as soon as we saw the first tank, and it was only seconds before the first T-34s stood shrouded in black smoke. Sometimes we had to take care of the Russian infantry riding on top of the tank in hand-to-hand fighting.

"Then, suddenly, there were 40 or 50 T-34s coming at us from the right. We had to turn and open fire on them...

"A T-34 appeared right in front of me when my assistant gunner yelled so loud that I could hear him without the headphones. 'Last shell in the barrel.' On top of everything else! I swivelled around to face the T-34 racing towards us at a distance of about 150 metres [164yd] when the next tragedy struck. The rear support for the gun collapsed and the barrel swung up to point at the sky. I used the force of swivelling the turret to bring the barrel of my 75mm gun down, managed to get the T-34's turret in my sights, and fired. A hit! The hatch opened and two men jumped out. One stayed put while the other hopped across the road between the houses. About 30 metres [33yd] in front of me, I hit the T-34 again.

"Everywhere, there were the shells of burning tanks, standing in a sector about 1500 metres [1640yd] wide; about 10 or 12 artillery pieces smouldering there, too. One hundred and twenty were supposed to have been in the attack, but there could have been more. Who counted!"

This was not the situation that the Germans had anticipated – a Russian attack had not been included in their plans.

From a command post, on a small hill south-west of Prokhorovka, Rotmistrov, Vasilevsky, the STAVKA representative and Kirichenko, commander of XXIX Tank Corps, had panoramic views of the battlefield. Having watched the air

▲ Senior-Lieutenant G.V. Ivanov whose antiaircraft gun crew shot down two *Luftwaffe* aircraft. By this stage, the soldiers of the Red Army were becoming more accustomed to the activities of photographers and their poses were consequently less stylized.

▼ Pictured here on its way to the killing grounds of Prokhorovka, a mixed group of T-34s of 1941 and 1943 vintage halts to check directions and take a breath of fresh air. Checking the tracks, as can be seen on the nearest tank to the camera, was essential during such a period of rapid movement.

battle from 06:30 hours and the 15-minute artillery bombardment from 08:00 hours, at exactly 08:30 hours Rotmistrov issued the codeword for the tank attack to begin.

With the words "*Stal, stal, stal*" (steel) ringing in their ears, Rotmistrov's formation commanders unleashed 500 tanks and self-propelled guns carrying tank *desant* men from the 9th Guards Airborne Division directly at the advancing Germans. The scene is graphically described in the Soviet official history:

"The battlefield seemed too small for the hundreds of armoured machines. Groups of tanks moved over the steppe, taking cover behind the isolated groves and orchards. The detonations of the guns merged into a continuous menacing growl.

"The tanks of the Fifth Guards Tank Army cut into the Nazi deployment at full speed. This attack was so fast that the enemy did not have time to prepare to meet it, and the leading ranks of the Soviet tanks passed right through the enemy's entire first echelon, destroying his leading units and sub-units. The Tigers, deprived in close combat of the advantages which their powerful gun and thick armour conferred, were successfully shot up by T-34s at close range. The immense number of tanks was mixed up all over the battlefield, and there was neither time nor space to disengage and reform the ranks. Shells fired at short range penetrated both the front and side armour of the tanks. While this was going on there were frequent explosions as ammunition blew up, while tank turrets, blown off by the force of the explosions, were thrown dozens of yards away from the twisted machines.

"Soon the whole sky was overhung with heavy smoke from the fires. On the scorched black earth, smashed tanks were blazing like torches. It was hard to determine who was attacking and who was

▼ A T-34 "brews up" on the Kursk battlefield. The Red Army tank crews displayed a reckless bravery during the battle, especially at Prokhorovka, where they fought the panzers at close quarters.

defending. The battle was going differently in the various sectors."

Rotmistrov later commented:

"Our tanks were destroying the Tigers at close range ... We knew their vulnerable spots, so our tank crews were firing at their sides. The shells fired from very short distances tore large holes in the armour of the Tigers.

" ...it turned out that both we and the Germans went over to the offensive simultaneously."

During the course of the morning the panzers of the *Leibstandarte* were driven back towards Oktiabr'skii, but the Soviet losses were grievous, approaching 50 percent. The incredible bravery of the tank *desant* men can only be marvelled at. Clinging to the metal grips on the turret of a bucking tank in a bullet-seared environment, gagging on the stench of exhaust fumes and cordite, then jumping off to fight on solid ground once more, their casualties were immense. Such fanatical bravery was equalled by the Soviet tank crews.To quote from the official Soviet history:

▲ The material losses. Taken shortly after the SS armoured units had been bloodily thrust aside, the Red Army photographed the battleground. The tanks here are mainly Panzer IVs, although to the left is a *Marder* III tank hunter which married a rechambered Russian 76.2mm gun with a Czech Panzer 38 (t) chassis.

► The long 50mm gun, pictured here, was the largest that the Panzer III could carry. The Panzer IIIs were to follow up the "panzer wedge" formed by the Tigers. However, the vicious, see-saw fighting at Prokhorovka was not a neat training ground exercise, and the Panzer IIIs suffered heavy losses.

◀ **The human cost of victory or defeat: the dead. Neither Stalin or Hitler had any interest in their men as individuals; they were simply the means to an end.**

"The 2nd Battalion of the 181st Brigade, XVIII Tank Corps, attacking along the left bank of the Psel, clashed with a group of Tigers, which met the Soviet tanks with fire from the halt ... Several Tigers opened fire on Skripkin's tank simultaneously. One enemy shell punctured the side, another wounded the commander. The driver-mechanic and radio operator dragged him out of the tank and hid him in a shell hole. But one of the Tigers was heading straight for them. The driver-mechanic, Alexander Nikolayev, jumped back into his damaged and burning tank, started the engine and rushed headlong at the enemy. It was as if a ball of fire careered over the battlefield. The Tigers stopped, hesitated, began to turn away. But it was too late. At full speed the burning KV smashed into the German tank. The explosion shook the earth. This ramming so shook the Nazis that they began a hasty withdrawal."

By the early afternoon the Soviet 170th Tank Brigade, despite having lost 30 of its 60 tanks, was heavily engaged with the *Leibstandarte*'s armoured reconnaissance battalion, which was fighting desperately to deny the Russians access to the division's rear. The Soviet pressure in this area threatened, by the late afternoon, to cut the *Totenkopf*'s links with the *Leibstandarte,* but a timely counterattack by *Totenkopf*'s Tiger Company restored the situation. By then the *Leibstandarte* had abandoned Oktiabr'skii and fallen back a further 1km (0.6 miles) to regroup.

As the day came to an end, the Soviets began to dig in. Kirichenko's men had held the SS before Prokhorovka, but the price had been high: the *Leibstandarte* alone claimed to have destroyed 192

▼ **A Hanomag Sd Kfz 251/10 variant that, judging by the warped, split-side armour, has suffered an internal explosion. The gun, a Pak 36/37 37mm piece, indicates that this was the vehicle of a platoon leader in a panzer-grenadier formation. The mounting towards the rear is for an antiaircraft machine gun. The tactical numbers are just visible on the upper-side plate.**

Soviet tanks and 19 antitank guns for the loss of as little as 30 tanks.

Elsewhere, the Germans had achieved more, particularly on the *Totenkopf* Division's front, south of the River Psel. Employing 121 tanks and assault guns the *Totenkopf* had, by midday, captured Hill 226, greatly weakening Rotmistrov's right flank. Happily for the Russians, *Totenkopf* was unable to advance further than Polezhaev, but in the thrust to Prokhorovka it had taken the longest stride.

On the *Leibstandarte*'s right flank stood *Das Reich*, with 95 tanks and assault guns; included in this figure were eight T-34s. A history of the division records its activities:

▲ A knocked-out Panzer IV smoulders on the battlefield near Prokhorovka. Manstein's panzer crews had done their best, but the Soviets had held and destroyed Hitler's dreams of final victory in the East.

▼ Outgunned and underarmoured, these Panzer IIIs paid the ultimate price in a battle that made no allowances for such weaknesses. The violence of the shelling has torn the *schurzen*, or side-armoured plates, away. Evidently the foremost tank was attempting to reverse out of danger when the track was ripped off.

"*Deutschland* Regiment [one of the division's two panzergrenadier regiments] continued to protect the flank of the advancing *Leibstandarte*, while the rest of *Das Reich*, still on the defensive, flung back a succession of infantry and tank attacks. One interesting incident was the employment against the Russians of T-34s, which *Das Reich* had seized from a factory in Kharkov. During the day a column of 50 Russian vehicles was seen driving along one of the balkas or valleys ... The direction of the column's advance showed that it was moving to attack *Der Führer* [the second of the division's panzergrenadier regiments].

▲ Victims of the *Shturmovik*. As the battle drew on, the panzers could no longer rely on the *Luftwaffe* to command the Russian skies. These three Panzer IVs have been spectacularly gutted in what is very clearly open country. With its combination of 37mm cannons and 82mm rockets, the *Shturmovik* was lethal.

"On the high ground above the Russian column stood the division's group of T-34s, which opened up a destructive fire upon the Russian tanks. The panzerman's tactic was one which they had learned early in the war with Russia: kill the enemy's command tank first. It was the only machine fitted with both a radio receiver and transmitter. The other vehicles had only receivers and could not communicate by wireless with one another. This was yet another weakness in the Red Army's tactics. Russian tanks carried on their rear decks a metal drum containing the reserve fuel

◄ Another classic piece of German military hardware, this time an 88mm, lies wrecked and abandoned in the wake of the Red Army's success at Prokhorovka. On the tube it is possible to make out 10 white "kill" rings. The tyres appear to have been removed, possibly for use on another gun chassis, as Germany was experiencing a chronic shortage of rubber.

supplies. A hit on the drum ignited the fuel and caused the tank to 'brew up'."

At 08:30 hours 120 tanks of General Burdeiny's II Guards Tank Corps went into the attack, effectively eliminating *Das Reich* from supporting the *Leibstandarte*'s assault on Prokhorovka and, more seriously, preventing it from defending the *Leibstandarte*'s right flank.

"Heavy fighting developed on the right flank of *Das Reich* Division. There the Soviet II Guards Tank Corps attacked repeatedly from the gap between Hausser's corps and Breith's divisions, which had not yet arrived. That accursed gap! 'The Russian attacks on our flanks are tying down half our effectives and taking the steam out of our operation against the enemy at Prokhorovka,' growled the regimental commander, Sylvester Stadler."

The Russian attacks against *Das Reich* ended in the afternoon, when a downpour turned the ground into a quagmire. Later on, the 26th Guards Tank Brigade was dispatched south to support Trufanov's group against III Panzer Corps.

As these mighty battles raged in the Prokhorovka cauldron, the German situation to the west was also deteriorating. With XLVIII Panzer Corps poised to cross the River Psel and push on to Oboyan, yet another of Vatutin's spoiling attacks burst over the Fourth Panzer Army.

Katukov's XXII Guards Rifle Corps had completed its hasty redeployment and placed 100 tanks in a position from which, at 09:00 hours, they burst through the 332nd Infantry Division's positions. By 17:00 hours, Kravchenko's V Guards Tank Corps, with 70 tanks, had reached Rakovo, and Burkov's X Tank Corps had driven the 3rd Panzer Division back towards Verkhopen'e and Berezovka.

The 3rd Panzer Division, reduced to less than 50 tanks, needed assistance if the western flank of the entire southern pincer were not to collapse. To counter this threat, *Grossdeutschland* was re-deployed to meet it. The knock-on effect of this move was to leave the 11th Panzer Division, itself only 50 tanks strong, in no position to do more than probe the Soviet defences. Then, late in the afternoon, the 11th Panzer Division was itself attacked by Russian tanks. Although the Soviets made some inroads, the 11th Panzer held firm, and finally Vatutin called off the attack as, once again, the skies opened and the ground became impassable.

▼ A Russian infantry squad inspects the shattered ruin of a Panther with curious caution. The much-vaunted Panther made an unspectacular debut during Operation Citadel. A Balkan cross is visible between the twin exhausts.

▲ **Russian infantrymen look at the results of the awesome destructive power unleashed by their artillery, tube and rocket units during the battle of Prokhorovka. Just visible through the distorted remains of this Panzer IV is the rear of the Russians' Willys Jeep.**

A day that had begun with a situation balanced on a knife's edge was concluded by forces outside any human control. By nature's intervention, the fighting was over. Heavy rain washed the surface clean of the blood spilt and cooled the heads of the wounded. All across the ruined fields of Prokhorovka lay the smouldering, torn remains of hundreds of tanks, self-propelled guns and the other detritus of mechanized warfare. Hundreds of grotesquely twisted and charred corpses stared sightlessly upwards, victims of their Führer's ruthless and obsessive ambitions.

But for those who remained alive after the fighting, there was still the next day's carnage to prepare for, as the epic of Kursk had not run its course in the charnel house of Prokhorovka. *Wehrmacht* and Red Army leaders took stock of the day's results. Vasilevsky agreed with Vatutin that the seriousness of the situation demanded only one course of concerted action: Soviet forces would continue to maintain the pressure all along the front. Vatutin subsequently ordered that all front forces should:

" ...prevent further enemy movement on Prokhorovka from the west and the south; liquidate the enemy groupings that had penetrated to the north bank of the River Psel by the joint operations of part of the forces of the Fifth Guards Tank Army and two brigades of V Guards Mechanized Corps [meaning the 5th Guards Tank Army]; liquidate units of the German III Panzer

▼ **The vast slab-sided shape of the *Ferdinand* is evident from this photograph. To the right of the missing rear hatch is an unidentified tactical marking. With the Germans being held at bay on the northern shoulder of the salient, it was possible for the Red Army's intelligence staff to inspect some of the new German weapons that had fallen into their hands during the fighting.**

Corps that had penetrated to the Rzhavets region; and continue the offensive of the First Tank and Sixth Guards Armies, and the right flank of the Fifth Guards Army."

Meanwhile, the Second Air Army was instructed to support Trufanov's forces in their determined thrust. Rotmistrov had ordered his men to prepare defences in anticipation of renewed German attacks, and these were expected to take place the following day. In the meantime, Trufanov was making preparations for an attack on III Panzer Corps. This would be a wholehearted attempt to stop III Panzer Corps' progress northwards, and to stop it once and for all.

That same evening, Vasilevsky was transferred to the South-Western Front in order to coordinate the forthcoming offensive, and Zhukov flew to join Vatutin for a similar purpose. The Russians were now moving into the offensive phase of their plan for the Battle of Kursk.

However, on the German side, the situation was now much less clear. The Anglo-American landings in Sicily and the opening of a Soviet offensive, Operation Kutuzov, which was aimed clearly at Orel, had that morning resurrected the doubts as to the value of Operation Citadel. Consequently Hoth ordered that offensive operations for the following day be considerably reduced, with the intention of closing the noose around those Soviet forces in the salient which had been formed between II SS Panzer Corps and III

▲ The Panzer III Ausf N, as seen here being towed into captivity, had been fitted with the short 75mm L/24 gun to enable it to carry out a close-support role. The barrel on this tank has a cover to protect it from the deleterious effects of dust. Production of the Panzer III ended immediately after the Kursk operation finished.

Panzer Corps. Both the *Leibstandarte* and *Das Reich* were to hold their positions, although the men from the *Totenkopf* were ordered to carry on the offensive in the following way:

" ...continue its right wing attack in the Psel valley to the north-east and is to move forces as strong as possible [at least one armoured force] onto the ridge of hills north of the Psel as far as the road from Beregowoje to Kartschewka. It is to force a crossing over the Psel in the south-east and to destroy the enemy forces south-east and south-west of Petrovka in cooperation with the *Leibstandarte*."

In an attempt at morale boosting, Hoth passed on a message to the troops from Manstein, who stated that that he wanted to:

" ...express his thanks to and admiration for the divisions of II SS Panzer Corps for their outstanding success and exemplary behaviour in this fighting."

Heartening words for the survivors, but of little consolation to the dead.

Withdrawal

Kursk had been fought and lost. Now the German armies on the Eastern Front were faced with a defensive war against a vastly numerically superior foe. For the Soviets, the battle marked a turning point in their war against Nazi Germany.

The date 13 July 1943 was a critical one for the Third Reich. Hitler summoned Manstein and Kluge to a conference at his headquarters, the *Wolfsschanze* (wolf's lair) in East Prussia.

As a result of the Anglo-American landings in Sicily, the possibility now existed that the Allies would invade somewhere else in the south of Europe. Consequently, Hitler received the commanders of Army Group South and Army Group Centre with a simple declaration of intent:

"I must prevent that. And so I need divisions for Italy and the Balkans. And since they can't be taken from any other place, apart form the transfer of the 1st Panzer Division from France to the Peloponnese, they will have to be released from the Kursk Front. Therefore I am forced to stop Citadel."

However, Hitler was also concerned about Operation Kutuzov, the Soviet offensive into the Orel salient. Model's Ninth Army had suffered 20,000 casualties and the panzer divisions were severely degraded. Kluge eagerly agreed with his Führer's decision to cancel Operation Citadel. On the other hand, Manstein was more optimistic, and spoke with the support of both Hoth and Kempf

▼ As the Russians advanced in the wake of the German withdrawal, scenes of destruction such as this became more familiar. With diminishing support from the *Luftwaffe* and the more confident and experienced efforts of the Red Air Force, panzers on the open steppe became prime targets for Soviet ground-attack aircraft.

when he requested that Citadel continue and ruled out the prospect of a Soviet attack south of Kharkov. Indeed, such was his conviction that Army Group South would succeed that Manstein had already moved XXIV Panzer Corps – consisting of the 5th SS *Wiking* Panzergrenadier Division and 23rd Panzer Division – into assembly areas around Kharkov in preparation for continuing the offensive. XXIV Panzer Corps would provide a further 104 tanks and 7 assault guns and, in Manstein's opinion, restore the momentum of the German attack.

At the very least, Manstein argued, his forces could inflict ruinous losses on the Red Army's strategic reserves. Interestingly in his postwar writings, he claimed Soviet losses at Kursk were four times those of his own, and that all Soviet reserves had been committed. Despite these arguments, Hitler remained adamant: Operation Citadel would be cancelled. But he conceded that Army Group South could continue operations of a reduced nature, with the aim of destroying the Russians' operational reserves and thus preventing them from undertaking any offensive operations that summer. Manstein retired to his headquarters, determined to render the Soviets incapable of taking major offensive action.

The reports from the southern edge of the Kursk salient were mixed. In the Prokhorovka region, the fighting was negligible. II SS Panzer Corps noted its tank strength as 250 tanks and assault guns, including 4 Tigers and 12 T-34s. *Totenkopf* was under severe pressure from the 10th

▲ These two photographs combine to form a searing image of the reality of war. Dead men, lying before uncut barbed wire defences, had been channelled into fields of fire and scythed down like chaff. In many ways, the Kursk salient resembled the battlefields of World War I

▼ The *Nebelwerfer* was the most widely used of the rocket launchers developed by the Germans. Each of the six barrels had a calibre of 150mm. The weight of shot that could be laid down was heavy in comparison with conventional artillery, but even so, it was far less accurate. However, the object was to saturate an area and demoralize the enemy. The range of a *Nebelwerfer* was 7000m (7330yd).

▲ **These two Soviet soldiers are members of specialized *Razvedchik* advance reconnaissance units. Here, they are taking directions from a local. The *Razvedchik* often worked with the increasingly large numbers of Soviet partisan units, and were well-versed in the use of captured Axis weapons.**

Guards Mechanized Brigade and 24th Guards Tank Brigade, and was not capable of making progress towards Prokhorovka. Nor had a supporting attack by the *Leibstandarte* made any significant progress. Soviet counterattacks were equally as unsuccessful:

"At 12:40 hours [14:40 Moscow time], the enemy attack collapsed at our main battle line. Our defensive success is to be ascribed primarily to the Artillery Regiment LAH, the 55th Rocket Launcher Regiment, and the concentrated fire of our heavy infantry weapons."

Although *Leibstandarte* and *Totenkopf* had failed, *Das Reich*, having regained its position, had recaptured Storozkvoe before going on to reach the outskirts of Vinogradovka. *Das Reich* at least was making some progress and moving towards the leading units of III Panzer Corps.

Trufanov's attacks had gone in as planned, but had coincided, in part, with the 19th Panzer Division's attempt to expand its bridgehead. Fighting raged for the whole of the day, with Trufanov's 26th Guards Tank Brigade and the 11th Guards Mechanized Brigade both sustaining heavy losses while attempting to contain Breith's panzers. However, by the end of 13 July the 7th Panzer Division was ready to join the 19th Panzer Division in a joint attack towards Prokhorovka at first light the next day. Manstein's limited continuation strategy still looked feasible. The name given to Army Group South's scaled-down activities was Operation Roland.

To the west, *Grossdeutschland* had finally completed its regrouping and, on 14 July, in concert with 3rd Panzer Division, counterattacked the Soviet V Guards and X Tank Corps, which had been reinforced by VI Tank Corps.The German counterattack drove the Russians back and, on 15 July, Vatutin asked Katukov to assume a defensive posture. Mellenthin would keep a balanced record of the efforts of XLVIII Panzer Corps, describing them in the following manner:

"All of this was certainly a success of some sorts; the dangerous situation on the left wing had been rectified, and the 3rd Panzer Division had

▲ These trenches could be anywhere in the Kursk salient. The dry, sandy soil would be difficult to dig and maintain. However, they had served their purpose well, and it only remained for the local population to return the land to its proper use.

▼ These twin windmills overlooked the land running towards Belgorod. Here, a Red Army security unit scrambles back to friendly lines, having completed a fruitless sweep for German stragglers.

been given some support. But *Grossdeutschland* was dangerously weak after heavy fighting lasting for 10 days, while the Russian striking power had not appreciably diminished. In fact, it seemed to have increased ... By the evening of 14 July it was obvious that the timetable of the German attack had been completely upset. Of the 80 Panthers available when battle was joined, only a few were left on 14 July."

During the evening of 13 July orders were issued by Army Group South for Operation Roland, the objective of which was to establish a continuous front in the Prokhorovka area and damage the Russians as severely as possible. In essence, III Panzer Corps and *Das Reich* were to link up, trapping as many Soviet troops as possible in the resultant pocket between the River Lipovyi-Donets and River Northern Donets. Mopping up of the encircled Russians would be left to the men of the 167th and 168th Infantry Divisions.

Zhukov and Vatutin accurately predicted the German course of action and took preventative steps. Strong forces were left to cover Prokhorovka

▲ Getting out and talking to the men was an essential morale-boosting exercise. In this picture, Army-General K.K. Rokossovsky and the Central Front's Political Commissar, Major-General K.F. Telegin, chat with a distinctly nervous enlisted man.

and all available armoured reserves were sent to relieve Trufanov and give General V.D. Kryuchevkin's Sixty-Ninth Army time to extract itself from the pocket.

Das Reich's attack began at 04:00 hours on 14 July; and the fighting was intense, as the history of *Das Reich* testifies:

"Stolidly they accepted casualties from the extensive minefields, across which they marched to gain the high ground south-west of Pravorot. The first houses in Belenichino, a village at the foot of the high ground, were taken by midday, when the fighting was from house-to-house and hand-to-hand. Twelve of the Russian tanks which intervened in the battle were destroyed by grenadiers using hollow-charge grenades, while overhead Stukas dive-bombed the Russians, destroying their resistance inside and outside the village. With Belenichino at last in German hands, the grenadier battalions regrouped under the protection of the panzer regiment whose counterattacks threw the Russians back in confusion. The panzer regiment then led the division's attack for what remained of the day and continued this throughout. But the attack which began with good success during the night of the 15th lost momentum as heavy rain washed away the road surfaces. Corps' other order, to regain touch with III Corps, was accomplished when the panzer regiment met the leading elements of 7th Panzer. That junction surrounded the enemy forces in the Gostischevo-Leski area and destroyed them."

But this optimism is followed by a much less positive outlook:

"Despite this successful operation it was clear that Citadel could not succeed, for on both the northern and southern flanks the German advances had not gained the ground expected of them and there was still more than 130 kilometres (80 miles) of trenches, minefields and Russian armour."

Although the Germans had sealed the pocket, the greater part of the Soviet forces escaped and the ranks of the panzer divisions were even thinner than before. The *Leibstandarte*, for instance, on 15 July counted 57 tanks and 28 assault guns.

▼ In the centre of this trio is Army-General I.S. Konev, commander of the Steppe Front, and to the right is Marshal G.K. Zhukov. It was Steppe Front, acting in concert with Voronezh Front, that was to strike at Army Group South in Operation Rumiantsev.

▲ **Pictured here, consulting a map with a local commander, General N.F. Vatutin is pondering his next move. Vatutin was highly regarded by both Stalin and Zhukov. During 1944 Vatutin was killed by Ukrainian nationalists.**

▼ **Guards Scout Sergeant Frolchenko is a typical veteran *Frontovik*, the Russian infantrymen who gave so much during the Kursk fighting. The summer of 1943 was a hot one, hence the leathery tan. However, Frolchenko seems more interested in lighting up than being photographed for posterity.**

Now Manstein had his continuous front and looked forward to shattering any Soviet riposte. Indeed, behind the Russian lines the Twenty-Seventh and Fifty-Third Armies of Konev's Steppe Front, plus the 400 tanks of XXXIV Guards Tank and I Mechanized Corps, began assembling near Oboyan and Prokhorovka, and the Forty-Seventh Army moved into position behind Shumalov's Seventh Guards Army. Zhukov and Vatutin were preparing to go over to the offensive, and this attack was timed to start on 17 July.

However, Hitler spared the Red Army the effort. At midday on 17 July he issued an order that II SS Panzer Corps should be withdrawn and await transfer to Italy. Thus Operation Roland and Manstein's hopes ended.

It was on 17 July that the Soviets launched their next offensive against the eastern extremity of Army Group South's defences along the Rivers Mius and Northern Donets near Izyum. The

purpose of this operation was to distract German attention away from the arrangements being made for the major Soviet summer offensive, Operation Rumiantsev. The Donets–Mius operation was extremely successful in achieving its objectives as the SS divisions *Das Reich* and *Totenkopf* were sent to the Mius, but the *Leibstandarte* departed to Italy.

However, it was the Soviet activities in front of Orel that posed the clearest immediate threat. Operation Kutuzov had begun on 12 July, conducted by the Briansk Front attacking the nose and southern flank of the salient, and the left wing of the Western Front attacking along the northern flank of the salient. Central Front was scheduled to join in on 15 July, having rested and re-equipped after its exhausting struggle with Model's Ninth Army. The German defence of the Orel salient rested on the shoulders of Lieutenant-General

▲ Surrounded by cameramen and reporters, Major-General A.G. Kravchenko, commander of V Guards Tank Corps, is presented with a medal by Army General N.F. Vatutin. To Vatutin's rear is Nikita Khrushchev, future Soviet Premier, who was at that time Member of the Military Council for the Voronezh Front. Khrushchev had played a significant, ruthless role during the Kursk fighting.

▼ This Guards tank crew, commanded by Junior-Lieutenant A.F. Nilov, is proudly walking to a medal award ceremony. The enamel badge worn over the right pocket of the *gymnastiorka* denotes the Guards status. To the men's left is a T-34 Model 1941, with its hatches and engine covers open for cleaning and maintenance.

Rudolf Schmidt's Second Panzer Army. The title Second Panzer Army was impressive, but its three army corps, XXXV, LIII and LV, consisted of 14 infantry divisions with the 5th Panzer Division in reserve, in total approximately 160,000 men and 350 tanks and assault guns. This was a drop in the ocean when compared with the Soviet forces ranged against them.

Whilst Operation Citadel had raged, General V.D. Sokolovsky, commanding the Western Front, and General M.M. Popov, commanding Briansk Front, had quietly gathered their forces to mount attacks against the Orel salient. Western Front had built up to 211,458 men, 4285 guns and mortars and 745 tanks and self-propelled guns. The Briansk Front had a spearhead of 170,000 men and over 350 tanks and self-propelled guns. Another newly formed tank army, Third Guards, with 731 tanks and self-propelled guns, was held in reserve. Stalin and his advisors decided it was time to launch Operation Kutuzov while the pressure on the Voronezh and Central Fronts was at its height.

At 03:30 hours on 12 July, Soviet artillery battered the German lines with a hurricane of fire. Complemented by air attacks, the guns and mortars of the Western and Briansk Fronts kept at their work until just after 06:00 hours. By the afternoon, the Eleventh Guards Army had pushed into the German lines, only to be held up by the 5th Panzer Division. Nevertheless, by nightfall the Soviets had forged 10km (7 miles) into the

▼ A very smartly turned-out group of Russian staff officers, looking more Tsarist than proletarian, listen as Army General K.K. Rokossovsky offers his thoughts on a captured *Ferdinand*. The efficacy of the *Ferdinand*'s armour is apparent from the three strikes it has taken. The broken track had meant the end for this vehicle.

▲ **This mine-detector operator is clearly an optimist considering his highly dangerous trade! As well as their own minefields, the advancing Red Army had to deal with freshly seeded German minefields. Many of the German mine cases were made of glass, plastic or wood to avoid magnetic detection.**

German lines. Rokossovsky's order of the day on 12 July read:

"The soldiers of the Central Front who met the enemy with a rampart of murderous steel and truly Russian grit and tenacity have exhausted him. After a week of unrelenting and unremitting fighting they have contained the enemy's drive. The first phase of the battle is over."

Fighting resumed the following day and further success attended the Russians' efforts. Although fighting desperately, the Germans had fallen back 15km (12 miles) along a front of 23km (17 miles). The northern flank of the German line in the Orel salient was in imminent danger of collapse.

Happily for Kluge, his local commander east of Orel, Major-General Lothar Rendulic commanding XXXV Corps, had prepared his defences well, and deployed: "6 of his 24 infantry battalions, 18 of his 42 artillery batteries, and 24 of his 48 heavy antitank guns opposite the narrow

▼ **A female combat engineer team cuts through barbed wire defences during the Red Army's pursuit of the *Wehrmacht*. The PPSh submachine gun lies in readiness for action.**

attack sector." Radio intercepts and aerial reconnaissance had provided Rendulic with an extremely accurate picture of the Soviets' axis of advance. The result of Rendulic's preparations was the destruction of 60 Soviet tanks on 12 July for the loss of 3 antitank guns. As the Briansk Front's Chief of Staff later wrote:

"The first day of the offensive did not produce appreciable success in the Briansk Front. In spite of the powerful artillery and aviation support of the attacking forces, on 12 July the front shock groups penetrated only 5–8 kilometres [3.1–4.9 miles] into the depths. The almost two years of enemy preparation of the Orel salient had a telling effect. Behind the first captured trench was a second, after each occupied position there was another, and beyond each line another appeared. We did not succeed in introducing the tank corps to battle on July 12."

▲ German prisoners as far as the eye can see. Stalin decreed that no German prisoner of war would return to Germany until Stalingrad was rebuilt. Millions of Axis POWs were engaged on reconstruction projects throughout the USSR.

Model, now commanding the Second Panzer Army as well as the Ninth Army, disengaged four divisions – including the 12th, 18th, and 20th Panzer Divisions – from his sector of Operation Citadel, and redeployed them to contain the Soviet breakthroughs.

On 15 July Rokossovsky's Central Front, rested and refitted, went over to the attack, and, although unsuccessful, proved yet another drain on Model's diminishing resources. The next day Model ordered work to begin on fortifying the River

▲ An essential element of the rearguard were the antitank batteries. This is an interesting gun as it is a hybrid Franco–German weapon. The gun itself is the French Model 97 married to the carriage of a German Pak (antitank gun). The shell could penetrate 83mm (3.5in) of armour plate at 822m (900yd). Manhandling was eased by the use of a castor wheel at the rear of the chassis. The perforated, drum-type muzzle brake was an instant identifying feature.

▼ For these Aryan supermen the war is over, and the Soviet *Untermensch* (subhumans) are triumphant. The *Wehrmacht*'s infantry were overstretched and outnumbered; surrender was preferable to a hero's death.

Desna at the base of the Orel salient to cover the vital rail junction of Briansk. This defence was to be known as the Hagen Line.

However, further difficulties were to come Model's way just two days afterwards. On 17 July the fresh Soviet XXV Tank Corps threatened the rear of his defences at Bolkhov. Two days after this, the forces of Rybalko's XII and XV Tank Corps attacked from the march and crossed the River Oleshen. In the process, Rybalko's two corps had gained a further 12km (9 miles) of territory on behalf of the Soviet Union.

In order to stiffen the *Wehrmacht*'s resolve, Hitler forbade any further withdrawals by Model's forces, issuing his directives in a Führer order dated 20 July. The absurdity of Hitler's instruction was made even more apparent when yet another Soviet army, Fediuninsky's Eleventh, began to batter away at the crumbling German line north of Orel on 21 July. On 22 July, Hitler's made a slight concession, and offered Model the power to conduct a mobile defence. With so many holes to plug, Model had

▲ This group of refugees is one of the luckier ones. The village to which they have returned looks relatively unscathed, and the Red Army appears to have lent a hand. There is a distinct lack of men, as the Red Army recruited all the males from liberated areas almost immediately after it had arrived.

already thrown into the line the 441st and 707th Security Divisions, but both of these units were incapable of resisting tanks.

By 25 July, the Third Tank Army had cut the Orel–Kursk railway and was probing for a weak spot in the German defences. However, STAVKA was forced to modify its plans as a result of Model's successful defensive operations. The direction of the Russian thrust to envelop Orel was changed from north and west to south-west. Rybalko's Third Tank Army, with over 450 T-34s, was redeployed to carry out this mission.

However, once again events in Italy intervened. On 25 July Mussolini was arrested. Hitler, determined to act rapidly, called Kluge once again to the *Wolfsschanze* on 26 July, where he announced that II SS Panzer Corps would leave for Italy immediately, and that several other divisions would follow on after it. To release these troops, the Orel salient was to be evacuated as quickly as possible. Despite Kluge's protestations, Operation *Herbstreise*, or Autumn Journey, would be authorized on 28 July.

Supported by the recently arrived *Grossdeutschland* Division, the Germans began to pull back to the Hagen Line. Despite innumerable partisan raids, the Germans managed to evacuate trains full of the wounded and fresh supplies. There was little threat from the Soviets at this point. The plethora of Soviet formations involved in Operation Kutuzov had led to a confusion in the command and control system, and the reorganization of their forces gave the Germans a small, but valuable, breathing space. On 5 August, Orel was finally evacuated.

Amidst the explosions of German demolition charges, the city of Orel once more became Soviet. Ten days later, the Germans had completed their withdrawal behind the Hagen line. As a result of Operation Kutuzov, the Red Army had eliminated the Orel salient, but had failed to trap Army Group Centre in what the Soviets had hoped would be a "Super Stalingrad".

Now Stalin and his staff could turn their attention to the main Russian offensive for the post-defensive phases of the Kursk battles. This offensive was called Operation Rumiantsev, and it was to be a far more ambitious project than Operation Kutuzov.

▼ As the Red Army liberated more and more of the Soviet Union, scenes like this were to become a familiar sight. The young soldier is holding his sisters whose village he has helped to free. On the original caption he has just been informed that his parents have died.

Aftermath

Defeat at Kursk meant Army Group South had no option but to retreat to the Dnieper. Despite the Führer's rantings that they not yield an inch of ground, German troops fled west, with hundreds of Soviet tanks in pursuit.

Hitler's removal of II SS Panzer Corps from the line allowed Manstein to shorten his front by returning to the positions occupied on 5 July. When the 3rd Panzer Division was sent south to support the River Mius' defences, the German forces before Belgorod and Kharkov were stretched perilously thin. With Manstein distracted by the Izium–Mius offensives, which had also drawn in the *Das Reich* and *Totenkopf* Divisions, the stage was set for Operation Rumiantsev.

The objectives for Operation Rumiantsev were breathtaking in scale, amounting to the total destruction of both the Fourth Panzer Army and Sixth Army by reaching the Black Sea coast behind them. The attacks by the Red armies were to be phased over a period of time to prevent the

▼ Armoured trains, although almost obsolete due to airpower, still played an important part by providing highly mobile fire support. Dressed for cold weather in greatcoats and fur caps, Russian infantry hurry past the remains of one of their own trains captured during 1941. The Red Army maintained the largest fleet of these weapons systems well into the Cold War era.

▲ **Despite the vast increase in the availability of motor transport, the Red Army still used large numbers of horses. Drawing the *panji* wagons, common throughout eastern Europe, the redoubtable Russian horses could survive, whereas those from the West perished in their thousands. This picture features a ford across the River Oka in central Orel.**

► **Following elaborate preparations, Operation Rumiantsev opened on 3 August. Three weeks of savage fighting later, Kharkov was once again in Russian hands. Here, a light tank drives beneath a banner whose proclamation reads: "Let us live in military harmony the USA, UK, USSR."**

Wehrmacht from drawing breath. The Soviet Union was now possessed of the men, equipment and experience to carry out such a rolling programme of attacks. The immediate tasks were to recapture Belgorod and Kharkov, and these devolved on the Voronezh and Steppe Fronts. The method of execution was to be simple; once again "Zhukov's bludgeon" was to be employed: massive hammer blows by artillery, tanks and infantry applied in such overwhelming numbers that no technological or tactical subtlety could stand against them. Stalin had hoped to launch Operation Rumiantsev on 23 July, by which time the *Wehrmacht* was back at the pre-Citadel jumping-off positions, but was persuaded otherwise by Zhukov, who argued that an eight-day delay was necessary to bring Vatutin's and Konev's forces up to strength.

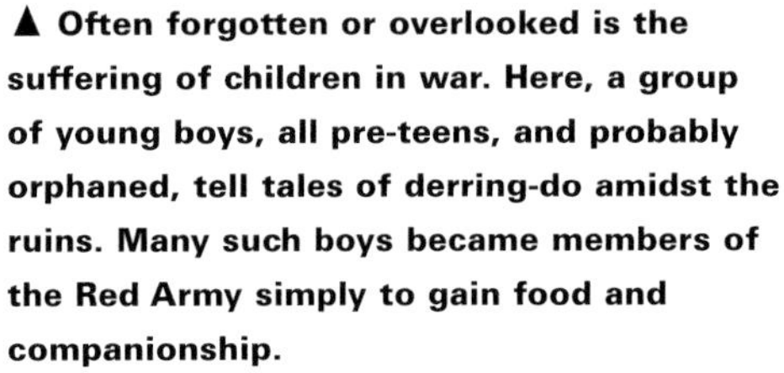

▲ Often forgotten or overlooked is the suffering of children in war. Here, a group of young boys, all pre-teens, and probably orphaned, tell tales of derring-do amidst the ruins. Many such boys became members of the Red Army simply to gain food and companionship.

◄ Yet more Lend-Lease vehicles, this time American White M3A1 scout cars manned by paratroopers of the 3rd Guards Airborne Division. This Red Army reconnaissance unit is about to move off towards the ephemeral German defences west of Orel – the Hagen Line.

▲ **Orel was successfully evacuated, despite the best efforts of the Central Partisan Bureau to coordinate sabotage activities during the first week of August. Orel was liberated, but many of the population had been forcibly evacuated by the Germans, along with 20,000 of their own wounded. The Russians made the most of the occasion, parading with flags and flowers.**

The postponement was granted and the time was used efficiently. Of the seven Soviet armies, four had been heavily degraded during the Kursk battles. The tank armies were now brought up to over 500 tanks each, and infantry replacements poured in. When Operation Rumiantsev began, Voronezh and Steppe Fronts had over 980,000 men, 2439 tanks and self-propelled guns, 12,627 guns and mortars and nearly 1300 aircraft, against 300,000 men, 250 tanks and assault guns, 3000 guns and mortars, and less than 1000 aircraft.

► **When the Red Army moved into Orel, they were led to this mass grave. The decaying corpses bear mute testimony to the brutality of the Gestapo's operations in occupied Eastern Europe.**

To further distract the *Wehrmacht*'s intelligence-gatherers, *maskirovka* (deception operations) were undertaken along the south-western flank of the Kursk salient. Dummy

▲ Collaborators? Fascist sympathizers? These men, all civilians, have been summarily executed for allegedly giving succour to the Germans. The advance of the Red Army provided an opportunity for some elements of the population to exact revenge on those who had worked for the Nazi authorities.

▼ A mine-clearance team moves cautiously through the rubble. The man on the left has a "prodder" which it is hoped will detect non-metal cased mines. The Germans were adept at littering areas with booby traps, as well as mines. The casualty rate amongst engineers such as these was unpleasantly high.

▲ The only really effective natural defence lines in the Ukraine were the waterways. This section of scouts are keeping well under cover. The western bank is noticeably higher than the eastern, giving the German defenders a considerable advantage. However, the speed of the Russian pursuit seldom allowed the *Wehrmacht* time to dig in.

positions, false radio transmissions and increased railway traffic diverted the 7th Panzer Division and 78th Infantry Division to the area, further weakening the already truly threatened part of the German line.

On 3 August, at 05:00 hours, the Russian artillery overture began playing along the German frontline. Three hours later, the Soviet artillery rolled on to bombard the German rear and allow the first ground attacks to go in. By the early afternoon, the German lines had been penetrated sufficiently for Vatutin to commit four tank brigades to exploit the breach, which they did to a depth of 25km (21 miles). By the end of the first day, the Russians had driven a 10km (7-mile) wedge between the Fourth Army and Army Detachment Kempf.

However, Steppe Front had not been so successful. Konev requested and received reinforcements – V Guards Mechanized Corps – to add weight to his attack. However, Manstein's reaction was swift. The SS panzer divisions *Das Reich* and *Totenkopf* were brought back from the River Mius and, along with the battered 3rd Panzer Division, were placed under III Panzer Corps. This force was given instructions to halt the Soviet armour north-west of Kharkov. Army Detachment Kempf was reinforced by the 5th SS Panzergrenadier Division *Wiking*.

If the Kursk battles had exhausted the *Wehrmacht,* so too had they the Red Army. Consequently, as the Soviet tanks pushed ahead while their infantry plodded in their wake, German formations dug in and fought the Red infantry. Gradually, the gap between the Soviet infantry and their tanks expanded dangerously. Nevertheless, on 5 August Belgorod was liberated. Coinciding as this event did with the recapture of Orel, Stalin ordered a salute to be fired by the guns of the Moscow garrison to celebrate these triumphs. This tradition was to continue with increasing regularity until the end of the war.

By 6 August the Sixth Guards Army had broken through in the west, and the ripple effect of Zhukov's plan spread wider. On 7 August Bogodukov was taken by the Soviets, as was Grayvoron. These penetrations threatened to encircle the 19th Panzer Division and the remains of the 57th, 255th and 332nd Infantry Divisions.

▲ Here, a Lend-Lease British Valentine tank escorts lorry-borne infantry to a crossing point. Finally, in the last days of September 1943, the Red Army once again stood on the eastern bank of the Dnieper River. The *Wehrmacht* hoped to defend this great river and gain time to rest and rebuild its strength, but the Red Army was not prepared to grant this respite.

Lieutenant-General Gustav Schmidt, commanding the 19th Panzer Division, was aware of the 50km (35-mile) gap between the Fourth Panzer Army and Army Detachment Kempf, but was unaware of just how deep the Soviet penetrations were. Schmidt's force moved out to realign between Grayvoron and Akhtyrka in a column several kilometres long. The column was covered by the *Luftwaffe*, which mounted mock attacks to convince any observers that it was a Soviet tank force.

The ruse worked for some time, but finally General Trofimenko, commanding the Twenty-Seventh Army in Grayvoron, realized that there were no Soviet forces in that area. Immediately an ambush was prepared in some woods through which the column had to pass. Varentsov, commanding Voronezh Front's artillery, directed the guns of the Twenty-Seventh Army and, with the aid of ground-attack aircraft, proceeded to destroy Schmidt's force.

By mid-afternoon the road was a mass of tangled lorries, tanks and guns shattered by the Soviets. Red Army men ranged through the woods, gathering prisoners. Schmidt was counted amongst the dead. Only a few survivors made their way through to link up with the elements of the *Grossdeutschland* which had returned from its "fire brigade" activities in the Orel salient.

On 8 August Manstein was visited by Chief of the Army General Staff Colonel-General Zeitzler. To Manstein, the only issue now was the Soviet attempt to destroy Army Group South. To deny the Russians this result, territory had to be given up and the line drastically reduced to enable the *Wehrmacht* to retain control of the southern River Dnieper. Zeitzler reported this viewpoint to the Führer.

Hitler's reply was to release the 3rd Panzer Division from the south as the Russian offences there had ended by 3 August. The 3rd Panzer Division joined the Eighth Army, formerly Army Detachment Kempf. The eastern suburbs of Kharkov were penetrated by tanks of the Seventh Guards Army, causing Manstein to consider the Roman punishment of decimation for the men of the 282nd Infantry Division that had collapsed and allowed the Soviet incursion. The 6th Panzer Division restored the situation. However, a similar breakdown in discipline took place on 18 August, when the 57th Infantry Division broke under Soviet artillery fire.

The *Totenkopf* had, by 12–13 August, arrived in sufficient strength to take on the overextended troops of Katukov's First Tank Army, and in the ensuing clash the First Tank Army lost 100 tanks. Although the SS panzers had suffered considerably at Kursk and the River Mius, *Das Reich* had received all of the *Leibstandarte*'s armour before the latter went to Italy. The increasing strength of the German forces kept open the roads and railway to Kharkov, and these Manstein hoped to use to evacuate the city. However, Hitler would not agree to let Kharkov go, as, he said:

"The fall of the city could have serious political repercussions ... the attitude of the Turks depends on it. So does that of Bulgaria. If we give up Kharkov, we lose face in Ankara and Sofia."

Manstein was not prepared to, as he put it, " ...sacrifice six divisions for doubtful political reasons ... I would sooner lose a city than an army."

In the face of Hitler's disapproval, Manstein ordered the evacuation of Kharkov on 22 August, along with the destruction of the city. Konev, in order to trap as many Germans as possible and to curtail the vandalism, ordered a night attack, but it was too late. The Soviets liberated only blackened ruins and took a handful of shell-shocked prisoners. But, symbolic as Kharkov was to Stalin and Hitler, to Manstein it was a concrete reality.

▼ Not the Andrews Sisters! These Guards tank men have just been awarded decorations for bravery. The curly hair effect is achieved by pulling down the sheepskin lining of their tank helmets.

▲ **The happy faces of these Russian children in a newly liberated village on the way to Belgorod need no further explanation. Two years of Axis occupation were now over.**

There was now nothing substantial to defend until the River Dnieper and Kiev. Now, Army Group South was faced with two grim choices: its men could either defend where they stood; or they could retreat as far as they could, all the while hoping that the much-vaunted Eastern Rampart was not simply an illusion which had been conjured up by Josef Goebbels' propaganda wizards.

The Eastern Rampart was the name given to a theoretically solid line of defences running from Melitopol on the Black Sea to beyond Gomel, some 800km (600 miles) to the north. For the greater part of that distance, it followed waterways, mainly the River Dnieper. It was described on propaganda leaflets thus:

"Germany has clad the west bank of the Dnieper in concrete and shod it with iron. We have created an Eastern Rampart there, impregnable as our Western Rampart on the

▼ **Throughout the autumn the Russians pressed on into the Ukraine. However, not everyone in the liberated regions welcomed the return of the Russians. Anti-Soviet Ukrainian forces continued partisan operations for almost a decade after the end of World War II.**

Atlantic. You [the Red Army] are being sent to your deaths. Death awaits you on the Dnieper. Stop before it is too late."

The section that ran from the Black Sea to the River Dnieper was known as the Wotan Line and protected access to the Crimea. However, although construction work had been carried out, mainly by forced, deported labour, it was the military engineering of fantasy, but one to which the scurrying *Wehrmacht* would cling with more and more desperation during the next few weeks.

With Kharkov back in Russian hands, the Soviets once more attacked along the River Mius, and this time the Germans did not hold. To the north, on the front of Army Group Centre opposite Smolensk, the Western and Kalinin Fronts opened their offensive, Operation Suvorov,

► K.K. Rokossovsky had served as a cavalry officer under the Tsar. During the years following the revolution, he rose to command a cavalry division, but was arrested as part of Stalin's purge of the Red Army in 1937. On his release from the Gulag in 1941, Rokossovsky was given command of a mechanized corps. The skillful leadership he demonstrated between 1941 and 1942 drew him to the notice of Stalin and Zhukov. However, his work at Stalingrad and Kursk brought him to international prominence. After the war, he was appointed Poland's Minister of National Defence between 1949 and 1956.

► G.K. Zhukov had served in the Tsar's cavalry. A firm supporter of communism, he rose steadily through the ranks, avoiding the horrors of the purges. Zhukov's military reputation was made by his crushing defeat of the Japanese in 1939. In 1941 he organized the defence of Leningrad and led the Moscow counteroffensive. Although Zhukov's offensives of 1942 were failures, the fighting at Stalingrad restored his reputation, and the success achieved by the Red Army at Kursk put him in an almost unassailable position of influence. Although regarded as one of the most successful leaders of World War II, Zhukov was marginalized by Stalin, who was jealous of his fame and popularity.

▲ In a scene that could be taken from Tolstoy's *War and Peace*, sabre-wielding Cossacks charge across the snow-covered steppe to harry retreating Axis troops. In the right circumstances, cavalry could prove surprisingly effective, particularly against groups of cold, hungry stragglers in the open.

▼ In the depths of the forest a pair of demolition experts lay charges to damage German communications. Throughout the latter months of 1943, partisan activities became more widespread, coordinated and effective. The Axis was forced to deploy more and more troops to counter such operations.

▲ **Abandoned German vehicles litter the streets of liberated Russian towns and cities. The speed of the Red Army's advance was, at times, so rapid that the Germans had no time to do more than abandon vehicles which could otherwise have been salvaged. The StuG III has been fitted with the wide *Ostketten* (east tracks) which provided better weight-distribution in mud or snow.**

on 7 August, to add even greater pressure to the now hard-pressed *Wehrmacht*.

On 27 August Hitler travelled to Vinnista in the Ukraine, where he was briefed by Manstein, and agreed to the transfer of troops from Army Group Centre to Army Group South. However, the situation of Army Group Centre made any transfers impossible. During the night of 27/28 August, two Soviet Corps broke through the Sixth Army's defences and struck south towards Mariupol which was on the Black Sea.

The date 3 September was the fourth anniversary of the outbreak of war, and also the day that Anglo-American forces landed on the mainland of Italy. It was also the day on which Manstein and Kluge met Hitler in East Prussia. The results of the conference were limited: Kluge was allowed to withdraw part of Army Group Centre to the River Desna; and Manstein was permitted to evacuate the Kuban bridgehead – the one German foothold in the Caucasus – and so abandon the River Mius line

Three days later, the Soviet Third Guards Army ripped a 36km (31-mile) wide hole between the First Panzer Army and Sixth Army, and the Central Front drove into the junction of Army Group South and Army Group Centre. It was at this point on 7 September that Manstein demanded "forces or a free hand for further withdrawal to shorter and more favourable sectors."

The next day Hitler arrived at Zaporozhye, Manstein's headquarters on the banks of the River Dnieper. Manstein suggested to the Führer the withdrawal of Army Group Centre across the River Dnieper to free troops that could man the Wotan Line. Hitler refused this proposal, but he did agree to transfer troops from Army Group Centre. Kluge promptly vetoed this. Communications from Manstein and Kluge to Hitler became increasingly pessimistic. Finally, on 15 September, Hitler capitulated and allowed Manstein and Kluge to withdraw behind the Rivers Desna and Dnieper. Only the Sixth Army would remain east of these rivers and engage in holding the Wotan Line.

From the moment the order to retreat to the rivers went out, the race to get across them was on. On foot, in lorries, by any manner of means, the *Landser* headed for the River Dnieper. Isolated German units were washed away like sandcastles on a beach by the flood tide of Russian armour.

It is perhaps fitting that the honour of reaching the eastern bank of the River Dnieper first went to men of Vatutin's 51st Guards Tank Brigade, who arrived there late on 21 September. Four Guardsmen paddled across and established a toehold which expanded during the next three days to a bridgehead of 31sq km (12 square miles). Men of Rokossovsky's Thirteenth Army reached the river north of Kiev on 22 September. During the next few weeks the Red Army busied itself with dispatching the last German pockets of resistance east of the River Dnieper, redeploying their by now depleted tank forces. Positions were established along the eastern bank of the River Dnieper and further bridgeheads set up on the western bank. At the end of October, Field Marshal von Kleist's Army Group in the Crimea was cut off from Army Group South as the River Shivash was crossed by Soviet troops.

The prize of Kiev

The next glittering prize for the Red Army was the Ukrainian capital of Kiev. Since the beginning of Russian history in the 11th century, Kiev had been a centre of Slav culture, and Stalin was determined that it should be returned to Soviet rule in time for the 26th anniversary of the Bolshevik Revolution on 7 November.

Kiev fell to the Russians in the early hours of 6 November. Men under Vatutin's command drove the T-34s that moved cautiously into the city. Four months and a day had passed since the opening of Operation Citadel. During that time, the Red Army had fought the cream of the *Wehrmacht* to a bloody standstill on ground of its own choosing, destroying forever the myth of German invincibility, and liberating vast tracts of Soviet territory from Nazi domination. The final German comments come from Heinz Guderian, Inspector General of Panzer Forces at this time:

"By the failure of Citadel we had suffered a decisive defeat. The armoured formations, reformed and re-equipped with so much effort, had lost heavily both in men and equipment and would now be unemployable for a long time to come. It was problematical whether they could be rehabilitated in time to defend the Eastern Front; as for being able to use them in defence of the Western Front against Allied landings that threatened for next spring, this was even more questionable. Needless to say the Russians exploited their victory to the full. There were to be no more periods of quiet on the Eastern Front. From now on the enemy was in undisputed possession of the initiative."

▲ Josef Stalin, pictured here in 1946, was the undisputed leader of the USSR throughout World War II. Unlike Hitler, Stalin had no frontline military experience to colour his strategic thinking, and furthermore, he placed more trust in his commanders, allowing them a greater degree of latitude in their operation, particularly after the crushing defeat they had managed to inflict on the *Wehrmacht* at Kursk.

Stalin's comment, made in a speech celebrating the 26th Anniversary of the Bolshevik Revolution on 7 November 1943, was equally apposite:

"If the Battle of Stalingrad signalled the twilight of the German-Fascist Army, then the Battle of Kursk confronted it with catastrophe."

The road to Berlin and ultimate victory was a long, hard one, and the men of the Red Army paid a shocking toll to take their first steps along it. The Battle of Kursk marked, to paraphrase Winston Churchill: "the end of the beginning."

German Army formations committed to Citadel

Army Group Centre (Field Marshal von Kluge)

Ninth Army (Colonel-General W. Model)

XX Army Corps (General of Infantry Freiherr von Roman)
45th Infantry Division (Major-General Freiherr von Falkenstein)
72nd Infantry Division (Lieutenant-General Muller-Gebhard)
137th Infantry Division (Lieutenant-General Kamecke)
251st Infantry Division (Major-General Felzmann)
XXIII Army Corps (General of Infantry Freissner)
78th Assault Division (Lieutenant-General Traut)
216th Infantry Division (Major-General Schack)
383rd infantry Division (Major-General Hoffmeister)
XLVI Panzer Corps (General of Infantry Zorn)
7th Infantry Division (Lieutenant-General von Rappard)
31st Infantry Division (Lieutenant-General Hassbach)
102nd Infantry Division (Major-General Hitzfeld)
258th Infantry Division (Lieutenant-General Hocher)
XLVII Panzer Corps (General of Panzer Troops Lemelson)
2nd Panzer Division (Lieutenant-General Lubbe)
6th Infantry Division (Lieutenant-General Grossmann)
9th Panzer Division (Lieutenant-General Scheller)
20th Panzer Division (Major-General von Kessel)
XLI Panzer Corps (General of Panzer Troops Harpe)
18th Panzer Division (Major-General von Schleiben)
86th Infantry Division (Lieutenant-General Weidling)
292nd Infantry Division (Lieutenant-General von Kluge)
Luftflotte 6 (Colonel-General von Greim)
1st Air Division (Lieutenant-General Deichmann)

Army Group South (Field Marshal von Manstein)

Army Detachment Kempf (General of Panzer Troops Kempf)

XI Army Corps (General of Panzer Troops Raus)
106th Infantry Division (Lieutenant-General Forst)
320th Infantry Division (Major-General Postel)
XLII Army Corps (General of Infantry Mattenklott)
39th Infantry Division (Lieutenant-General Loenweneck)
161st Infantry Division (Lieutenant-General Recke)
282nd Infantry Division (Major-General Kohler)
III Panzer Corps (General of Panzer Troops Breith)
6th Panzer Division (Major-General von Hunersdorff)
7th Panzer Division (Lieutenant-General Freiherr von Funck)
19th Panzer Division (Lieutenant-General G. Schmidt)
168th Infantry Division (Major-General C. De Beaulieu)

4th Panzer Army (Colonel-General Hoth)

II SS Panzer Corps (SS-Obergruppenfuhrer Hausser)
1st SS Panzergrenadier Division *Leibstandarte Adolf Hitler* (SS-Brigadeführer Wisch)
2nd SS Panzergrenadier Division *Das Reich* (SS-Gruppenführer Kruger)
3rd SS Panzergrenadier Division *Totenkopf* (SS-Brigadeführer Priess)
XLVIII Panzer Corps (General of Panzer Troops von Knobelsdorff)
3rd Panzer Division (Lieutenant-General Westhoeven)
11th Panzer Division (Major-General Mickl)
167th Infantry Division (Lieutenant-General Trierenburg)
Panzergrenadier Division *Grossdeutschland* (Lieutenant-General Hoerlich)
LII Army Corps (General of Infantry Ott)
57th Infantry Division (Major-General Fretter-Pico)
255th Infantry Division (Lieutenant-General Poppe)
332nd Infantry Division (Lieutenant-General Schaeffer)
Luftflotte 4 (General of the *Luftwaffe* Dessloch)

Losses at Kursk

The vast array of statistics that claim to represent accurate measurements of the losses suffered by both sides make for a study in their own right. I readily acknowledge my debt to David Glantz and Jonathan House for plundering their highly scholarly work, *The Battle of Kursk*, in pursuit of recent, well-researched figures.

Glantz and House quote, with reservations, from Soviet and German records and freely state: "no comprehensive tally has been made on the German side...", and "...the circumstances of Soviet record keeping were so chaotic that actual loss figures may never be fully known." With these points in mind readers are left to judge for themselves as the figures provided can only be treated with circumspection.

Soviet Front	Establishment	Losses
Central	738,000	33,897
Voronezh	534,000	73,892
Steppe	———-	70,058
Total	1,272,700	177,847

The above figures include formations not directly engaged in battle. When these formations are discounted the percentage increases from 14 percent to between 20–70 percent in some heavily engaged formations. When assessing tank and self-propelled gun losses the Soviet sources give a figure of 1614 lost out of 5035 committed to action.

German losses between 5 and 20 July are:

Ninth Army: 20,720 men

Army Group South: 29,102 men

giving a total of 49,822. Again, the formation commitment alters actual unit percentage losses.

German tank losses are also calculated by the calendar. II SS Panzer Corps' tank and assault gun strength fell form 494 on 5 July to 251 on 13 July, 50–60 being lost at Prokhorovka alone.

By 13 July XLVIII Panzer Corps numbers, again including assault guns, had dropped from 601 to 173. Those of Army Detachment Kempf during the same period fell from 326 to 83.

These figures can be deceptive, as not all armoured vehicles were "total losses": many were recovered and repaired. A rule of thumb calculation suggests that between 15 and 20 percent would be actual write-offs. Thus, Fourth Panzer Army had 629 damaged armoured vehicles of which about 126 would be total losses and Army Detachment Kempf would have suffered 336 damaged and 67 total losses. Ninth Army figures would read as 647 damaged and 130 destroyed.

The total German panzer loss for Operation Citadel, using the method outlined above, would be 1612 damaged and 323 irreparable losses.

Calculated in the same manner, Soviet tank and self-propelled gun total losses would be 1614, five times those of the *Wehrmacht*.

Losses for both sides during the post-Kursk operations were roughly in the same proportions: one German for five Russians. However, the Soviet Union was far more capable of sustaining this ratio than the Third Reich.

Major Red Army formations committed to Citadel

Western Front (Colonel-General V. D. Sokolovsky)

Fiftieth Army (Lieutenant-General I. V. Boldin)
Eleventh Guards Army (Lieutenant-General I. K. Bagramian)
First Air Army (Lieutenant-General M. M. Gromov)
Front strength: 211,458 men, 4285 guns and mortars, 144 rocket launchers, 745 tanks and self-propelled guns and 1300 aircraft

Briansk Front (Colonel-General M. M. Popov)

Third Army (Lieutenant-General A. V. Gorbatov)
Sixty-First Army (Lieutenant-General P. A. Belov)
Sixty-Third Army (Lieutenant-General V. A. Kolpakchi)
Fifteenth Air Army Lieutenant-General N. F. Naumenko)
Front strength: 433,616 men, 7642 guns and mortars, 160 rocket launchers, 794 tanks and self-propelled guns and 1000 aircraft.

Southwestern Front (Army General R. I. Malinovsky)

Fifty-Seventh Army (Lieutenant-General N. A. Gagen)
Seventeenth Air Army (Lieutenant-General V. A. Sudets)
Front strength: 65,000 men and 80 tanks. The number of aircraft is unavailable.

Central Front (General of the Army K. R. Rokossovsky)

Forty-Eighth Army (Lieutenant-General P. L. Romanenko)
Thirteenth Army (Lieutenant-General N. P. Pukhov)
Seventieth Army (Lieutenant-General I. V. Galanin)
Sixty-Fifth Army (Lieutenant-General P. I. Batov)
Sixtieth Army (Lieutenant-General I. D. Chernyahovsky)
Second Tank Army (Lieutenant-General A. G. Rodin)
Sixteenth Air Army (Lieutenant-General Rudenko)
Front strength:s 711,575 men, 11,076 guns and mortars, 246 rocket launchers, 1785 tanks and self-propelled guns and 1000 aircraft

Voronezh Front (General of the Army N. F. Vatutin)

Thirty-Eighth Army (Lieutenant-General N. E. Chibisov)
Fortieth Army (Lieutenant-General K. S. Moskalenko)
First Tank Army (Lieutenant-General M. E. Katukov)
Sixth Guards Army (Lieutenant-General I. M. Chistyakov)
Seventh Guards Army (Lieutenant-General M. S. Shumilov)
Sixty-Ninth Army (Lieutenant-General V. D. Kriuchenkin)
Second Air Army (Lieutenant-General S. A. Krasovsky)
Front strength: 625,591 men, 8718 guns and mortars, 272 rocket launchers, 1704 tanks and self-propelled guns and 900 aircraft

Steppe Military District (Steppe Front from 9 July) (Colonel-General I. S. Konev)

Fifth Guards Tank Army (Lieutenant-General P. A. Rotmistrov)
Fifth Guards Army (Lieutenant-General A. S. Zhadov)
Fourth Guards Tank Army Lieutenant-General G. I. Kulik
Twenty-Seventh Army (Lieutenant-General S. G. Trofimenko)
Forty-Seventh Army (Lieutenant-General P. M. Khozlov)
Fifty-Third Army (Lieutenant-General I. M. Mangarov)
Fifth Air Army (Colonel-General S. K. Goryunov)
Front strength: 573,195 men, 8510 guns and mortars, 1639 tanks and self-propelled guns. The number of aircraft is unavailable.

The numbers quoted do not include Front reserves and are taken from the returns for 1 July, four days before the offensive began.

German tank aces at Kursk

That the German panzer force was technologically more advanced than that of the Red Army is beyond doubt. The capacity of the Tiger to absorb punishment, combined with the range of its main gun, provided the men who operated it with the opportunity to achieve great things. The battle for Kharkov during the early months of 1943 had earned the SS panzer troops an excellent reputation. Kursk and the subsequent fighting during the Soviet counteroffensives from August to November 1943 confirmed their status as an élite fighting force. From the ranks of these men there were many who found fame and glory, but there were a few who were elevated to the pedestal of tank ace. There is no similar section for Russian tank heroes as theirs is a story that remains to be told.

Michael Wittmann

Of all the German tank aces, one stands as first among equals: SS-Untersturmführer (Second-Lieutenant) Michael Wittmann, who commanded a Tiger troop of the *Leibstandarte* during Operation Citadel. On the first day of Citadel Wittmann's Tiger destroyed eight Soviet tanks. It was Wittmann's troop that shattered the attack of the 181st Tank Brigade at Prokhorovka on 12 July, a remarkable achievement. During the Kursk battles Wittmann and his crew claimed to have destroyed 30 tanks and 28 antitank guns. Before his death in Normandy on 8 August 1944, Wittmann had accounted for 138 tanks and 132 antitank guns, almost 20 percent of which were gained during Operation Citadel.

Manfred von Ribbentrop

SS-Obersturmführer (Lieutenant) Manfred von Ribbentrop, son of Hitler's Foreign Minister, fought in the *Leibstandarte*'s panzer regiment at Prokhorovka. On 12 July Ribbentrop's tanks were attacked by a large group of T-34s. As the range reduced to less than 175m (200yd) the effectiveness of the German guns was neutralized. The fighting was vicious and carried out at close quarters. The claim of Ribbentrop and his crew, for that day alone, was 14 Soviet tanks.

Franz Staudegger

It is to SS-Unterscharführer (Sergeant) Franz Staudegger that the most remarkable performance in the Kursk salient must be credited.

On 8 July Staudegger's Tiger was under repair at Teterevino. A report arrived that some 50–60 Soviet tanks were approaching. Staudegger and his men hurried the repairs and set off to meet the Russians. During the course of the morning this lone Tiger fought for two hours, destroying 17 enemy tanks. The Soviets withdrew to regroup. Staudegger followed and, catching the Russians bunched in a gully, proceeded to destroy a further five T-34s. With his ammunition gone Staudegger withdrew. On 10 July Staudegger became the first Waffen-SS Tiger commander to be awarded the Knight's Cross.

Bibliography

Ailsby, Christopher. *Images of Barbarossa*. London: Ian Allan, 2001.
Bartov, Omer. *Hitler's Army: Soldiers, Nazis and War in the Third Reich.* Oxford: Oxford University Press, 1992.
Brett-Smith, Richard. *Hitler's Generals*. London: Osprey, 1976.
Carell, Paul. *Hitler Moves East, 1941–1943*. Boston: Little, Brown & Co., 1964.
Carell, Paul. *Scorched Earth*. New York: Ballantine, 1971.
Cooper, Matthew, and Lucas, James. *Hitler's Elite*, London: Grafton, 1990.
Cooper, Matthew, and Lucas, James. *Panzer*. London: Macdonald, 1976.
Cooper, Matthew, and Lucas, James. *Panzergrenadier*. London: Macdonald and Jane's, 1977.
Dunnigan, James. *The Russian Front*. London: Arms and Armour, 1978.
Forty, George. *German Tanks of World War Two*. London: Blandford Press, 1987.
Glantz, David M., and House, Jonathon. *When Titans Clashed: How the Red Army Stopped Hitler.* Lawrence, KS: University of Kansas Press, 1995.
Glantz, David M., and House, Jonathan. *The Battle of Kursk*. London: Ian Allan, 1999.
Glantz, David M., and Orenstein, Harold S. (translated and edited). *The Battle of Kursk 1943: Soviet General Staff Study*. London and Portland: Frank Cass, 1999.
Guderian, Heinz (translated by Christopher Duffy). *Achtung-Panzer!* London: Arms & Armour, 1992.
Guderian, Heinz. *Panzer Leader*. London: Joseph, 1952.
Haupt, Werner. *Army Group Center*. Atglen, PA: Schiffer, 1998.
Healy, M. *Kursk 1943*. London: Osprey, 1993.
Jentz, Thomas, Doyle, Hilary, and Sarson, Peter. *Tiger I*. London: Osprey, 1993.
Jukes, G. *Kursk: The Clash of Armour*. London: Purnell's History of the Second World War, Battle Book No 7, 1968.
Lehman, Rudolf. *The Leibstandarte*. Manitoba: JJ Fedorowicz, 1990.
Lucas, James. *Grossdeutschland*. London: MacDonald and Jane's, 1978.
Lucas, James. *War on the Eastern Front: The German Soldier in Russia 1941–45*. London: Greenhill, 1979.
Luck, Colonel Hans von. *Panzer Commander: The Memoirs of Hans von Luck*. Westport, CT: Praeger, 1989.
Mellenthin, F.W. von. *Panzer Battles 1939–45: A Study in the Employment of Armor*. London: Cassell, 1955.
Newton, Steven H. *German Battle Tactics on the Russian Front 1941–45*. Atglen, PA: Schiffer, 1994.
Nipe, George. *Decision in the Ukraine*. Manitoba: JJ Fedorowicz, 1996.
Reynolds, Michael. *Men of Steel*. Staplehurst: Spellmount, 1999.
Rokossovsky, K., *A Soldier's Duty*. Moscow: Progress Publishers, 1985.
Sadarananda, Dana. *Beyond Stalingrad*. New York: Praeger, 1990.
Seaton, Albert. *The German Army, 1933–1945*. London: Weidenfeld & Nicolson, 1982.
Sydnor, Charles. *Soldiers of Destruction: The SS Death's Head Division, 1933–1945.* Princeton, NJ: Princeton University Press, 1977.
Williamson, Gordon. *The SS: Hitler's Instrument of Terror*. London: Sidgwick and Jackson, 1994.
Ziemke, Earl F. *Stalingrad to Berlin*. Washington, D.C.: US Government Printing Office, 1968.

Index